£2

INDIAN
SCHOOL ROAD
Legacies of the Shubenacadie Residential School

CHRIS BENJAMIN

D1471628

NIMBUS
PUBLISHING
— NIMBUS.CA —

Nimbus Publishing Limited
P.O. Box 9166, Halifax, NS, B3K 5M8
(902) 455-4286 nimbus.ca
Printed and bound in Canada
NB1077

Interior design: John van der Woude Designs
Cover design: Heather Bryan
Cover photograph: Sisters of Charity, Halifax, Congregational Archives

"I Lost My Talk" by Rita Joe, from *Songs of Rita Joe: Autobiography of a Mi'kmaw Poet* reprinted courtesy of Breton Books.

Images on pages 37 and 41 Copyright Government of Canada. Reprinted with the permission of the Minister of Public Works and Government Services Canada (2013).

Library and Archives Canada Cataloguing in Publication
    Benjamin, Chris, 1975-, author
    Indian school road : legacies of the Shubenacadie Residential
    School / Chris Benjamin.
    Includes bibliographical references and index.
    Issued in print and electronic formats.
    ISBN 978-1-77108-213-6 (pbk.).—ISBN 978-1-77108-214-3 (mobi).—ISBN 978-
    1-77108-215-0 (html)

1. Shubenacadie Indian Residential School. 2. Micmac Indians—Nova Scotia—Residential schools. 3. Abused Indian children—Nova Scotia—Shubenacadie. 4. Indians of North America—Nova Scotia—Shubenacadie—Residential schools. I. Title.

E96.6.S58B45 2014   371.829'97343071635   C2014-903184-X
                                      C2014-903185-8

 Canada Council Conseil des arts
for the Arts   du Canada

Nimbus Publishing acknowledges the financial support for its publishing activities from the Government of Canada, the Canada Council for the Arts, and from the Province of Nova Scotia through Film & Creative Industries Nova Scotia. We are pleased to work in partnership with Film & Creative Industries Nova Scotia to develop and promote our creative industries for the benefit of all Nova Scotians.

This is for my children. Because even at its ugliest,
the truth is less repulsive than lies.

I Lost My Talk

I lost my talk
The talk you took away
When I was a little girl
At Shubenacadie school.

You snatched it away;
I speak like you
I think like you
I create like you
The scrambled ballad, about my world.

Two ways I talk
Both ways I say,
Your way is more powerful.

So gently I offer my hand and ask,
Let me find my talk
So I can teach you about me.

—Rita Joe

CONTENTS

FOREWORD

BY DANIEL PAUL, AUTHOR OF
WE WERE NOT THE SAVAGES

When despotic Caucasian aristocrats ruled over most European nations to maintain their positions, they used terrorism to keep their citizens controlled, which was paramount for their very existence. Thus, when their representatives "discovered" non-white civilizations where the people ruled it was in their best interests to destroy such civilizations before their democratic ideals spread to their own populations. To make the eradication seem really desirable among their subjects, they undertook steps to dehumanize the populations of such democracies by demonization—implanting in the minds of their subjects a picture of bloodthirsty, mindless savages. Such practices were used brilliantly in the Americas; so thoroughly implanted was the white supremacist propaganda that the grotesque negative effects are still being felt by Canada's First Peoples today.

To refute the aforementioned propaganda, I'll simply relate some of what the Mi'kmaq Nation didn't have and what it did have. Five hundred years ago the Mi'kmaq did not burn people at the stake, did not use humans as work-animals, did not have bedlams and poor houses for their sick and disadvantaged, did not castrate young boys so that their sweet voices could be heard by the elite for a longer period, did not have debtors' prisons, did not practice any kind of intolerance, and so on. They did have democracy. There was no poverty among them, divorces were available and a female was not beheaded to dissolve a marriage, there were no dictators and no elite: the people ruled, freedom and justice for all, and so on. I'll leave it to the reader to decide which was the most desirable civilization.

In the early stages of the European invasion of the Americas, out-and-out genocidal practices were liberally used to exterminate indigenous populations, for instance the Beothuk were wiped out and proclamations for the scalps of Mi'kmaw men, women, and children were issued by Massachusetts governor William Shirley (1744) and Nova Scotia governor Edward Cornwallis (1749).

By the time Canada was created in 1867, such barbarous practices had been replaced with a gentler methodology: severe malnutrition was permitted to be quite common among the tribes and medical assistance was minuscule. Thus, even minor illnesses more often than not proved fatal. This neglect worked toward the goal of eliminating what Caucasian politicians, bureaucrats, and citizens deemed "the Indian Problem." Indian Commissioner Dr. Duncan Campbell Scott in 1920 stated, "I want to get rid of the Indian problem...Our objective is to continue until there is not a single Indian in Canada that has not been absorbed into the body politic...." But progress was slow.

In the late 1800s new tools to expedite the process were devised: Indian residential and day schools. The sole reason for their establishment was to take "the Indian out of the Indian." This story by Chris Benjamin about the Shubenacadie residential school is your story, not ours. It reveals a sin that is to Canada's everlasting shame, an attempt to exterminate its Indigenous peoples by assimilation. Not even South Africa's apartheid rivals the effort: apartheid was invented to separate the races; Canada's assimilation policies were implemented to exterminate.

Chris's book reveals the pain that white supremacist racism can inflict upon a people of colour. It demonstrates vividly that the wounds and scars accumulated by the incarcerated children will not heal in their lifetimes.

WHY AND HOW

*Oppressors always expect the oppressed to extend to them
the same understanding so lacking in themselves.*
—Audre Lorde

UNSETTLING

Here is what I found first: a recurring nightmare. Me wandering the black
and white halls of the old building, as seen only in photographs, pristine but
steeped in an old rotten stench. The facts playing hide-and-seek within the
walls. Finding only a sense of lurking, dishonest evil. What fool's mission
was this? What right did I have to come here?

Dorothy Moore lived here as a girl. Sister Dorothy Moore she's now
called, a well-known Mi'kmaw Elder who once said to a luncheon at St.
Mary's University that white people owe First Nations people an explana-
tion for residential schools. Now, a couple decades after she said it, most of
the creators of the system and its schools are dead or very, very old. But I'm
alive, and fairly young. I have questions about residential schools, particularly the one that ran in my home province of Nova Scotia. The big one is:
what the hell were we thinking?

In her probing book, *Unsettling the Settler Within*, Paulette Regan wonders why, with all the talk of the Aboriginal peoples' need for healing, aren't
more of us looking at "what it means to be a colonizer and our own need to
heal and decolonize." European-Canadians committed what John S. Milloy,
a Canadian Studies professor at Trent University, calls a "national crime," in
his book of the same name. He quotes a residential school survivor who told
researchers in 1966, "This is not my story but yours." Milloy adds, "It is *our*

history, *our* shaping of the new world." For white writers to solely treat residential schools as someone else's story is to miss the chance to learn about ourselves, to live in a society better able "to deal justly with the Aboriginal people of this land." We tried to erase hundreds of cultures across the country. To open ourselves to that history is to feel crippling guilt and daunting responsibility. Maybe that's why we avoid it, or why we treat the residential school system as if it's only in the past, ignoring its living legacy and the ongoing divide between Euro-Canadian and Aboriginal cultures.

This state of denial allows Euro-Canada to continue its oppression, with settler Canadians taking from Aboriginal peoples instead of living in partnership. I am writing this book in the hopes of better understanding the crimes Euro-Canadians committed and are committing against the First Nations of the Maritime region, and to push myself to be a better ally in the struggle against oppression by white society. As educator Paulo Freire one wrote, "Washing one's hands of the conflict between the powerful and the powerless means to side with the powerful, not to be neutral." The only way I can avoid participating in oppression is by participating in the struggle against it. To do this I need to move past learning and become a witness, to tell others what I've learned.

Despite all the media coverage—since allegations of sexual abuses in the early 1990s and more recently as a result of testimonies at Truth and Reconciliation Commission sessions across Canada—the majority of non-Aboriginal people still don't know about residential schools. A 2008 survey conducted by the research firm Environics found that only one-third of Canadians were "familiar with the issue of Native people and residential schools," and only 5 percent said they were "very familiar" with these issues. More than one-third had heard about physical and sexual abuse, but just 20 percent realized that children had been separated from their families, and only 10 percent knew that these children weren't allowed to speak their mother tongues. "We still know very little about this period of history or about the reasons why residential schools had such a lasting impact on Aboriginal people," Marie Brunelle told an audience at St. Francis Xavier University in Antigonish in 2011. A human rights and equity advisor at the university, she added: "Each of us has a role to play in this reconciliation process. This cannot happen if only one party is involved."

In my own conversations with other white people about this book, most are familiar with the concept of an Indian residential school and are sad that such a thing once existed and caused so much hurt. But only about half are aware there was such a school in the Maritimes, and few know anything about it beyond a general sense of tragedy. A few shake their heads and tell me what they think needs to happen now with Aboriginal peoples, unaware that they are doing exactly what our ancestors did. They are trying to fix "the Indian Problem."

As Paulette Regan wrote, there is no Indian Problem. There never was. What we have here is a settler problem, a deep-seated belief that one culture is better than the other. Only from the place of cultural arrogance can we proclaim solutions for another peoples' problems—problems defined and created by that same arrogance. Too often we hear, and tolerate, criticisms of the Mi'kmaq for failing to "get with the times" or "stop whining about the past." In other words, assimilate into our ways; forget their history, tradition, and culture. Give up who they are and become us instead. The inherent assumption is that we are better.

To root out that arrogant seed we need to look more closely at our own history, which includes the Shubenacadie Indian Residential School. I am not Mi'kmaq or Wolastoqiyik (Maliseet) or Peskotomuhkatiyik (Passamaquoddy), and the experience of surviving this school is not my story. This book is my attempt to better understand what happened and convey it to you, based mostly on existing testimony from many different sources. I hope it is an honest version, based on the facts as best as I can find and interpret into story.

If European-Canadians don't know these stories, we will continue to treat the First Nations peoples and cultures of this region as inferior, and with the assumption that they need to adapt to the now predominant Euro-Canadian culture. This would be the continuation of a tragedy. I hope this book will contribute knowledge and perspective to help light a path of respect for the first cultures of this land.

THE STORY OF THIS BOOK

This is the first published account of the Shubenacadie Indian Residential School from the varied perspectives of its founders, teachers, and survivors. I've drawn from many sources for information and photographs. Whenever possible I've noted the source of these in the text and in the Further Reading section.

Despite a lot of gaps in the official records, there is enough documentation in Library Archives Canada to give a sense of how the Shubenacadie Indian Residential School came to be and who was involved. The children's and parents' stories emerged later, in the media, beginning with a three-part 1978 series in the *Micmac News* by Conrad W. Paul, for which he interviewed more than thirty survivors. In the 1980s freelance journalist Heather Laskey researched and wrote a short documentary on CBC Radio as well as a feature for *Atlantic Insight* about the school. But media coverage exploded in the 1990s after Phil Fontaine, head of the Assembly of Manitoba Chiefs, went public with the sexual abuse he experienced in residential school. The school received heavy media coverage again in 2011 when the Truth and Reconciliation Commission hosted several events in the Maritimes. Shubenacadie survivors told their stories publicly, many for the first time.

I have read as much material as possible, including every piece of media coverage I could find, to get a sense of life at the school and of TRC events. I have mostly avoided first-hand interviews with survivors for several reasons. The stories, as you will see, are painful. For many, telling these stories reopened old wounds and extracted long-buried memories. Given that so many of these stories have just been told publicly at the Truth and Reconciliation Commission, commonly called the TRC, I saw more harm than good in trying to convince Mi'kmaw Elders to put themselves through it again for my sake.

The exception was Wayne Nicholas, a band councillor at Tobique First Nation and Shubenacadie residential school survivor. I called Wayne to ask about key changes at the school in the 1950s and he told me his whole story. He'd told it many times before and said it was important to share so that others would know the truth. I'm glad he did because it gave me at least one direct, compassionate voice of survival. But as I will explain, while there are important themes common to all the Shubenacadie school survivor stories, no two are completely alike.

For the most part, in relaying these stories, whether I've found them in media coverage or in the archives, I generalize in order to give the reader a better idea of what life at the school may have been like. When talking about school survivors I often leave out names to respect the privacy of individuals and their descendants. The names are available on public record, but were put in the archives without the consent of the individuals affected; when they spoke with the media it wasn't with the understanding that their names would end up in a book. There are a few exceptions, particularly concerning survivors who published their own stories and have thus made the courageous and informed choice to be a public voice about the school. In particular I found detailed expressions of life at the school in Rita Joe's autobiography, *Song of Rita Joe,* and Isabelle Knockwood's account of the school, *Out of the Depths.* I also use the names of some residents who died while incarcerated at the school, because I feel that these instances are severe and important enough that the public should be aware of the names of these individuals to honour their memories.

MISSING PUZZLE PIECES

In talking about how the school came to be I've looked whenever possible at the original source, mostly consisting of archival letters between government officials and school principals. But there are holes in this information. More than one-third of the files on the school are locked up in Library Archives Canada. The public is legally prevented from seeing them. The files that *are* available to the public mainly cover the 1930s and '40s. The government's and church's views on the school's last twenty years are murky.

One reason for these gaps in the records on Shubenacadie may be that the government intentionally destroyed its own documents on this and other schools. According to a 2006 report by the Shingwauk Project of Algoma University in Sault Ste. Marie, which is based on archival documents, many government documents were intentionally burned or pulped between 1936 and 1973. Indian Affairs's Records Destruction Teams eliminated monthly reports, accounts, correspondence, diaries, and medical and attendance records to free storage space. The government denies these purges. As an internal Aboriginal Affairs document claimed in 2009, "The admission of the deliberate destruction of student records and documents might spur further legal action against the government of Canada."

Isabelle Knockwood writes of a mini-purge at Shubenacadie during the late 1960s, when the school was winding down. Father Paddy Collins, the principal, asked a First Nations janitor to burn the school's records.

But the man refused, afraid he would be breaking the law. So instead, Collins bought off a white employee with a bottle of rum, and the white man did in the paper trail with a bonfire. Knockwood also notes that the Audette Report, the result of a 1934 federally commissioned public inquiry into the severe beating of nineteen boys at Shubenacadie Indian Residential School, is mysteriously difficult to locate. Only one copy of the original seven remains. "Other evidence surrounding the March 1934 beating seems also to have been destroyed," she writes, including the formal complaint about the beatings filed by an Indian Agent. These are part of a four-month gap, from December 1933 to April 1934, in the Shubenacadie Indian Residential School files of Indian Affairs at Library Archives Canada.

There were other fires, and floods too. The Sisters of Charity (SOC), a congregation of nuns in Halifax, taught at the school, and the Catholic Archdiocese of Halifax ran it. SOC's original mother house burned down in 1951, likely taking school records with it. But the Sisters don't have many documents from the school after 1951 either. Much of whatever survived the 1951 fire may have been burned by Father Collins, or with the school itself when the building, closed in 1967, burned down in 1986. The Archdiocese and the Sisters say they sent whatever they did have to the TRC, which has a court-ordered mandate to uncover and publish all information about residential schools.

That leaves little to go on in understanding the story of the nuns who taught at the school. Their perspective has always been a bit of a mystery. SOC offers no journals and only minimal records of who taught at Shubenacadie. There was a book of Annals—sort of a collective journal of the goings-on at the school, kept by all the Sisters who taught there—but they didn't enter their names, their record keeping was inconsistent, and the book was open to the Sister Superior or the principal, so the Sisters likely didn't record their truest feelings. Still, the Annals should provide clues. But SOC refuses to let me see them. The material is too personal. SOC did allow Marilyn Thomson-Millward to see the Annals as part of her Ph.D. research in the mid-1990s. And so with Thomson-Millward's permission I've relied heavily on her interpretation of the full Annals, which she wrote about in her 1997 dissertation "Researching the Devils." With the help of SOC's communications director, I also interviewed three active Sisters to get their thoughts on the Shubenacadie school and the reconciliation process.

Only three of the Sisters who taught at the school are still alive. Two still live in Nova Scotia, but are elderly and declined being interviewed for this book. Even when they were alive, none of the Sisters who taught at the school spoke with researchers from the media or academia. Instead, various SOC communications professionals have acted as the main spokespersons about the organization's involvement in the school since its closure.

The government records in Ottawa are rich but incomplete. Daniel Paul, who worked for Indian Affairs from 1971 until 1986, recalls accessing records that were illegible due to water damage. "A lot of the records from the Shubenacadie Indian Agency were destroyed by flooding in the 1960s," he says. The information challenge is a national one. Even the TRC had to take the Government of Canada to court in 2013 to get access to millions of archival records. This fight happened several years after a settlement had been reached between residential school survivors, associated churches, and the federal government, obliging the feds to disclose all relevant documents to the TRC.

The TRC was originally supposed to complete its work by the summer of 2014, a deadline that was extended a year when Library and Archives Canada released nearly one hundred thousand previously withheld Indian Affairs documents in April 2014. By that time, little had changed since Aboriginal Peoples Television Network (APTN) reported earlier that year, "nearly three years after the work began and with a year left before the money runs out, no one knows how much it will cost to gather all the historical documents, who will pay for it or what materials are even 'relevant' for the project." APTN journalist Jorge Barrera estimates that it could take ten years to find and digitize all the documents. That estimate seems conservative. Aboriginal Affairs is one of more than thirty federal government departments and agencies with somewhere between 5 and 50 million files—that's one hundred thousand boxes of documents—that may or may not be relevant. Then there are the various provincial, university, and museum archives. There are also eighty-eight church archives to go through. Not only have the churches often resisted the TRC's efforts, but according to several sources, the Catholic Church is infamous for not being forthcoming with its records on the residential schools, repeatedly making claims of privacy. "I'd be surprised if the TRC has been sent everything," says Jennifer Llewellyn, a Dalhousie University law professor who has been deeply involved in the truth and reconciliation process.

Once the documents are gathered, historians and database archivists need to review and organize them and make them searchable and accessible. In the meantime, TRC isn't sharing. I spoke to Peter Houston, a TRC archivist. He wanted to share Shubenacadie records with me, he said, but his manager told him not to. The records are officially closed, sealed off from the public and from researchers until the National Research Centre, or NRC, on residential schools is established as a permanent memorial. On Llewellyn's advice I also called Paulette Regan, TRC's research director, to ask for help. She did not return my phone call.

Besides archival information, I've consulted several published and unpublished accounts and analyses—by journalists, government workers, research firms, students, and university researchers—of the Canadian residential school system, Mi'kmaw history and contemporary issues, and the Shubenacadie Indian Residential School itself. You can find information about these works in the Further Reading section at the back of the book. Every one of them is fascinating and educational. For the latter sections on Mi'kmaw children in state care and Mi'kmaw and Wolastoqiyik (Maliseet) education and language resilience and renewal, I interviewed experts from within the education system, provincial government, and local universities.

My Language Choices

Almost all of the children at the Shubenacadie Indian Residential School were Mi'kmaq. It was the only federally funded Indian residential school in the Maritimes during the residential school era, which ran from the late 1800s until the last school closed in 1996. A much smaller number were Wolastoqiyik, who are often called Maliseet, a Mi'kmaw word meaning "broken talkers." And a very few were Peskotomuhkatiyik (Passamaquoddy) or of another First Nation. Whenever possible, I use the most specific and respectful terms.

I have also used the Smith-Francis orthography, which is officially recognized by Mi'kmaw chiefs in Nova Scotia and by the Mi'kmaq-Nova Scotia-Canada Tripartite Forum, with respect to the spelling of "Mi'kmaq" and "Mi'kmaw." So, "Mi'kmaq" is used as a noun, singular or plural. "Mi'kmaw" is used as an adjective and also as the name of the language of the Mi'kmaq. When I'm writing about more general, Canada-wide policies, I revert to terms like "Aboriginal peoples" and "First Peoples" to describe all those descended from the original human inhabitants of what is now Canada. I use the term "Indigenous peoples" to describe First Peoples of all nations, including Canada. "First Nation" is another general term I use to describe all Aboriginal peoples of Canada with the exception of the Inuit, who are not First Nations people.

I use the outdated general term "Indian" only when quoting people or documents, describing their perspectives, or discussing official terms, like the name of a school or the Indian Affairs branch of the federal government. The branch was first founded in 1880 and has been housed within different government departments ever since, under different names. I tend to use "Indian Affairs" or "the Department," and when speaking of contemporary issues, "Aboriginal Affairs." Another common usage of the word "Indian" in this book is when discussing various Indian Agents, local low-wage employees of Indian Affairs who managed various issues like education, employment, and health care on reserves for the Department. The term lasted until the early 1950s, when the Department changed it to Agency Superintendent, then later to District Superintendent and then again to District Manager. In 1971 Indian Affairs got rid of Indian agencies altogether and simply had a District Superintendent in each province. But "Indian Agent" remained in common usage.

When describing the children who went to the Shubenacadie Indian Residential School, I most often use the term "survivors." I sometimes use the word "residents." I avoid the term "student" because it sounds too much like a typical young person going off to learn and grow. Even the most positive accounts of life at Shubenacadie do not match that image. Some children who went there did indeed go on to become first-class scholars, in part through sheer force of will, but their path to success was quite different from what most students experience. The word "survivor" is not perfect, and as you'll see not everyone survived the school. But it honours, I hope, the resilience of the people who went there, and their culture.

I

BEFORE
SHUBENACADIE

A SUPERIORITY COMPLEX

FIRST NATIONS KNOWLEDGE

Mi'kmaw is a language shaped, as Isabelle Knockwood puts it, by "the sounds of the land, the winds and the waterfalls." In *Out of the Depths*, Knockwood recalls learning from her mother how to listen to her own footsteps in the woods so that when she returned home she would notice any difference if she strayed from the proper route. The first Europeans to arrive in Mi'kma'ki benefited from this learned ability to navigate by the senses. And yet, by the time Mi'kma'ki became part of the new nation of Canada, Euro-Canadians saw the Mi'kmaq as an inferior people. A 1947 Bachelor of Education thesis for Mount Allison University, called "Indian Education in Nova Scotia," begins: "Determining the relationship between the Indians and the whites became an immediate problem with which the latter, because of their superiority, were forced to contend."

A. A. Currie, who wrote this thesis more than six decades ago, shared the attitudes of the day, arguing that it was up to white Canadians to turn First Nations cultures around, so that they could adjust to new realities. Only education—Euro-Canadian education—could accomplish this, as evidenced by the fact that North America's Indigenous peoples had failed to do the job themselves in thousands of years, and could never equal European culture, remaining "three millennia behind," as Currie wrote. The Mi'kmaw and Wolastoqkew Elders likely could have told Currie different, had he talked to them. But few Euro-Canadians had bothered to ask, and they remained ignorant of the richness of the first human cultures of this land. Even in 1965, Indian Affairs bureaucrats shared Currie's perspective: "The culture with the more advanced technology, the superior body of knowledge, and the facility for adapting to the accruing exigencies is invariably the one that dominates," the chief superintendent of vocational training wrote that year.

The Mi'kmaq of Mi'kma'ki—which now includes the Maritimes, Newfoundland, northeastern Maine, and the Gaspé Peninsula (Gaspésie)—recognized seven districts, likely based on water drainage and river systems, with several distinct communities in each district. Extended intergenerational familial relationships were, and are, paramount. Because familial relationships extended beyond individual communities, children often lived in multiple homes, picking up skills from different adults on their travels. Adult mentors—including older siblings, parents, grandparents, and Elders—taught children skills like hunting, fishing, trapping, preparing fish, and curing caribou and moose hides. Parents were providers, but aunts, uncles, and grandparents could be disciplinarians. Everyone was a teacher and student, and children were not seen as burdens because the responsibility for raising them was shared among many. Women held positions of high esteem as givers of new life and caregivers.

Early Europeans were amazed by the kindness the Mi'kmaq showed their children, and wrote much of their incredible freedom and egalitarianism. The explorers were perplexed that these people lived more or less equally, with leaders taking on more power but also far more responsibility. The land was absent of dictators. Leaders seemed to have the genuine respect of their people. Yet there was complexity in their governance, which had three levels: local bands, district leadership, and band council. Modern democracies were modelled after indigenous systems.

In their 2012 book, *The Language of This Land, Mi'kma'ki*, Trudy Sable and Bernie Francis explore the culture and world view expressed by the Mi'kmaw language. It is a complex, challenging language evoking an active relationship with the environment, extended family, and community. Sable and Francis describe a pre-European-arrival Mi'kmaw perception of the landscape as alive, aware, and dynamic. "The Mi'kmaw language has its own language of science, language of spirituality and language of governance and law, which were sung and danced into being," they write.

That Mi'kmaw science is well documented, increasingly so thanks to academics at Cape Breton University. Stephen Augustine, the principal of Unama'ki College at CBU, is a nationally recognized expert on traditional

Mi'kmaw knowledge, something he started learning from Elders at a young age. Much of this knowledge was practical: "How to take a tree down and turn it into a basket or another kind of tree into a canoe," he explains. Or moccasins, or a toboggan. "Understanding the elasticity of the wood, how to use it when wet." Long before Europeans arrived in Mi'kma'ki the Mi'kmaq had learned, through meticulous observation and experimentation, about math, astronomy, physics, biology, and chemistry. They used this knowledge in fishing, trapping, hunting and gathering, as well as in their practice of medicine. Modern pharmaceuticals owe much to the advanced understanding of plants that existed in the "New World" before Europeans arrived here.

The need to heal the sick also necessitated proper use of plant medicine, which involved understanding a wide array of species. Laurie Lacey chronicles more than seventy plants used by the Mi'kmaq for medicine—likely a tiny portion of the total—that he learned from Mi'kmaw Elders. "Mi'kmaq knowledge of natural medicines was as effective as the knowledge of their European counterparts," Lacey writes, "and in some instances surpassed it." In his 1977 book, *Micmac Indian Medicine*, Lacey writes of "constant exchange of medical knowledge between the Europeans and the Indians." Beyond understanding the properties of plants, skillful preparation was needed, whether it was boiling, steeping, or using the plant raw. Often a plant had to be broken into separate components, each of which was prepared differently. Many were mixed with an animal-fat base, also a medicinal ingredient, creating compound medicines that were either drunk, eaten, or applied as a poultice or salve. Some plants worked when masticated—chewed by mothers—mixed with antibodies, and fed to the children.

There were also specialized medicine people who played a spiritual and medical role and were able to make and read sacred markings on birchbark, cataloguing detailed rituals. Scholars, including Mi'kmaw author and educator Marie Battiste, have pointed out that with few exceptions European immigrants largely ignored this Mi'kmaw literacy, preferring to maintain the "myth of the illiterate savage." Despite having learned much from the Mi'kmaq about health care, missionaries also discredited traditional medicine. When anthropologist Frederick Johnson visited Mi'kmaw communities in 1930, no one would admit to practicing shamanism, once a revered ability to heal people and interpret the spirit world.

Mike Isaac, a student services consultant with the Mi'kmaq Liaison Office of Nova Scotia's education department, speaks of the Mi'kmaw story Muin and the Seven Bird Hunters, about a single part of the night sky. It contains detailed instructions on constellations and shows that patterns in the sky are connected to patterns on Earth, giving us a calendar, a measurement of time on a grand scale. The story identifies several of the same constellations identified by the ancient Greeks as well as the North Star and its circumpolar stars. "You take that story and match it with other cultures doing the same study and there's nothing different, from the Milky Way to the Big Dipper," Isaac says. "We just interpret it differently through our stories but the knowledge and concept of it is universal—the understanding is equal."

Lisa Lunney Borden taught math in a Mi'kmaw community school in Cape Breton for ten years, and did her doctoral research with Mi'kmaw Elders on the math they've used their entire lives. Whenever she asked questions like, "how many?" or, "how much?" they would say, "*tepiaq*," which means, "enough," and then make a gesture demonstrating a certain size. She eventually learned that they did so because, to them, the gesture more precisely showed "how much" than a number could. Space and shape were more important than enumeration. Lunney Borden remembers talking with the late Dianne Toney, a renowned quill box maker who learned geometry by making boxes with circular lids. "To find the centre, I just fold it in half twice," Toney told Lunney Borden. Intersecting diameters. Then, to make a perfectly round ring, "You need to go across the centre of your birchbark three times and allow about the width of your thumb."

And then it hit Lunney Borden: "My God that's pi!"

Pi (π) is roughly 3.14. When multiplied by diameter ("across the centre") it gives you the circumference (the perfectly round ring). Only in Toney's pi, the 0.14 was judged by the width of her thumb. If she'd been making a hamper instead of a box, she'd have used a hand width instead of a thumb width.

Lunney Borden now teaches in the education department at St. Francis Xavier University and runs Show Me Your Math, a program exposing Mi'kmaw children to traditional math. She says there is an "inherent spatial reasoning" in the Mi'kmaw language, which she describes as a process-, action-, or movement-oriented, verb-based language. It is focused on relationships—between people, animals, plants, objects, and spirits. This is perhaps why the language quantifies things spatially, by the distances between them.

Without an earnest attempt to understand Mi'kmaw culture and language—and with a deep-seated belief in its inferiority—it is not surprising that the people who founded the Shubenacadie Indian Residential School didn't see these mathematical skills in their wards. They had no clue, for example, that counting in Mi'kmaw is complicated by the use of three different sets of number-words, depending on whether you are counting animate or inanimate objects, measurements of time, or age.

Like Mi'kmaw science, Mi'kmaw math is practical, driven by need. Both subjects are connected to the language. They evolve together within the culture. The Elders Lunney Borden learned of used math to navigate difficult waterways and to build tools and housing, to calculate complex spatial geometry, fractions and angles—all in their heads. They call it common sense. Western science, on the other hand, is more abstract—sometimes finding application after the fact. It thrives on the analysis of component pieces of systems, understanding how they work individually with less attention to the relationships between things. It's easier to understand things that way, to measure them and be certain of their individual importance. But you can miss the big picture.

A MODEL RESIDENTIAL SCHOOL

The concept of a residential school in what is now Canada goes all the way back to the spring of 1616, a year after three Récollet—members of an order of Franciscans focused on meditative practice—priests and one unordained brother landed in Québec City with Samuel de Champlain. It had been Champlain's idea to turn the children of the "heathen savages" of New France into new Frenchmen. Supported by a royal edict, he had asked the Récollets to send some of their best men to find Catholic converts. Their superior was Denis Jamet, who influential Récollets in France had chosen for his administrative experience and astute political leadership. Joseph Le Caron, a thirty-year-old charismatic priest, Jean Dolbeau, a thirty-year-old mystic priest, and Pacifique Du Plessis, an apothecary (pharmacist) and unordained Récollet brother, joined Jamet. The four men established an ad hoc friary in Québec City, which Champlain had founded seven years earlier, and wandered the surrounding woods in search of "savages." They were the first of the Catholic missionaries, signalling a shift from partnership with the First Nations to an attempt to change them and bring them under colonial control.

Le Caron and Dolbeau got together again the spring following their arrival in Québec City to chat about winter. They'd been busy baptizing Montagnais Innu and Wendat (Huron) folks as soon as possible so as not to risk losing them to Protestant competition. But they were frustrated by how quickly the converted relapsed into "savagery," risking their immortal souls and those of the priests who had baptized them. The Récollets created several strategies for ensuring more permanent conversions. One of these was to focus on the children, whose culture, they believed, hadn't set in yet. In their eyes, the children were a blank slate. The problem with giving adults the gift of Catholicism was that they took it and melded it with their previous beliefs, a religion-by-design that predated postmodern hippies by four centuries.

Paramount to this youth-focused religious and cultural education was to gain control and authority over the children. Youth—boys in particular—would need to be isolated from the influence of their elders, French-ified and Catholicized, then released back among their people as missionaries. The Récollets would teach these children just as young French children were taught: adhering to rigorous schedules and beaten upon any failure to obey and learn. The Récollets, failing to appreciate that both Innu and Wendat cultures garnered wisdom not from youth, but from Elders, founded a boarding school in Québec City, headmastered by the unordained, young Brother Pacifique. They called it their *séminaire* (seminary). There, sheltered from the dangers of their own communities and Protestant traders, a handful of Wendat boys were taught French and Latin, as well as the Catholic world view.

The Récollet school became an unintentional model for the Jesuits, who would replace the Récollets in 1629, and for the eventual Canadian residential school system. The Récollets recognized their failure to "civilize the savages," and in their place the Jesuits built a schoolhouse farm with livestock in 1635 for Wendat and French children. The Jesuits also involved another institute of the Catholic Church: the Ursuline nuns, who established a convent upon the arrival of Mère Marie de l'Incarnation in 1639. She, along with Marie-Madeleine de Chauvigny de la Peltrie made a point of learning the Wyandot language. The nuns taught at Jesuit day schools as well as the boarding school, and were among the first to teach Wendat girls how to become "proper" housewives for French bachelors. (Their efforts, funded directly by the governor of New France, may have been in vain; it was more common that Frenchmen joined Wendat communities.) From there, just like First Nations and Inuit captives at future residential schools, the children would often flee, preferring their own homes and cultures. When the first bishop of New France, François de Laval, opened the Petit Séminaire in the fall of 1668 on the orders of the king, there were eight French and six Wendat students. Within a few years, there were no Wendat students.

ACADIA'S MI'KMAW SCHOOL

Not long after the Récollets started their school, in the early summer days of 1632, three members of a new and small Franciscan order of monks, the Capuchins, set sail from Auray, France, on the *L'Espérance en Dieu* (Hope in God). Isaac de Razilly, the new lieutenant general of New France, captained the ship. Three more Capuchins followed on another ship later the same day. Their job was clear: convert the locals to the true faith and make sure the French didn't "go native."

By this time, the Mi'kmaq had officially adopted Catholicism. Grand Chief Mouipeltu (Membertou) and 21 of his relatives, along with another 120 Mi'kmaw volunteers, agreed to let Father Jessé Fléché baptize them in the early summer of 1610—this after the French Jesuits apparently cured him of a terminal illness. Mi'kma'ki adopted Catholicism as its faith—though the Mi'kmaq have always remained free to choose Catholicism or their traditional faith, and many practice both. As Marie Battiste observes, "Micmac spiritual culture and sacred view of nature were broadened, not altered, by the Catholic theology...Micmac society embraced the two spiritual worlds as one, enlarging the rituals but not changing the ideological foundation." But the Capuchins wanted to make sure Catholicism remained the religion of choice.

They landed at Port-Royal, now Annapolis Royal, centre of New France on what they called "la Baie Frangaise," now the Bay of Fundy. Razilly was determined to establish a French, Catholic colony, and he would soon write to Cardinal Richelieu that "the savages obey all the laws one may impose upon them, divine and human." Port-Royal had a large log church, decorated on the outside with evergreens and flowers, where Mi'kmaq and French worshipped and sang together, but the missionaries had yet to teach Mi'kmaw children French ways. It took several years, but with money given by Cardinal Richelieu (who was known as the king's "first minister") and Charles de Menou d'Aulnay, the governor of Acadia, the Capuchins created a *séminaire* boarding school, where they taught about thirty Mi'kmaw boys and thirty Mi'kmaw girls. The Capuchins had two houses built: the boys' dorm was attached to their monastery; the girls' was separate. The school was headed by Father Pascal de Troyes, whose letters to the Capuchins back in France show an unhappy time. He was unimpressed on the potential impact of his mission; he had hoped for a larger population to convert. Letters from others in the colony requested that de Troyes be removed. He drowned in 1649 and was replaced by the much more popular Father Léonard de Chartres.

De Chartres, now canonized, had been a monk for nearly twenty years and despite his reputation for oration was a true Capuchin, a great lover of silence. On his arrival at Port-Royal, de Chartres made the rounds of the local Capuchin posts and baptized Mi'kmaq. The Capuchin Friars' website tells a tale of de Chartres being shot in the back with an arrow while administering the sacraments to a dying Mi'kmaw child. He lived, and was sent to Port-Royal to replace Father de Troyes. "Peace and happiness filled his life as he taught his red skinned scholars about the God who was his and theirs," the website reads. "It was an inspiring scene to see the humble, brown clad friar with the Indian boys and girls sitting at his feet in open mouthed wonder and admiration."

Several other friars taught at the school, including Fathers Cosmas de Mentes and Gabriel de Joinsville, the most experienced missionaries among the Capuchins. Many of the brothers learned to speak decent Mi'kmaw, something that would one day be discouraged at the residential school in Shubenacadie. Madame de Brice, a widow and the mother of two Capuchins, arrived in the summer of 1644 to teach the girls and recruit new students. I can only speculate as to what the Mi'kmaq thought of this school, but the French were thrilled with it. Governor d'Aulnay wrote reports to King Louis XIV that the school was a success, thanks to the dedication of the teachers and students. While the goal was to raise Catholics, it seems the students were already believers. Many of them had already been baptized, while others were preparing for the sacrament.

The school's undoing started in 1650, when Governor d'Aulnay died in a boating accident. Emmanuel Le Borgne, a merchant who had lent the governor 260,000 livres, demanded repayment. In a dispute over the sum, Le Borgne had Madame de Brice, Father Cosmas, and Father Gabriel jailed for five months. When released, they caught the next ship back to France. Two years later, a small fleet of English ships on Port-Royal Harbour signalled big trouble for the French, and the Mi'kmaq too. The English sacked Port-Royal without resistance, shuttered the school, and expelled everything French. The friars were marched to the beach and thrown aboard English ships. Only Father de Chartres refused to leave, saying that his Mi'kmaw students—the boys—needed a spiritual father. The other Capuchins wanted to stay with him, but he told them to leave. As the ship headed to England and an unknown fate, de Chartres's students and the other teachers heard the shot that killed their schoolmaster back onshore.

THE NEW ENGLAND COMPANY

Was it better for the Indians to integrate with the growing white settlements, or to maintain separate Indian communities? This serious issue has dogged all plans and efforts to assist the original inhabitants of North America, even into the present.
—The New England Company, 2002

It wasn't until the end of the Seven Years' War, with the Proclamation of 1763, that the English took complete control of New France, from Newfoundland to the Rockies and from the Hudson Bay to the Gulf of Mexico. In Mi'kma'ki, the Brits had never taken up the effort of the French to provide the Mi'kmaq with formal education. From the closing of the Port-Royal *séminaire* in 1654, it would take more than a century until the idea cropped up again. When it finally did, it was ugly.

The New England Company opened the second residential school—though it wasn't called that at the time—in Sussex, in the colony of New

Brunswick in 1787. It was a disastrous experience, but one that would be largely forgotten by the twentieth century. The New England Company, a conservative Protestant organization with Puritan roots, was founded by Oliver Cromwell's parliament in 1649 to spread the gospel "amongst the heathen natives in or near New England." They believed that Christians had the responsibility to bring their faith to all races through teaching Indigenous peoples to read and write. Wealthy MPs, aldermen, and bankers—often with the Bank of England—sat on the board of directors. They bought up cheap land in New England, which had been taken from the same people whose souls they hoped to save, and used interest and rental income to fund their missionary work.

After the American Revolutionary War, English missionaries found themselves unwelcome south of the new border. The company moved its work to friendlier territory, specifically Nova Scotia and New Brunswick. Its man in New Brunswick, Edward Winslow, wanted to open a series of Indian schools there. Settlers had by this point driven the Mi'kmaq and Wolastoqiyik into a state of deep poverty. The settler response was to try to convince the Indians to be less Indian, to stop moving seasonally to new hunting grounds and start farming. In the company's previous missionary efforts in New England, teachers had generally made an effort to learn and teach in local languages. But in New Brunswick this wasn't the case. The goal was to "civilize" Mi'kmaw students, equipping them with the English language, the Protestant faith, and the skills to farm, so they could in turn "civilize" the rest of their communities.

Though the land issue had largely been settled, the Catholics and Protestants still fought for Indian souls, and would continue to do so throughout the residential school era. More members meant more donations to the cause. The Catholics in New Brunswick had two major advantages: first, the Mi'kmaq were already Catholics and had been for nearly two centuries; second, the Catholics made every effort to learn the many Algonquian languages. This made for a better, more reciprocal—if still unequal—relationship with the Mi'kmaq and Wolastoqiyik. The fact that the Mi'kmaq had already been Catholic for more than 180 years only encouraged John Coffin, headmaster of the New England Company's school. By 1787 Coffin produced a list of seven possible sites for Mi'kmaq and Wolastoqiyik schools, succeeding in all but four of the locations, where company representatives failed to convince parents to send their children to the school, even after showering them with bribes.

The company had schools built in 1791 at Sussex Vale, Meductic, and Maugerville, but within a couple of years the board decided to save money by consolidating at Sussex Vale, where the treasurer, George Leonard, lived. Eight First Nations children attended the school along with twenty to thirty whites. Leonard invited the parents to squat on a small plot of land by the school and gave them clothing, blankets, tobacco, and supplies. But the parents had their own lives to lead, traditional territory and hunting grounds, and when they left their children went with them. The ones who stayed did poorly. They were supposed to apprentice in white homes, but Leonard failed to place any. Worse, he embezzled funds from the English backers. Three board members quit when they realized what was going on.

John Coffin took charge. He swore he would civilize the Indian children by removing them from their parents' influence. "If you do not take the children early they are not only complete Indians but complete Catholics," he wrote. His opinion was popular: his supporters wanted segregation; they felt the families' influence undid the good work of the school. Company officials in England felt that taking children from their families was too harsh. In 1803 they shut down the school.

Two years later, Coffin wrote the board saying the Indians had a change of heart and wanted their children to be apprentices. In reality he had offered them gifts in exchange for their children. Families were too weakened, pushed to the point of desperation to say no. Twenty boys and girls, aged seven to twelve, were placed with white families, attended nearby schools, and apprenticed in a trade. Coffin even took infants and sold them to white families. Girl "apprentices" were often treated as slave girls were treated by white masters in the South. They were commonly raped and impregnated, birthing more children for the New England Company to take. Coffin was aware of the situation but brushed it off in correspondence with the English backers.

The board gave a grant of £20 to anyone willing to take a Mi'kmaw apprentice and teach him or her to farm. Apprentices did the work for free; farm labourers got £25 per year. This sweet deal didn't impress the backers in England, who were concerned that a farmer could make more for taking an apprentice than he would pay a labourer. At the time, workers willing to do the hard labour of farming were scarce. After their apprenticeships, some graduates would be given eighty hectares of land to farm. This enfranchisement would become another lasting tactic in the attempt to assimilate Aboriginal people long after the creation of Canada.

The apprenticeship system was as big a failure as the residential school system that would eventually follow. Graduates became lost between two cultures. Rather than "civilize" their own people, they rejected the Mi'kmaq completely. They could not have easily re-entered Mi'kmaw culture anyway; they had lost their language. And the whites rejected them, leaving them with no one. Many became despondent and turned to alcohol. Also like the residential school system that would follow, the Sussex Vale school's misdeeds did not go unnoticed. Even the governor of New Brunswick, Sir Howard Douglas, energetically argued that Indian families be kept together, that they be given adequate reserves for hunting and gathering or farming, and that Catholic missionaries be sent to live with them rather than taking them to live with Protestants as parents. In the end, the Company sent Captain Walter Bromley, who was known to push for better conditions for the Mi'kmaq in Nova Scotia, to assess the situation. He reported that the families taking on apprentices from the school were motivated only by money and brutally mistreated their wards. In yet another feature prescient of future residential schools, the apprentices rarely had a chance to return to school and spent much more time doing menial labour than learning.

In a follow-up to Bromley's visit, Reverend John West noted that half the students at the school were actually white children taking advantage of a free education, though they were likely treated much differently than their Mi'kmaw counterparts. West was particularly disturbed that men of faith were sexually abusing the children. He described one priest as being more "like a mad dog—after his prey—than a Clergyman in the habit of praying for things requisite and necessary." The students had learned very little, and could not read or understand the Bible. Coffin said it was the Indians' own fault. They had never been enthusiastic about the chance their children were given, he said. Unconvinced, English backers pulled the plug on the school in 1826. More than a century later, the Canadians responsible for the education of the Mi'kmaq and Wolastoqiyik would fail to heed history's lessons. The New England Company still exists today as a grant-giving charity, paying "each year for two Native Indians to travel to the Centre for Anglican Communion Studies" in Virginia.

MARITIME INDIAN SCHOOLS

It wasn't until decades after the Capuchin *séminaire* closed, with the Siege of Port-Royal in 1710, that Britain took permanent control of peninsular Acadia. They renamed it Nova Scotia. While the French had tried to teach the Mi'kmaq their ways, for more than a century the British showed no interest in Mi'kmaw education. In *We Were Not the Savages*, Mi'kmaw historian Daniel Paul shows that while the French had made efforts to trade and coexist with the Mi'kmaq and other First Nations, by comparison the British saw them as obstacles to be subdued or eliminated. Treaties were one tactic of subjugation. The first was signed in 1725 and made King George "the Rightful Possessor of the Province of Nova Scotia." But the Mi'kmaq and the king's representatives had different ideas about what they were signing, and the treaties have stayed contentious for nearly three hundred years. For the British, the treaty meant that, among other things, they owned all the land and whatever they gave the Mi'kmaq was a kindness. The Mi'kmaq would be "granted" the worst pieces of their own land, and over centuries new settlers would chip away at even those allotments. Throughout the 1730s, colonial authorities granted Mi'kmaw land to newcomers, sometimes granting as much as four hundred hectares to a single family.

"Centralizing" the Mi'kmaq, moving them onto fewer plots of land for easier management, would become a British then Canadian obsession. When Edward Cornwallis arrived as the new governor of Nova Scotia in 1749, he wrote to the Board of Trade arguing for a final solution to what would more broadly become known as "the Indian Problem." He wanted to wipe out the Mi'kmaq, and he put a bounty on their heads. That year, 150 men went into the forests to find and kill any Mi'kmaq they found. Cornwallis only wished he could do more, believing that with naval reinforcements he could "root them out entirely." At this point the Mi'kmaq were suffering and had become outlaws in their own home. They found themselves without their traditional hunting lands, exposed to new illnesses from the Europeans, and at risk of state-sanctioned murder by mercenaries. By 1752 there were only twenty thousand Mi'kmaq left. There had been at least two hundred thousand before European contact. Their situation only worsened when their allies, the Acadians, were expelled three years later. The Mi'kmaq had little choice but to accept whatever form of peace, and accompanying rules, the British imposed.

Over the next few decades, boatloads of poor European Protestants arrived to flesh out Nova Scotia, each having been promised at least 20 hectares of land, tax-free for a decade. It was a giant leap in social class in exchange for the work of clearing land. Higher-ranking military personnel could take 240 hectares. What was promised to the Mi'kmaq, via treaty, was further subdivided and given to the newcomers. Tracts of Mi'kmaw land were torched to drive them out.

In 1801 the colonial government created 3,442 hectares of "Indian Reserves," on "swamps, bogs, clap pits, mountains and rock piles," Daniel Paul writes. The traditional hunting grounds that had sustained the Mi'kmaq for centuries were no longer accessible. Settlers drove the Mi'kmaq population downward to fewer than one thousand by 1848. Those who survived did so in abject poverty, often forced into begging. This situation forced the British to show some interest in Mi'kmaw education. In an effort to halt starvation and disease, the province passed in 1842 an Act to Provide for the Instruction and Permanent Settlement of the Indians. It appointed a part-time commissioner of Indian Affairs to establish schools for Mi'kmaw children, with a tiny budget of £300—only £50 less than the province's governor had paid for twenty-five Mi'kmaw scalps in 1744.

The 1842 act was a half-hearted measure and did nothing to stop the loss of land and food that was killing the Mi'kmaq, who would have preferred to learn to read and write on their own terms, and use such knowledge to transmit their own culture rather than that of the British. But it did result in a few education efforts, thanks in part to the work of Reverend Silas Tertius Rand. The Protestant minister, who arrived from London in 1845, found that many Mi'kmaq had already taught themselves to write using an English-style script that read like French. A passionate believer in the value of formal education, Rand spent several years raising money to set up day schools on reserves throughout the province. As a Protestant, he had to rely on Joe Ruisseaux Brooks, a Frenchman fluent in Mi'kmaw and English, for assistance. Mi'kmaw children could attend school in the day while still living in their communities, learning to read and write a new Mi'kmaw roman script that Rand had developed. They also learned the virtues of the Protestant faith over their own. While the schools were poorly funded and closed within a few years, Rand was satisfied that many Mi'kmaq had learned to read.

It took the passing of another couple of decades and the creation of Canada for day schools—twenty-eight in all—to become more permanent features in the Maritimes. In 1872, day schools, now paid for by what would become Indian Affairs, were once again established on three reserves: Bear River, Whycocomagh, and Eskasoni. Once again, low attendance was a problem and the Bear River school was shut down within two years. In 1876 the Shubenacadie Band asked Ottawa for a day school. They wanted their children to learn English and other skills that would eventually help improve conditions on the reserve—and they weren't the only ones asking. Aboriginal communities across Canada were requesting day schools. Treaties from this period included a promise by the Canadian government to provide on-reserve schools "whenever the Indians shall desire it." But this promise was quickly broken due to a chronic lack of funds for education. Indian Affairs considered the day schools that did exist "very inferior" to the dozen or so residential schools it funded in Ontario, Northwest Territories, and the western provinces, where students lived permanently in off-reserve schools. The Department was deliberating closing day schools altogether. And yet, low-quality day schools continued to be built in the Maritimes until most Mi'kmaw children could walk to one in 1900, by which point, Aboriginal parents across Canada had come to see residential schools as a bad idea.

Shubenacadie did not get its day school until 1894, nearly two decades after the Band first asked, mainly because the cost of a building was too high. The school was eventually built for $600 and was drafty, dark, and full of leaks. This poor quality would prove typical, as Maritime day schools often lacked the money to buy books or desks, let alone weatherproofing. Twenty-five children enrolled for the Shubenacadie day school, but the average daily attendance of just twelve students did not

Silas T. Rand, c. 1880, Amherst, Nova Scotia.
Nova Scotia Museum

impress the Department. While the rate wasn't far off the Nova Scotia public-school average of 58 percent, over the next twelve years attendance declined steadily. Indian Affairs shut down the school in 1906, reopened it in 1911, and closed it again in 1912.

Most of the day schools in the region suffered a similar fate at the hands of a department always reluctant to spend money. But Duncan Scott, the superintendent of Indian education, was hopeful that the day schools would help young Mi'kmaq overcome their difficulties, despite their parents being "prone to wander about from place to place, selling their baskets or squatting in the vicinity of towns...." In his 1911 report, Scott noted that on "several of the reserves successful day schools have been established."

The day school at Shubenacadie was reopened once again in 1913 and stayed open until 1930 (with a two-year hiatus from 1920 to 1922 when the Department couldn't find a teacher), with an attendance rate of about 33 percent, which was typical of day schools across the Maritimes. When Indian Agents and others began lobbying the federal government in the 1920s for a residential school in Nova Scotia, they usually mentioned the low attendance rates at day schools. Not surprisingly, no one thought to ask Mi'kmaw parents if there was a better way to provide an education for their children, such as modifying the school calendar to work around hunting and harvest seasons. No one at Indian Affairs seemed to consider the fact that parents didn't want to send their children to schools with no desks, books, or heat. Often they lacked even a teacher—the pay was so low that anyone qualified chose to work elsewhere.

Martha Walls, a professor at Mount Saint Vincent University specializing in Atlantic Canadian First Nations history, argues in a compelling paper in the *Canadian Journal of Native Studies*, "By allowing Maritime day schools to languish, the federal government was better able to compel students' attendance at the more strongly assimilative Shubenacadie residential facility." Walls also points out that many school inspectors didn't bother with the day schools. "I used to visit them till I found that I had little or no influence," one wrote in 1912. This lack of inspection continued for years after the Shubenacadie Indian Residential School opened, when a lone inspector was responsible for dozens of day schools across the Maritimes and central Canada. Some were literally falling over, yet Indian Affairs would not spend the money to fix them.

THE CANADIAN RESIDENTIAL SCHOOL SYSTEM

INDUSTRY AND KNOWLEDGE

The idea of a school for Aboriginal children that mimicked a European settler community, with short-haired kids in European clothes learning to farm, was established in what is now Canada during early experiments in New France and Acadia. An earlier model of European industrial or reform schools for young people who broke the law or came from poor families influenced these early efforts in the "New World." Similar schools also existed in the West Indies and United States, and like the Indian residential schools, became best known for rampant child abuse.

Robert Bagot was the first to make the concept official. As Governor General of the Province of Canada in 1844, he proposed that Aboriginal children be separated from their parents and the "half-civilized" reserves, and absorbed into Canadian culture. "To civilize, Indians need industry and knowledge," he wrote. Three years later, Egerton Ryerson, the colony's most influential educator, added that the focus in these schools should be religion, to build moral character. Ryerson had already founded English Canada's public school system with similar aims of improving attendance and "inculcating loyalty and patriotism, fostering social cohesion and self-reliance... the acceptance of the established authority." Learning practical farming skills was to be part of the program at both public and residential schools. The big difference was that Indian children would be forced to live away from their families, with nuns and priests as fearsome parental replacements.

The response from Aboriginal leadership was, at first, positive. Many communities set aside treaty payments to help pay for the schools. But the first residential schools, founded in Upper Canada soon after Bagot's report, suffered from low enrollment, runaways, and graduates who went straight back to the reserve. The colonial government tried to sweeten the lure of "civilized" life with the 1857 Gradual Civilization Act. While offering residential school graduates twenty hectares of land, they would also be forced to give up their legal rights as registered Indians, and thus their cultural identities. This act was paired with a scheme of building planned communities around the schools for married graduates, but almost no one was interested in living there.

Churches worked with governments from the earliest days to run Canadian schools for Aboriginal children. They used the same per capita system later adopted for the residential school system, in which government paid the churches a set dollar amount for each student. The more students a school had, the more money the church had to work with. This system would become the cause of much overcrowding and death. In early 2013 researchers from major national Aboriginal organizations, a national organization representing survivors, churches, the federal government, and academic John Milloy examined the number and causes of deaths, illnesses, and disappearances of children and the locations of burial sites. From one million government and school records—only one-fifth of the documents known to exist—they identified three thousand deaths at residential schools. The school principals hadn't bothered naming almost a quarter of those children, and there were likely many more in the records that researchers weren't allowed to access. The schools also stopped reporting deaths in 1917—thirteen years before Shubenacadie opened.

Deaths at residential schools often went unreported even to the families, who were left to wonder why their children didn't come home. And Indian Affairs refused to cover the cost of sending the bodies home. Children died mostly of disease, but also due to malnutrition and accidents, the researchers found. Some committed suicide and others died trying to escape. Death was always part of the plan at residential schools: architectural blueprints often included cemeteries. In February 2013, researchers had found fifty burial sites. There are rarely grave markers or names, and they have mostly grown over. In some cases, like at Shubenacadie, the government sold the land to private owners after the school closed.

For the most part, the churches were the ones pushing for residential schools, which they saw as a tool for indoctrinating new believers and lifelong members. Sometimes the missionaries would take a role negotiating treaties and have chiefs request schools as part of the process. They would often go so far as to build a school and then beg funding from the government. The schools built by churches without government funding were usually rush jobs with low-quality materials and poor design. They were badly lit and lacked proper drainage, heat, and ventilation. They often burned down, and many didn't have fire escapes.

The government paid for the schools it chose to support, putting a portion aside to build schools, buy books, and pay teachers every year from 1838. Less than a decade later, the federal government decided to stop paying for gunpowder for reserves, instead putting that money toward Aboriginal education. Gunpowder would be used to hunt, a pre-civilized activity. For any funding other than for schooling and farming—the civilized way to get food—Aboriginal people would now have to make a special application.

AFTER CONFEDERATION

The effort to assimilate Aboriginal peoples was made official with the British North America Act, which created Canada in 1867. The country's first prime minister, John A. Macdonald, stated that an important goal for the new nation was "to do away with the tribal system and assimilate the Indian people in all respects with the inhabitants of the Dominion." With this end in mind, the act gave the federal government the power to legislate on behalf of Aboriginal people, taking control of their property. They became federal wards and the government became the parent, responsible for their care and education. The federal government would educate Aboriginal people and the provinces would educate everybody else.

But it wasn't until the federal government created the Indian Affairs Department in 1880 to solve the "Indian Problem" that the strategy of "taking the Indian out of the child" was formalized. By this time, the First Nations had outlived their usefulness to the English and French as potential military allies and trading partners. They had become, quite literally, a liability, an expense to be minimized. The purpose of Indian Affairs was to figure out what an Indian was, who qualified, how many there were, and how much they would cost. The idea was that they'd be cheaper if they were "civilized"—they had to disappear into the fabric of Canada and become like everyone else.

The hodgepodge of schools on and around reserves had already begun to gel into a system of day and residential schools in 1879. John A. Macdonald hired thirty-nine-year-old Nicholas Flood Davin, a writer for the *Globe and Mail*, to write a confidential report on industrial schools for "Indians and Half-Breeds" in the United States. He was to determine whether such a system would make sense for Canada. Davin visited with the US Secretary of the Interior and Commissioner of Indian affairs in Washington. They told him of "happy results which had attended the industrial schools wherever established." The American schools included livestock and crops, and the boys learned farming, carpentry, or blacksmithing from a resident expert. Davin wrote that the farm revenue would soon cover all costs of running the schools.

Davin regurgitated the wisdom of the day that "the day school did not work, because the influence of the wigwam was stronger than the influence of the school." He noted that in the American system, an amount is paid per pupil, per year, by government to the church running each school, a system that deprived the children of sufficient food. Davin recommended against it. He included design plans for a school "of the cheapest kind" to build. He was enthused by the potential of the schools to prepare "the native populations of the North-West" for their new reality under Canadian rule. But he was cautious, noting that industrial schools would take "a generation or two" to work. One thing was for certain: "If anything is to be done with the Indian, we must catch him very young." Davin urged the government to use existing missionary schools and set up four new industrial boarding schools right away.

Davin's report hit the mark with government. From the beginning, the residential school system defined itself with the violent idea that the government had to "catch" young Indians. The annual reports of Indian Affairs that year espouse the need for "emancipation" of young Indians from "the condition of ignorance and superstitious blindness" of reserve life.

Lawrence Vankoughnet, the deputy superintendent—now called deputy minister—of Indian Affairs, was particularly enthused by the residential school concept. Going against the advice of the Americans, he suggested that Prime Minister Macdonald grant funds to churches based on the number of students in each school. Soon after, Vankoughnet took over all the costs of the missionary schools in the west. It took all the Department's funds. Vankoughnet pushed that students be punished for speaking their own language through starvation and solitary confinement. English and French educators believed that Aboriginal languages were incapable of expressing European ideas and concepts. Vankoughnet's successor, Hayter Reed, pushed this concept even further, instituting an official policy in 1896 that all teaching, and even recreational activities, be done in English. The policy was still in place, inscribed into the Programme of Studies for Indian Students decades later, when Shubenacadie's first students arrived in February 1930.

A decade after Davin's report, thousands of students nationwide, aged six to sixteen, attended schools far from their communities, traditions, and the public eye. The federal government provided land, buildings, fences, equipment, books, and police to hunt down escapees. Churches helped pay for repairs and medicine and kept detailed records of attendance and expenses. The government's constant worry about costs meant that buildings were badly designed, poorly constructed, and lacked proper lighting, heat, and ventilation. Each school was essentially identical, following the same bland industrial design that allowed for quick, cheap construction. The children were poorly fed, despite most of the schools having livestock and crop operations on-site, run on student labour.

The Shubenacadie Indian Residential School, which opened in 1930, was a relative latecomer to this national system. It was one of more than 150 government-sponsored, church-run schools that existed between the 1870s and 1996. In all, more than 150,000 Aboriginal children attended these schools.

BATTLE OF THE BUREAUCRATS

In 1907 Frank Pedley, the superintendent general of Indian Affairs, asked the Department's chief medical officer, Peter Bryce, to examine the health of residential school students. Pedley wondered if the schools were fully Canadianizing Indian children. A report of a few years earlier had shown that only 40 percent of graduates went on to any kind of success in life. The other 60 percent were either dead or had "turned out badly."

Bryce spent three months examining students and talking to staff members at thirty-five schools in Alberta, Saskatchewan, and Manitoba. He found that one in four children had died of tuberculosis at school or soon after leaving it. He estimated a death rate at the schools of between 35 and 60 percent. Bryce, who had co-authored the Ontario Public Health Act in 1884, resisted popular but unproven ideas. As a result he butted heads with his superiors until they forced him out. At a time when most white people assumed their inherent superiority over others, Bryce looked scientifically, to environmental factors, to explain the difficult situations of non-whites and immigrants. He used his position to conduct extensive studies over many years of how urbanization was creating poverty for these groups, making them dependent on others to earn low wages, and putting them at greater risk of disease and of committing or becoming a victim of crime.

The "inadequate government funding, poorly constructed schools, sanitary and ventilation problems, inadequate diet, clothing and medical care" disgusted Bryce. School staffers usually shut off the ventilation in the winter to save on heating costs. Sick students were commonly admitted without a medical checkup, despite rules requiring they see a doctor first. He noted a complete lack of exercise other than forced farm and domestic labour. In all, students put in fifteen-hour days including classroom time and labour. Disease spread in overcrowded dorm rooms. The churches tried to maximize the number of students—well beyond building capacity—to get more funding. Bryce recommended what he thought were low-cost solutions, including hiring nurses familiar with tuberculosis to work at the schools.

Bryce sent his report to Pedley, as well as Duncan Campbell Scott, then superintendent of Indian education (and whose only child had died in a boarding school in France two years before Scott had taken charge of the residential system in Canada), and several MPs and church officials. Frustrated by the lack of response from his superiors, Bryce published articles about the residential school deaths in the *Ottawa Citizen* and *Saturday Night Magazine*. The Indian Agents weren't surprised; they knew the conditions at the schools were bad. But the churches got defensive because Bryce had partially blamed the deaths on the confusing arrangement between church and government, whose roles were usually unclear—and who had a history of blaming each other for any problems.

Duncan Scott was also annoyed. At forty-five years old, he was a discreet career bureaucrat who had worked his way up from junior copy clerk and would eventually put in fifty-two years, growing the residential school system to its peak. But he was also an avid outdoorsman, poet, and piano player, a Renaissance man of sorts. His well-loved "Indian poems" lamented the very effort to eliminate indigenous cultures that he was responsible for. In his poem "The Half-breed Girl" he wrote of one, "free of the trap and the paddle" yet for whom, "something behind her savage life / Shines like a fragile veil." Lines like these had made him famous, the toast of high culture.

Scott's day job would earn him a different reputation among his wards, the Aboriginal peoples of Canada. He was a well-known fiscal conservative, a real penny-pincher. Disturbed by the high cost of the treaties between Canada and First Nations, he was determined to cut every corner possible. He cut the salaries of Indian Agents, clerks, and residential school farming instructors. Even Bryce's modest recommendations got Scott's goat. He figured they'd cost a great deal, which he was "not able to recommend." Indian Affairs *did* create a maximum enrollment rule, increased funding by twenty-five dollars per student to improve facilities, and asked schools to keep a room available to isolate tuberculosis patients, but Bryce was infuriated by these meagre responses to a crisis situation of tragic proportions: children were dying by the hundreds if not thousands. He wrote to Scott's superiors, claiming that Scott was "counting upon the ignorance and indifference of the public to the fate of the Indians."

At this point, Indian Affairs stopped using the phrase "industrial schools," which had developed a poor reputation. The Department published statistics showing attendance below capacity, but medical observers visiting the schools noticed a different reality. The heat of the sensational newspaper articles cooled away, but at least the growth of the residential school system had slowed. There were now nearly four thousand students at seventy-four schools: about one in every five Aboriginal children between six and fifteen.

Bryce wasn't the only one complaining. A group of well-known lawyers, church officials, educators, and Indian Affairs bureaucrats worked to have the worst of the schools shut down. They argued that the Department could save a lot of money by getting rid of them. Higher-ups in the churches and government shut down their efforts, and the deaths at schools did not stop, even as reports from Bryce and other doctors flooded the Department. In 1914,

Scott, now deputy superintendent of Indian Affairs, had "the troublesome Mr. Bryce" removed from "Indian work" to focus on immigrant health. "The cost of compiling such statistics far outweighed the benefit of the information," he wrote of Bryce's most impassioned work. Dr. O. I. Grain replaced Bryce and found the residential schools in satisfactory condition.

After Bryce was forced to retire, he wrote *The Story of a National Crime*. In this booklet, published in 1922, he accused Scott of having a cold indifference to the health of his wards, to their lives and deaths. He cited several efforts on his part to convince his superiors they were dealing with a humanitarian crisis. He gave statistics backing his belief that the federal government didn't care about Aboriginal health. He pointed out that the City of Ottawa, with a population about the same as the nation's Aboriginal population, spent more than three times the total budget of Indian Affairs on tuberculosis patients.

Bryce's publication embarrassed the government further, which responded by asking the churches to list the kind and quantity of food served each day, an attempt to more closely monitor nutrition levels. But little changed at the schools, and by the early 1920s Aboriginal leaders had mostly turned against them. They'd wanted an education for their children, not a cultural makeover and forced removal into a disease pit. Some leaders petitioned instead for more day schools, where at least the kids could come home at night for deprogramming and a traditional meal. Despite growing evidence that it was killing children rather than culturally assimilating them, the residential school system was strengthening with the enthusiasm of Duncan Campbell Scott.

In 1920 Scott urged the government to make school attendance mandatory for Indian children between the ages of seven and fifteen. Parents who tried to keep their children close would be penalized. "I want to get rid of the Indian problem," Scott told a parliamentary committee. "Our objective is to continue until there is not a single Indian in Canada that has not been absorbed into the body politic, and there is no Indian question, and no Indian Department."

THE SHUBENACADIE INDIAN RESIDENTIAL SCHOOL

A SCHOOL FOR MARITIME INDIANS

THE TARGETS WERE CHILDREN

In its thirty-seven years, more than two thousand children were taken to the Shubenacadie Indian Residential School. Many were traumatized by the school's environment of fear and self-loathing. As a school, Shubenacadie fails any modern academic standard, and any similar test of its day. The records that weren't destroyed and the testimony of its survivors show that the institution was really a self-sustaining work camp, complete with livestock and produce, for much of its existence. The real reason for the institution wasn't education. It had two main functions: house poor or parentless children and assimilate Indians into the dominant culture.

Although Indian Affairs had officially dropped the goal of getting Indians to give up life on the reserve and become part of Euro-Canadian society in 1899, comments from Department officials show that the Shubenacadie residential school was at least partially designed to assimilate the Mi'kmaq. Officials hoped to eliminate Aboriginal cultures and languages by creating a break between young people and their families and communities. This process has been called cultural genocide.

More than many other residential schools, Shubenacadie was closer to an orphanage—with all the worst connotations of that word—than a school. The targets were children from the poorest eastern First Nations families, mainly Mi'kmaw, Wolastoqkew, and Peskotomuhkatiyik—orphans and foster children who had limited means to resist. Children without access to on-reserve day schools were also targeted—even though many reserves lacked schools because Indian Affairs would not pay for them. The creation of the Shubenacadie residential school went hand in hand with Indian Affairs's ongoing attempt to centralize the Mi'kmaq into as few locations as possible. It was seen as the cheapest and most effective way to deal with them. But the assimilation effort was too poorly funded to work. A lack of funding resulted in overcrowding: the school was built for 125 students, but its enrollment numbers were never so low until its final decade. Sickness and injury were rampant. For the students, who were not allowed to leave and were punished seemingly at random, it was a prison. The conditions were so bad that one resident, who later became a POW during the Second World War, told CBC that of the two experiences, one was no worse than the other.

THE ONLY REGION WITHOUT A RESIDENTIAL SCHOOL

It was a strange time to open an Indian residential school. The Mi'kmaq population continued to struggle, with only around two thousand left in

Political cartoonist Michael de Adder's astute depiction of the Shubenacadie Indian Residential School as it was seen by the outside world versus the experience of its child residents.

the region. Recent studies had shown that most of the youth leaving residential schools in the rest of Canada returned to their reserves, having lost their mother tongues, and had no chance of finding employment in white Canada.

The United States, whose residential school system had initially served as a model for the Canadian system, was now moving away from it, or at least reforming it to instill more respect for Indigenous American cultures. This change was based on three years of research by a team of legal, economic, health, educational, agricultural, and social work experts led by Lewis Meriam. In their 847-page report, entitled *The Problem of Indian Administration* and often referred to as "The Meriam Report" (published in 1928), the researchers wrote: "Provisions for the care of the Indian children in boarding schools are grossly inadequate." Specifically, it detailed that the children were malnourished and their health poorly cared for. Teaching standards were low and culturally insensitive. The schools only stayed open on the backs of student labour. Meriam recommended an education system based on integrating children into mainstream public schools, a policy Canada would adopt within twenty years. The report moved some white Americans to push for reform and greater respect for First Nations cultures within the education system. The idea of removing children from their homes, parents, and communities was suddenly being called out in the mainstream. In practice though, the American residential school system would survive another forty years, and Canada's for longer.

In Canada, the fifty-four-year-old system had long suffered criticism for its failure to educate or care for its wards. In short, it was doing a better job—at great financial expense—of infecting them with tuberculosis and other deadly illnesses than teaching them about the White Man or anything else. The Department of Indian Affairs was also well aware of allegations of physical and sexual abuse in many of the schools by this time. For the most part, these were either ignored or dealt with by moving the accused to another religious assignment or residential school. Despite losing their mother tongues, the children who attended the schools still had weak English skills. The focus on "vocational training," via slave labour, to help supplement the costs of running a boarding school had not made the residents employable. It was clear that they'd have done better learning practical skills in their own communities.

Years before Shubenacadie opened, residential schools had come to be seen in most of Canada as places of disease and death, a failed experiment. Minor changes were made. Teachers received raises. Residents got one warm meal a day and got to play games sometimes. More than five thousand children lived in seventy-one residential schools across Canada, but First Nations children in the Maritimes had so far avoided that fate. And yet, there were rumblings here. Even back in 1885, John A. Macdonald had lamented that "Maritime Indians" didn't make their children go to school and thought perhaps a residential school was the answer. Edgar Dewdney, the superintendent general—now called deputy minister—of Indian Affairs, said the same thing to the Governor General a few years later. By this point, the Maritimes was the only region in Canada without one. Two decades later, a low-level bureaucrat and man of faith came to the same conclusion.

Father F. C. Ryan was the New Brunswick supervisor of Indian schools in 1911 when he wrote to Ottawa urging Indian Affairs to establish a residential school in the Maritimes. Without it, he believed, the Mi'kmaq and Wolastoqiyik were unfit for "the battle of life." He mostly worried for the boys. The girls at least learned sewing and knitting in day schools. The boys had nothing. They needed to learn useful skills, like carpentry, blacksmithing, tailoring, and farming. Father Ryan's petition was ignored.

Eight years later, another New Brunswicker took up Father Ryan's call. H. J. Bury was the supervisor of Indian timber lands for the region, whose job it was to help make money off what was left of reserve lands. He wrote regular memos and reports to his superiors in Ottawa between 1919 and 1934. In numerous letters to his superiors, Bury noted that hundreds of Mi'kmaq in Nova Scotia were squatting in shacks, especially in the Halifax area. The owners of the land had told them to beat it, but they found it impossible to make a living on reserve.

Nova Scotia Indian Superintendent A. J. Boyd had long been pushing the Department to buy land for off-reserve Mi'kmaq, but Bury didn't trust the Mi'kmaq to stay put. He wanted them relocated to Indian Brook reserve, near Truro, for the time being. Like many at Indian Affairs, Bury believed in putting the Mi'kmaq onto just a few large reserves. He suggested selling off the reserves with poor land and buying new, more arable land around Truro, Shubenacadie, and Whycocomagh. In 1924 he estimated that there were about 2,400 Mi'kmaq in Nova Scotia, with 1,500 living on the province's twenty-six reserves. Many were still nomadic, but about 540 Mi'kmaq were squatting near the city. Bury was convinced that if the Mi'kmaq were given better land and taught farming as well as other trades, they'd be much better off.

Like centuries of "Indian workers" before him, Bury saw farming as the only way to civilize the Mi'kmaq. The first missionaries had seen that the nomadic Mi'kmaw lifestyle made it impossible to keep pace and spread the word of Jesus. To the government, farming was the European, and later Canadian, way. And Indian farmers were as good as Canadian. Ironically, while federal government workers pushed farming on the Mi'kmaq, the Nova Scotia government profited on the image of the Indian woodsman. It toured elaborate displays in large American cities depicting Mi'kmaw hunting guides in buckskins. One guide demonstrated his moose-calling skills on NBC.

Bury, on the other hand, suggested a residential school on a farm as the means to contain roving Mi'kmaw children in one place, to learn farming in a caring environment. Agricultural education in public schools was being phased out, but Indian Affairs still supported the concept in residential schools. The proposed school was a small ingredient in Bury's larger plan to amalgamate the reserves, a process that would save a bundle by employing three full-time Indian Agents—who would presumably be better qualified—instead of nineteen part-timers. He suggested both of these things in a report to Duncan Scott. Bury noted with some envy that there were more than seventy residential schools nationwide, and none in the neglected Maritimes. He suggested Truro as the ideal location.

Bury wasn't alone in this opinion. Cameron Heatherington, the Indian Agent for Guysborough, had already written to Indian Affairs requesting a residential school for those who didn't live near a day school. A. J. Boyd, superintendent of Indian Affairs for Nova Scotia, also supported a residential school. He felt that Canada's education policy was failing the Maritime Indian. He'd been to Western Canada to study the residential school system and found the schools "highly successful." He had apparently missed much of the recent news on Peter Bryce, who had exposed the schools as death traps, rife with disease.

Boyd submitted a May 1925 report urging Indian Affairs to build a residential school and farm in Nova Scotia. "The current [day school] system is unacceptable," he wrote. "It keeps the Indian down and does not advance him in any way towards becoming a self sustaining and useful citizen." A residential school would isolate the young Indian from bad influences on the reserve, he argued, and teach him the "proper way of life." It was essential to educate the Indian out of the Indian.

Father Ryan, perhaps sensing the momentum shift, resumed his campaign of fourteen years earlier. He again wrote to the Department advocating for a residential school in the Maritimes, mainly to house and school "delinquent Indian children," particularly orphans. He argued this time that the building of the school was a matter of justice, that without it all Maritime Indian children were being dragged down into a life of delinquency. Ryan felt that nothing good had come from having "prosecuted Indian after Indian." The school was the progressive thing to do. He wrote that the current "educational system is only good for a few, and these few are soon overcome by the conduct of the delinquent...all due to the want of this one institution." His letter was ignored.

The next year Father Ryan tried again, this time using an economic report arguing that while a new residential school might seem expensive, the government actually couldn't afford *not* to have one. The government was paying Mi'kmaw families to look after Mi'kmaw orphans, "a grave financial drainage," and because those payments were making the families lazy, the government could solve the Maritime "Indian Problem" by sending those kids to residential school instead. "The Indian question in the Maritime Provinces will then, and only then, be solved for all time," he wrote.

IT'S OFFICIAL

A. J. Boyd wasn't a popular figure among the Mi'kmaq. They had petitioned Duncan Scott in Ottawa several times to fire Boyd. Ben Christmas, chief of Membertou First Nation, accused Boyd of drawing two salaries while the Mi'kmaq lived in poverty. He also said Boyd rarely visited the reserves and was "not capable to protect an Indian," having let the reserves become "deplorable and a disgrace." Nevertheless, given his position as superintendent for the province, Boyd's voice of support for a Maritime residential school was hugely influential. In fact, his esteem with the Mi'kmaq, and their opinion in general, was of no concern to Indian Affairs. Despite the fact that Ottawa was just beginning to acknowledge the failure of the residential school system to assimilate Aboriginal peoples, Indian Affairs Deputy Secretary J. A. MacLean took Boyd's letter seriously enough to tour the Maritime reserves in the fall of 1926. When he returned to Ottawa, MacLean wrote Boyd to say he agreed wholeheartedly with the need for a residential school "convenient to the railway and sufficient in size to accommodate 80 children under the Catholic Church as virtually all Indians in the area belong to that faith."

Duncan Campbell Scott, the sixty-four-year-old deputy superintendent of Indian Affairs, was also a supporter. In the previous few decades Scott had opened dozens of new schools, and he considered starting one on the East Coast a primary career goal. "When we have this school established one of the desires of my official life will have been accomplished," he wrote to the Halifax Catholic Archdiocese in 1926. Doing so would make the residential school system coast-to-coast-to-coast, with schools in the west, north, and east. He also wanted the school within view of the highway and rails, "so that the passing people will see in it an indication that our country is not unmindful of the interest of these Indian children."

Scott officially announced his intentions to build a "home and school" in Nova Scotia nine months later, in another letter to A. J. Boyd. "The children will receive academic training, as well as instruction in farming, gardening, care of stock, carpentry in the case of boys, and for the girls, domestic activity," he wrote. There would be a barn and henhouse on site. A farm instructor and carpenter-engineer would be hired. A year before it opened, Scott wrote to the *Halifax Chronicle* about the school: "For some time it has been known at Ottawa that a school of this kind was needed in the Maritimes… the time has come when something should be done."

Now the Department would be able to take Maritime First Nations children living in foster homes and in various other institutions—as many as 125 of them, anyway—and put them in a central location. The school would "consolidate Indian education work in the Maritimes," the *Halifax Chronicle* trumpeted. Finally a home for the "underprivileged Indian child of Nova Scotia and the other Maritime Provinces." It would "mould the lives of the young aborigines and aid them in their search towards the goal of complete Canadian citizenship." No Mi'kmaq were interviewed for the article. Scott also wrote to the local Liberal Minister of Parliament,

James Lorimer Ilsley, who was originally from the Annapolis Valley but had been a lawyer in Yarmouth and Halifax, explaining the many benefits of the school and its goal, which was to ensure that graduates "will become self-supporting and not return to their old environments and habits."

Shubenacadie was the 78th federally funded residential school in Canada, the only one east of Ontario and one of the last built. The number of schools peaked at 80, with more than 8,200 children attending, in 1931. Just like the other residential schools, the church would run the Shubenacadie Indian Residential School. The government would provide the building and pay $150 per child per year to cover expenses. The school farmer would sell the produce to supplement the grant and cover repairs, food, clothing, and fuel. Indian Affairs would cover the cost of classroom supplies and medical services.

THE SITE

Once Scott was on board, things moved quickly. The Department of Indian Affairs had its own architect, R. Gurney Orr, who designed the building. That is, he copied the design of every other residential school in the country. It would cost $172,500. By June, the Department was looking for a location. At this time Charles Stewart was the minister of the Interior and Mines, which included Indian Affairs. He had a lot on his plate regarding the Nova Scotia Indians. Indian Affairs was following through on Bury's centralization plan, which went hand in hand with the creation of the residential school. Stewart was overseeing the forced movement of Mi'kmaq from other reserves to Millbrook. He told the Montréal *Gazette* that by summer's end he'd have them all "comfortably housed, with school accommodations provided on the reserve."

In reality, neither of these things happened. In March 1932 Indian Affairs finally axed eighteen Nova Scotia Indian Agents "for reasons of public economy." But half the population of Mi'kmaq were still living spread out across fifteen different reserves. Indian Affairs was forced to hire nineteen new agents to replace the eighteen they'd laid off. Ten years later Indian Affairs tried again, but despite promises of jobs, housing, food, and schools, many Mi'kmaq refused to leave their homes for a new reserve. Of those who did move to the Shubenacadie reserve, many were parents of children in the residential school who wanted to be closer to them. Their new houses were, as per Indian Affairs policy, built as cheaply as possible. The foundations were of low-quality concrete, which soon crumbled. The lumber warped badly and after a few years houses had to be demolished. The school, once built, suffered similar problems.

But first a site had to be chosen. Stewart assigned provincial Indian Superintendent A. J. Boyd to find some land. Boyd got help from a local landowner, Robert Gass, who offered to sell the Department "one of the finest farms in the Province, within sight of the Town, less than 1/2 mile [1 km] from Ry Depot, on the main highway, at a good elevation overlooking the Shubenacadie River and in full view from the Railway...." Gass repeated several times that he had "no axe to grind" and no particular desire to sell his land. He wanted only that the endeavour be popular, he said. He felt that Shubenacadie Village was the best place for the school, "situate [sic] on the CN [rail line] and on the main highway from Halifax to Truro, exactly in the centre of the Province, the best farming community...and the Indian

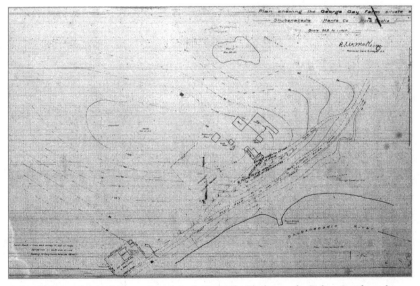

A hand-drawn sketch of the newly acquired site for the Shubenacadie Indian Residential School, which includes a portion of the Shubenacadie River, c. 1928. LIBRARY AND ARCHIVES CANADA/DEPARTMENT OF INDIAN AFFAIRS AND NORTHERN DEVELOPMENT FONDS/REEL C-8161

Reserve of some 1800 acres [730 hectares] is only 5 miles [8 kilometres] distant." For good measure, Gass suggested several other landowners—S. J. Etter, George Gay, Fred Etter, and Joseph Flemming—who had good locations worth considering.

Boyd passed the recommendation on to his superiors. Later that summer, J. L. Ilsley, the local Liberal MP, met with Orr, the architect, in Shubenacadie. Together they visited four potential sites for the school, including Fred Etter's and George Gay's farms as Gass had suggested. Gass's property wasn't in the running. They were looking for at least twenty hectares of good farmland with space for twenty healthy milk cows. (The cows would be milked and the milk drunk by the children or churned into butter.) The location also had to be close to the hospitals and not too far from the Archdiocese in Halifax. In the end Ilsley and Orr chose Gay's farm, about seven kilometres from Shubenacadie/Indian Brook First Nation. Its vegetable gardens and fertile fields abutted Snides Lake and Nova Scotia's largest river, the Shubenacadie, or in Mi'kmaw, *Sipekne'katik* or *Sikipne'katik*, "land of wild potatoes." The site would provide "ample opportunity for excellent drainage and water supply," Orr wrote in his report to Duncan Scott.

"I did not in any way influence or try to influence the decision," Ilsley wrote to Stewart. It was one of the few times in the early life of the school that Ilsley did not make specific recommendations on how to spend Indian Affairs's money. He did, however, advise against plans to hire Gay and his son to work on the farm until the school principal arrived because they were Conservatives: "I am inclined to think that any such arrangement would be undesirable from the political standpoint," he wrote. "The payment of government money to Conservatives is resented by Liberal workers in this province." Ilsley also took pains to say he supported the purchase of the Gay property despite the fact that it was "bitterly resented by...the leading man in our party in the district, who called me up last night and indulged in much menacing talk about the support I would lose next election." He concluded his letter by asking that he be consulted "in detail" about future property purchases and hiring for the school.

At this time, many farmers were eager to sell land and livestock, and the federal government was a reliable buyer. These were Ilsley's constituents; he also took pains to recommend several other service providers for the school, including providers of bedroom, dining room, and living room furniture, kitchen utensils, and dry goods. Gay's sixty-hectare farm and house was the best choice, they figured, in every way but one: its land wasn't as productive as the Etter farm. But it was less than a kilometre from the train station, which would save a fortune on the costs of moving hundreds of children, plus the staff, to and from the station over the years, and about seven kilometres from the Shubenacadie reserve.

Indian Affairs paid $11,000 for twenty-six cultivated hectares, twenty hectares of woodland, four hectares of pasture, and seven hectares of wetlands that could be used to make hay, and the farmhouse. The site also had easy access to electric—a twenty-four-hour service from Avon River Power Co.—and telephone hookups. It was an easy decision, being $2,500 cheaper than the only other viable option. On top of being closer to the train station, it also had better amenities, including a road. Although it was rumoured to flood on occasion, Orr asked around and found that "the road was flooded for an hour or two a day in the spring of certain years only, but that it was not impassable even when flooded." Eventually it must have posed a problem, because in January 1930, a month before children arrived, the school principal insisted that the Department of Highways of Nova Scotia bring in crushed gravel from its plant in Debert to fix the road, at a cost of more than $400—about half of what the job was actually worth.

Once the site was selected, Ilsley happily recommended R. W. McKenzie of Enfield to survey the site to ascertain acreage and elevations. He later recommended Stewart J. Etter of Shubenacadie be hired as resident farmer to lead the young boys working the fields. It is unclear whether they knew that they were digging at their ancestors. "At Shubenacadie, the Abanakees used to hold every year a ceremonial meeting," the Catholic Diocese of Nova Scotia wrote in its 1936 directory. "Here, fittingly enough, the Department of Indian Affairs decided to build a residential school for their descendants." It was, in fact, built over a sacred Mi'kmaw burial ground, which some say was why the school was cursed from the start.

THE BUILDING

Indian Affairs invited tenders in the spring of 1928 and immediately received a flood of unsolicited letters from companies offering their services in plumbing, refrigeration, barn building, well drilling, lightning-protection systems, coal supply, cream-separating equipment, and furniture supplies. Local businessmen were thrilled to have a new potential federal government customer in town. The Department chose a bid from the Rhodes Curry Company in Amherst, which promised a school "with all the modern convenience of a three-storey structure of brick and granite...spacious and well lit." As per Indian Affairs policy, it was the low price that got Rhodes Curry the job. Its bid of $153,000 was $790.50 lower than the runner-up, a Moncton company. Rhodes Curry was a reputable business with a four-decade history building train stations and mansions. On Ilsley's advice, Duncan Scott hired James Crowell of Windsor to inspect the company's work. During construction, which was delayed several times and eventually came in nearly $75,000 over budget, Crowell gave handwritten updates, always starting with, "Regarding the progress of the work I might say..."

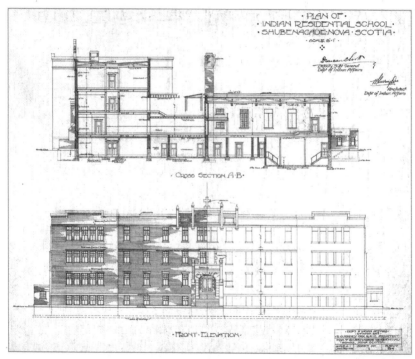

Architectural drawings for the school by Indian Affairs staff. LIBRARY AND ARCHIVES CANADA

The school was built at the highest point on the property, atop "quite an abrupt little hill," as the school's first principal, Father Jeremiah Mackey, put it. The hill began its descent toward the riverbank about twenty metres from the school, leaving little room for a lawn. There were no trees, opening the building to wind and rain from every direction, creating a whirlwind effect. For fifteen years, water would be pumped uphill from the lake seven hundred metres to the northeast of the school. Well water was hard and unpalatable but the lake was free of contaminants. A subcontractor, Canadian Fairbanks-Morse Co., installed an automated pump at the lake and a pump house halfway up the hill, four metres above water level. Getting water up to the school was a challenge. The architect, Orr, and the inspector, Crowell, wrote to Rhodes Curry several times on the subject. "It is very necessary that a water supply be put into that building before the ground freezes," Orr wrote in early November 1928. "We will appreciate an answer stating just

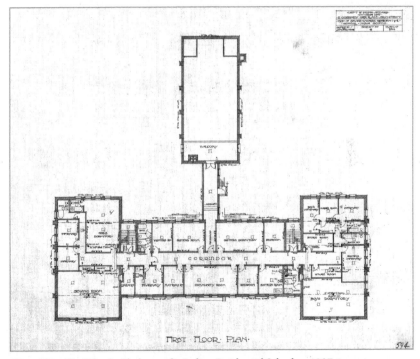

"First Floor Plan" for the Shubenacadie Indian Residential School, c. 1927. LIBRARY AND ARCHIVES CANADA/DEPARTMENT OF INDIAN AFFAIRS AND NORTHERN DEVELOPMENT FONDS/REEL C-8161

what your intentions are regarding water supply." Several months later, the company president, A. Curry, wrote to Orr saying that the building would not be completed on time because the granite trimmings and flooring he'd ordered were months late arriving. He blamed the Department for switching to a cheaper material after he'd already placed the order, forcing a delay as he reordered.

In the summer, when Rhodes Curry declared the school complete, Crowell completed a final inspection with Principal Father Mackey and reported that "the only finish the floors have received was a coat of linseed oil & gasoline mixed," applied unevenly. "Every strip seems to be a different shade." This report started a lengthy battle between Indian Affairs and Rhodes Curry, during which at least one law firm was engaged. Curry, the company president, argued that he hadn't budgeted on a "floor the same as a first class." He claimed that due to delays in the project "beyond our control," his company had made no money. "He seems to think this is a 2nd or perhaps a 3rd class job…as this school is only for Indians," Crowell concluded.

More importantly for the people who had to live in the building, the roof leaked. A roofer had come to fix it, but it would remain a problem for at least another three decades. Orr was brought in to do his own inspection

The school's exterior was glorious or ominous, depending on the viewer.
COLLECTION OF ELSIE CHARLES BASQUE, NOVA SCOTIA MUSEUM

in fall 1929, and he concurred that the floors had not been properly laid. Indian Affairs informed Rhodes Curry it was withholding the final payment until the floors were fixed. Curry wrote the Department again on Halloween demanding payment. The Department paid all but the last $1,000 owed. Finally, in the new year, Curry hired a lawyer, J. A. Hanway, to dog Indian Affairs for the final payment. Hanway argued that the Department had never specified the floors needed to be waxed. Seven months later, Indian Affairs still hadn't made the final payment. By this time the unfinished floors were being trampled daily by more than a hundred pairs of little feet.

In July 1930 Curry visited the building along with Mr. Dunn, the project foreman. "Father Mackey pointed out the bad places—there was only one—about four feet square in the Girls Play Room and one about the same size in the Dining Room," he wrote to Orr. He blamed wear and tear. "I have not seen a better concrete floor than what we have put in that building." But he agreed to go over the windows with a cement putty to reduce leakage. In the end, Indian Affairs paid Curry in full and the principal had to finish the floors with Hippo oil.

The press was thrilled with the facility. The *Halifax Chronicle* reported that it "rated as one of the best institutions of its kind in Canada." The Catholics called it a "striking, semi-fireproof edifice of brick and granite." Its accommodations for students and staff, they said, "leave nothing to be desired." The paper described the classrooms as "large, attractive, and well equipped" and noted the well-lit, airy devotional chapel for two hundred worshippers and a sanctuary furnished by friends and colleagues of the principal.

In fact it was the standard residential school design: a three-storey (plus a finished basement) brick and granite structure, forty-eight by twenty metres. The front door was ornate and appealing, but for the most part the building was a simple, inexpensive boarding school. In the basement were a playroom and three dining rooms (one each for the children, teachers, and male staff), laundry, and furnace rooms. The three classrooms, workshop, principal's office, chapel with grand crucifix, parlour room, kitchen, children's washroom, and principal's office were on the ground floor. Upstairs were dorm rooms—the boys' facing southeast and the girls' northwest—a sewing room, four classrooms, and student washrooms. And on the top floor were the Sisters' washrooms, bedrooms, and community room featuring a full-scale cross on the wall. Outside were two barns, a shed, cold storage, and outhouses.

The building was atop a windy hill. SISTERS OF CHARITY, HALIFAX, CONGREGATIONAL ARCHIVES

Many of the residential schools ended up burning to the ground. Like Shubenacadie, they were poorly constructed of cheap materials. Some even lacked fire escapes. But many were much older than the Shubenacadie building by the time they met their fiery fate. The Shubenacadie residential school nearly burned to the ground in the fall of 1936 after a fire started in the boiler room. A Sister knocked on Principal Father Mackey's door just before noon. He ran to the basement and was quickly joined by several older boys. They ran a hose down to the boiler room, but it had to take several sharp turns to get there and the water wouldn't go through. Mackey ran a second hose from the first floor straight through a basement window. Edward McLeod, the school's carpenter-engineer, went out to the pump house and cranked the second pump to its highest pressure. Still the hose wouldn't work.

Eventually the townspeople of Shubenacadie arrived with two RCMP officers, and started a hand-to-hand bucket brigade to douse the flames. But the fire had spread from the boiler room through cracks in the surrounding metal and had gotten into a wooden beam. They had to cut open the chapel floor to find and douse the slow burn. Mackey blamed the older boys for the fire. He said they made a habit of smoking in the boiler room. In his report to Indian Affairs, Mackey promised to check into things with the boys. It's unclear if he ever found satisfaction.

THE MEN IN CHARGE

FATHER MACKEY

The government couldn't run the schools without the churches, which provided administrative and teaching staff on the cheap. For the priests and nuns, working at Shubenacadie was to be a labour of love, part of their service to God. Other teachers expected competitive salaries and benefits suited to their education level, but Fathers and Sisters, having taken vows of poverty, were able to work on the minimal salaries offered by Indian Affairs.

In the summer of 1927, A. J. Boyd and architect R. Gurney Orr met with a committee appointed by the Archbishop of Halifax, Edward Joseph McCarthy, who was personally unavailable—his health had been failing and he would pass away a few years later after twenty-five years as archbishop. Monsignor MacManus of St. Mary's Cathedral led the Archdiocese committee. Boyd wrote to Duncan Campbell Scott saying the Archdiocese was eager to cooperate. Archbishop McCarthy waited until the next spring to appoint a principal. It was a difficult choice. The principal would be king of Shubenacadie. He would need to command the respect of the nuns who would teach there and the child-learners. Yet he needed the skills of an accountant and had to finesse a penny-pinching government department. He would have to be absolutely dedicated to the cause; the position offered few rewards. There would be no glory, no high society, no fine wines or delicacies. It would be a life of remote poverty and constant frustration.

McCarthy chose thirty-three-year-old Jeremiah Mackey, a dedicated priest from Springhill, Nova Scotia, a mining town of about five thousand residents and already famous for disaster. The Reverend Father from the small town had done well for himself, graduating St. Francis Xavier University in Antigonish and Holy Heart Seminary. He'd been an ordained priest for ten years, having worked as a curate in Annapolis for two years and at St. Mary's Cathedral, the second cathedral built in Halifax and the church's historic flagship of the province. He was described as a "slight man of medium stature," but he enjoyed boxing. Duncan Scott approved of the appointment, immediately sending the archbishop a letter saying he was impressed with Mackey, who he found to be a "youthful, energetic priest." In Scott's experience, the Catholics had always done a better job running residential schools. He asked Mackey to come live on the site before the school was built and to keep an eye on construction. He had high hopes for Mackey's administrative abilities, and he wouldn't be disappointed. "His zeal, energy and devotion to duty are unflagging," states the church's 1936 directory. "It is thanks chiefly to his administrative ability that the school enjoys the prosperity it does."

Mackey was the school's first and longest-serving principal, putting in well over a decade at the school. His low-paid administrative efforts were just short of superhuman. But what drove him? A 1939 *Halifax Chronicle* article called "Indian Boys and Girls Get Valuable Training at School at Shubenacadie" described Father Mackey as having humanitarian and democratic principles. "We don't know whether we are teaching them or they are teaching us," the principal said in the interview. In 1937 he stuck his neck out, recommending a Mi'kmaw teacher for a day school in Cape Breton. When the local Indian Agent refused to consider it, Mackey demanded angrily that the agent be fired. The teacher was not hired. The public perception of Mackey while he was principal—in the church, with government bureaucrats, and in the media—was of a man dedicated to his work because he loved the children. He was reported to be a kind man of gentle disposition.

The surviving wards of Shubenacadie's early years remember Father Mackey very differently, and many of his letters show he held the same contempt for the Mi'kmaq as so many other white men, believing them to be unreliable liars and con artists. He himself refused to hire Mi'kmaw men at the school. Isabelle Knockwood wrote that some of the boys called Mackey "Scratch" because he lit a match for his pipe with the seat of his pants, leaving a permanent scratch. But she also recalled that "Scratch" was one of Satan's nicknames. Some have called Mackey's time as principal a reign of terror, and many of the thirty survivors interviewed by the *Micmac News* in 1978 remembered him as a sadist who "loved to dish out punishment" simply because "he was that type of person."

The punishments were severe, ranging from beat downs that left life-long physical and emotional scars, to locking kids in one of two small closets—which the children called "the hole" or "the dungeon"—for days at a time. Some survivors recall that Mackey practiced "scourging," the term originally used to describe the beatings Jesus Christ took while carrying his cross to his own crucifixion. In Mackey's case, it involved taking a metre-long piece of polished horse harness, wrapping it around his wrist, and hitting children with it. Occasionally, people who didn't live at the school heard tales or saw signs of Mackey's viciousness. Donald Reid, who grew up near the school, told journalist Heather Laskey that after he reported some Shubenacadie boys throwing rocks, Mackey invited his father to "come up to the school to see how they know the way to beat things out of Indian children."

Mackey also used psychological torture, turning children against one another if he could. He forced boys to box against each other and if the one he liked less was winning, he would step in, put on the gloves, and hammer on the winner. Knockwood wrote of a time that Mackey, in front of a full classroom, threw a fat fist into the jaw of a fifteen-year-old boy, knocking him unconscious. Other survivors recall him doing the same to girls, sometimes using both fists, ordering his bloodied victims to get up again for more. The children watching cried and screamed. Sisters stood and watched in silence.

Several survivors have also accused Mackey of sexual assault, including raping boys. "I went up to Father Mackey's office and he penetrated me," one Elder told the Truth and Reconciliation Commission at Indian Brook. These allegations did not arise until long after Mackey's death in 1957, when the victims were mostly still young and the school was still open. Survivors never had a chance to confront Mackey, and he never had a chance to respond. But survivors of his reign as principal have never forgotten him. Many still have scars to remember him by.

BUREAUCRATIC STRUGGLES

The Shubenacadie residential school opened during hard financial times for Canada and for Indian Affairs in particular. Budget cuts were chronic.

Toward the end of its second year, the Department told Father Mackey it was cutting his budget by 10 percent. "With the Sisters receiving only three hundred a year, with ten days allowed for their retreat, to reduce their income seems absurd," Mackey responded. "For the past year there has not been any money spent by the Department for this school."

The Great Depression landed hard on Shubenacadie. Budget cuts were an annual event, predictable as Christmas carols. Sometimes Indian Affairs took away as much as 15 percent of the school's annual budget. But the churches lobbied against the Department until the cuts were completely reversed by 1939. Just in time for the Second World War, when the government quickly re-established the budget cuts as every resource was put toward the fighting in Europe. Generations of Shubenacadie's residents would suffer leaks and creaks, insufficient space, and worse as moisture built up between the walls, the floors and plaster warped, compromising the air quality.

Mackey needed to justify every expense not already covered in the annual budget. Approvals were unpredictable. In one request to Indian Affairs, Mackey explained why the school needed a forty-four-dollar attachment for the farm's manure spreader. The attachment was approved, along with replacements for seven sewing machines that had been in constant use for

In sewing class, children made their own clothes. LIBRARY AND ARCHIVES CANADA

eleven years (students made hospital gowns, pajamas, scarves, and sweaters for servicemen during the war), but his request to replace a twelve-year-old fridge was denied. At one point, toward the end of his term as principal, Indian Affairs surprised Mackey with a new car. His old one was notoriously in need of repairs, and the Sisters had joked about it in their school Annals. "Dear Phil," Mackey wrote by hand to Philip Phelan, the head of Indian Affairs's training division. "Just a line to thank you and to let you know the Ford has come. The first trip was out for blueberries, not to [*sic*] plentiful." Other years, the Department denied requests to have children's cavities filled, tonsils removed, or medicines provided. Indian Affairs couldn't be accused of overspending, but it certainly took better care of some of its wards than others.

The Department sent Mackey plenty of letters in return, including instructions on the running of the school. At first the information focused on his responsibilities to the children. There was little to indicate how cost-conscious he was expected to be. But when the cost of maintaining or repairing the building, or of various medical expenses, came up, Indian Affairs was quick to remind Mackey of its limited budget. It took him some time to get a handle on reporting every expense to the Department. His first accounts, once the school opened, were returned for being "full of errors." Duncan Scott sent Mackey a letter sternly reminding him that he was responsible for preparing a quarterly fiscal statement with receipts, and that there would be a monthly school inspection and annual audit of the books. Perhaps overreacting to earlier admonishments, in his first year running the fully operational school Mackey sent a request for a potato peeler and was informed, "It is not the policy of the Department to supply this type of equipment."

One of Father Mackey's first duties was the hiring of school staff members. Indian Affairs made it clear that staff should be from Hants County, where the school was located. His hires included a doctor (Dr. McInnis), farmer (Stewart Etter), assistant farmer (Mr. Parker), carpenter-engineer (Edward McLeod), and a night fireman. At least, they were his hires in theory. Indian Affairs policy said the churches would hire and supervise the staff and the Department would step in only if there was a problem. But for the most part, Duncan Scott asked J. L. Ilsley whom to hire and Father Mackey followed through on the MP's advice.

One such political appointee, Dr. D. F. McInnis, the school physician, arrived at the school to find it already populated by several dozen children who had not yet been examined. His job was to examine each child twice a year and do any minor surgeries they needed, but the pay did not impress him. "Your prices offered are contemptible," he wrote to Indian Affairs, "you must be taking me for a boob." Dr. McInnis compared the Department's offer to what an unskilled labourer might earn. He said that any decent general practitioner could do better, and wondered how they expected to get good doctors interested in "Indian work" at that rate. Regardless, Dr. McInnis took the job. Indian Affairs also employed a nurse who travelled the reserves and institutions with various medicines.

With staff in place, Mackey turned his attention to the farm. He'd assumed the new barn would be built long before the students arrived, but the Department had still not approved the budget eight months before the school was to open. In the meantime Mackey had given permission to a neighbouring farmer to use the dilapidated barn already on-site. Without a new barn forthcoming, Mackey lacked a place to store seventy-five tonnes of hay, plus potatoes, oats, and turnips from six hectares of harvested land. Mackey went ahead and had a new barn built, paying the labourers with his own wages. Then, hoping to catch Indian Affairs in the Christmas spirit, or at least a piteous mood, he asked for more money in December. "Please let us have more money," he wrote, "otherwise it is the poorhouse or jail for Yours Truly, Father Mackey."

Mackey also required a henhouse, hog house for twenty-five pigs, dairy house for twenty-five cows, tool shed with blacksmith shop and workshop, root cellar, and storage barn for flour and feed. He requested these in a single letter the month after the first children arrived. Indian Affairs responded, asking Mackey to prioritize the building needs as "only limited funds are available for improvements at your school this year." Mackey decided the root cellar and tool shed were most important—a lot of the potato and carrot crop had already gone bad—but, he said, "It would be very convenient to have a dairy. So I cannot say which is more urgent." He offered to buy flour and feed in small quantities. The children would go without eggs and milk. Mackey got his approval for the root cellar and tool shed and built them using lumber from the old barn. He had money left over and spent it on fixing leaks in the school building.

At the end of the school year, Mackey wrote another request to the Department for funds for the other buildings. T. R. L. MacInnes, the acting secretary of Indian Affairs, approved $1,000 to build a hog house and dairy. Mackey built a smaller hog house than planned, along with the ice house and the dairy. As usual, the older boys helped with the carpentry work to save money and to give them a learning opportunity. The buildings were far from satisfactory. For many years after the school opened, Mackey finagled small sums of money when he could to expand facilities, always relating his hopes of producing more food for the children. Most of his requests were denied or ignored.

At times Mackey made requests on behalf of his employees. When the carpenter-engineer, Edward McLeod, announced his engagement in 1930, Mackey asked for $2,500 to build the new family a cottage on school grounds. There had been a fire in Shubenacadie Village and no rental homes were available. A. F. MacKenzie, secretary of Indian Affairs, suggested the happy couple live in the school building. Mackey asked again in 1931 and then once more in 1933, calling the situation "very trying." Indian Affairs approved $3,500 for the house, but suggested Mackey use it instead for the pig barn, henhouse, tool shed, root cellar, and storage facility he'd asked for earlier. However, after an Indian Affairs official visited the school and reported back that, indeed, the house was needed because McLeod helped on the farm and did all the minor repairs, saving the Department a lot of money, Mackey finally got approval to build McLeod's house.

Mackey's relief didn't last long. A year later, in 1934, Mr. Parker, the assistant farmer, asked for a house at the school. Parker needed to be at the school farm for morning milking by 5:15 A.M., otherwise the boys would be alone in the barn. It had happened before, and "Needless to say that things do not go well," Mackey wrote. Parker had been renting a house three kilometres down the road, but the owner wanted to live there himself, and there were no other livable buildings nearby. But by this time the school building was leaking all over, and there wasn't the budget to deal with both problems, so Mackey requested funds to build a house for Parker and left the leakage for another year. Indian Affairs denied the request anyway, due to there being "no funds available...during the current fiscal year." The acting secretary advised Mackey to try again the next year. Mackey did so, and also asked for a budget for general repairs. Indian Affairs approved "$1,000 for a residence for the assistant farmer and $300 for general repairs." But as usual, it wasn't enough money to cover labour, even though Mackey had already explained that there were no boys that year big enough to help.

The school building continued to have problems. Mackey soon discovered that Rhodes Curry had used the cheapest, softest brick they could find, a brand called Bluenose facing bricks (provided by C. W. Stairs of Nova Scotia Clay Works Ltd). They leaked in the rain. Mackey and a building inspector climbed between the top-floor ceiling and the roof after a rainstorm and found no water coming in: it was going right through the wall. The leaks were damaging or destroying the plaster on every floor and seeping into the basement, causing damp spots. Mackey also found dampness around many of the windows. He and the Sisters had to put basins and towels under them to catch the drip. Mackey got a quote for having the exterior windows caulked—there were more than two hundred of them—and asked Indian Affairs for the money in two separate letters over a two-year span. There are no records of a response from the Department, and Mackey eventually took the money from another budget item.

On the advice of Indian Affairs's architect, Mackey hired Western Waterproofing Company in Montreal to fix the brick problem for $2,000. Orr inspected several other new buildings in Halifax that had had the same leakage problems, including the Nova Scotia Hotel, Bell Telephone Co., Capitol Theatre, Nova Scotia Light & Power Co., Bank of Montreal, and Moirs Factory. Western Waterproofing, which guaranteed its work for five years, was making a killing in Nova Scotia, thanks in part to Bluenose bricks. "Practically every brick building erected in the Province for the past twenty-five years has had the same trouble," Mackey would later write.

But none of these other buildings were on a high, exposed hill. Their leaks weren't as bad. Western's work on Shubenacadie failed within two years. When Dr. Thomas Robertson visited the school to assess its health for Indian Affairs in 1936, his report was mostly positive. But he noted the poor condition of the boys' rec room, which was "not a good example of the white man's standard of living to keep before the eyes of those Indian children." Robertson said that unless the problem was fixed right away it would lead to "irreparable damage" and "heavy expenditure." Indian Affairs responded to Robertson's report by granting Mackey $400 for repairs and improvements. But within two years the leaks were back, pouring in through the top windows during a cold rain. The problem would haunt the school all its days, with Indian Affairs steadfastly ignoring it all the while. Even more than a decade later, when the chief of Indian Affairs's training division joined the Sister Superior Mary Charles and Indian Agent Rice for a tour of the building, all the plaster on the upper floor was destroyed by ongoing leakage.

Corrosion in the pipes also gave Mackey fits. In 1934 a pipe burst after a January cold snap. There were many years when such problems left the building without hot water. This was the first time Mackey asked Indian Affairs to cover a repair bill. The work required "dies, vice, pipe-cutters, and three foot wrench," expensive tools he didn't have. The following year the pipes were clogged. They couldn't handle the pressure needed to pump water to upper floors. To have baths, the students had to lug hot water from the laundry room. Within another two years, the clogging was so bad that the girls' bathrooms weren't getting any water. The pipes were brittle and broke easily; they'd need to be replaced with new copper pipes.

Mackey also discovered that the pump and pump house installed by Canadian Fairbanks-Morse Co. wasn't working. It didn't seem to be powerful enough for the slope and distance the water had to travel. Mackey took a train to Fairbanks-Morse's Halifax office to meet the manager. While he couldn't explain why the pump wasn't working or how to fix it, the manager did write a sympathetic and critical letter to his head office counterpart in Montreal: "I understood Father Mackey to say that last winter he carried water for several months and they are almost entirely without fire protection," the manager wrote. "Father Mackey is an unusually fine type of man...it is something that you should have thoroughly investigated." But the school went without an effective water pump—relying solely on a smaller emergency pump—for more than a year before the Montreal office wrote Orr, the Indian Affairs architect, to say that the problem was two missing nuts. For several years Mackey went on taking older boys to the reserve to fetch water. Luckily the school would not experience a fire until years later.

One thing Mackey managed to get fixed quickly was the school's chimney. Soon after the children arrived, the cook made it clear the oven was no good. "A mad cook is not a pleasant animal," Mackey wrote. "Rice pudding and apple pies in the oven for three hours and not cooked is to say the least a bit provoking." Much worse was the gas that filled the kitchen. The solution was to build the chimney higher, a labourious and expensive task, to better catch a draft and fan the flames. For the sake of not gassing school residents, or perhaps to save Mackey from the cook, Indian Affairs promptly approved this request.

HEALTH CARE

A year before the children arrived, Mackey received a letter from E. L. Stone, director of medical services for Indian Affairs. Stone reminded Mackey that as principal he was the legal guardian of the children, even during summer vacations, and thus responsible for their welfare. He was to ensure that every child was vaccinated on arrival and to "resolutely refuse…any pupil who has tuberculosis in any form." TB had killed residential school children by the thousands already and embarrassed Indian Affairs. Stone told Mackey that above all else, "kindness, good feeding, good ventilation, vigilance against contagious diseases and tuberculosis, and last of all and least, medicine," were the secrets to healthy children. He recommended a diet of brown bread, fish, meat, cheese, and beans—plenty of protein.

But in the coming years, Indian Affairs failed to give Mackey the funds needed to meet his responsibilities, denying the children even basic dental care. Instead, the Department hired Dr. McInnis in March 1930 as school physician. He made $480 a year to do checkups on the children every six months, conduct all minor surgeries, and remain the physician on call. Each year McInnis gave Mackey a list of children needing glasses, dental work, x-rays, and tonsillectomies. McInnis was willing to do the tonsillectomies at $5 per child and provided his own operating table, something other doctors did not.

Mackey faithfully sent the lists to Indian Affairs. Twice a year he received a response from a secretary saying there was no money. "Our funds being extremely limited, it will not be possible…." In a good year, the Department would pay for the most urgent cases. Mackey was then supposed to contact parents of affected children for permission to conduct any surgeries. But in some cases this wasn't necessary. Really it was up to Mackey to decide. A dentist would then visit the school to do any fillings that were approved using "cheap material." If the children still had their baby teeth, the offending tooth was pulled; no point spending money to fill a temporary tooth. For the most part though, all dental work was denied.

McInnis usually completed the tonsillectomies and other minor surgeries at the school. It was a horrible experience for staff and students: setting aside the space, quarantining students, dealing with medical waste and curious children, and living with the anxiety that something might go wrong. Tonsillectomies disturbed the school day and night for at least a week. When Mackey complained, the Department responded by cancelling the surgeries altogether.

Keeping the school disease free was an impossible task in an overcrowded, drafty, leaky building. Despite warnings from the director of medical services and the Department's own rules against it, Mackey, Indian Agents, and Indian Affairs made matters worse by repeatedly admitting to the school children with tuberculosis, venereal, and other contagious diseases. Mackey and the Sisters were also sent children who were deaf, epileptic, and mentally or physically disabled. The principal and teachers were not trained in working with these special needs, and Mackey did all he could to send them away again. But those with infectious diseases usually went unnoticed until it was too late.

Only two months after Shubenacadie opened, five children under the age of twelve told the Sisters they were feeling very ill. McInnis examined them and diagnosed tuberculosis in each case. As the children lay in their beds, still in their shared dormitories, their white caregivers went half mad trying to figure out what to do with them. McInnis called the Nova Scotia Department of Public Health. On hearing the details, the Department said to send four of the children to a sanatorium to be treated, and to keep the other child for observation and study. McInnis checked with the NS Sanatorium in Kentville. They told him no, they could not take children under twelve. The Lourdes Sanatorium in Pictou *did* take very young children, but refused to take Indian children. McInnis called the Province again and was told to put the children "on the cure in a section of the school," and not to return them home.

The children stayed at the school in their own beds, though they were moved away from the other children. Indian Affairs was not impressed. A. S. Williams, the acting assistant departmental secretary, ordered Mackey to keep looking for an institution that would take the contagious children.

It took Mackey another two months to convince the Kentville sanatorium to help, and in the end they took only the two worst cases. When Mackey told the Department the good news, he received an angry letter criticizing him for letting tuberculosis into the school. Strangely, the letter reminded the principal of their policy of sending sick children home. Mackey did just that, in one case, two months later. The last two children with tuberculosis got better at the school. More than a decade after Peter Bryce's exposé on tuberculosis and the Indian population, little had changed. The disease was still running rampant on reserves and was common among children. Dr. J. Blecker of the Children's Hospital in Halifax wrote on one prospective student's medical report, "the only Indian child I have ever had under my care free from tuberculosis."

During the winter of the school's second year there was an outbreak of mild flu. McInnis was not called in but wrote to say the children probably caught it from visiting parents, although the first cases were in children who had not had visitors. In March, a Sister fell sick with scarlet fever and three children were diagnosed with syphilis. McInnis wanted to give every child a blood test. A. F. MacKenzie wrote to the Nova Scotia provincial health officer asking them to provide blood tests. He offered a "nominal fee" of fifty dollars. MacKenzie assumed the Province would provide use of its labs for free as it had done in the past. He also hoped the Province would provide access to free treatment for any child testing positive for syphilis.

Having not received an answer, MacKenzie offered the $50 to McInnis, who accepted but wanted $5 per treatment in addition. Mackey went ahead and paid McInnis $10 for the first treatment of two of the first three cases, but many treatments were required for each case. "It would cost $120 per child for three months treatment," Mackey wrote to the Department, "which is two thirds of what you are allowing for their full years keep." Mackey had to request permission for this expense, but there is no response on record. A month later, four children came down with enlarged glands due to bacterial infections and there was another case of scarlet fever. McInnis sent three children to the Victoria General Hospital in Halifax, which was a common occurrence.

McInnis saw at least twenty-five children with syphilis that year. When Mackey reported the outbreak, a senior bureaucrat at Indian Affairs replied that Shubenacadie was "a good place to have it." More than a decade later, when five children got sick with diphtheria despite Indian Affairs's vaccine program, McInnis placed the whole building under quarantine for a month. No one could visit or leave.

Early in the 1932–33 school year, Mackey, frustrated by constant struggles over funding for minor but necessary medical treatments, wrote a flippant letter to the Department wondering what was the point of doing checkups twice a year if there was never money to pay for tonsil and dental procedures. To his surprise, Indian Affairs agreed. Checkups would now happen only once a year. In the fourth year Mackey grew desperate and offered to pay for the medical work from the school's regular budget. He took the money from travel expenses, meaning fewer students would go home for the summer. Indian Affairs allowed it and didn't fund any tonsillectomies, glasses, or dental work, for another three years. In his May 1936 denial of tonsil and dental work, Secretary MacKenzie wrote that the Department "would be pleased to [provide the work], except that your pupils had the advantage of very considerable work of this kind last fall." At Shubenacadie, seven children had mucous coming out of their ears because of infected tonsils; some had rotten teeth and couldn't chew. But other schools had been waiting longer.

Tuberculosis hit the school again in the late spring of 1938, when McInnis diagnosed a girl with an active case and Mackey immediately asked to send her to the NS Sanatorium because she had no home. Indian Affairs approved, but reminded Mackey that Doctor McInnis should have used the proper form for medical examinations to keep her from entering the school in the first place. The following school year, nine new children arrived. One boy complained that his neck was sore. Soon a gland in his neck was discharging. McInnis was called in to examine him. "Evidently someone has mistaken our Residential School for a TB sanatorium," he wrote. "Please arrange with the Department for his removal." In this instance, the Indian Agent had actually followed guidelines and sent a signed application form with a medical, which clearly noted that the boy had tuberculosis. But Indian Affairs had admitted him to Shubenacadie, where no one knew of his illness. Regardless, the Department instructed Mackey that the boy "should be disposed of in accordance with the regulations for disposal of tubercular Indians." The policy was to have a room available for infectious cases. Mackey reported that the boy responded well and his gland stopped discharging.

However, when the boy came down with a bronchial infection immediately afterward Mackey wrote to Nova Scotia Public Health. He received no answer. As winter set in, the boy caught a cold and bronchitis. A Sister sent him to see McInnis, who sent him on to the Victoria General. The VG refused to take him because he clearly had active tuberculosis. The doctor there wanted to transfer the boy to the Sanatorium in Kentville. However, the Sanatorium would only take the boy if Indian Affairs reassured them that the Department would cover the expense. In November McInnis finally sent the boy to a Halifax hospital, where it was confirmed he had active TB and should be at the Sanatorium. To send him there, Mackey still needed the permission of Indian Affairs. The boy stayed in Halifax until he died ten days later. His admission to the school had been "a clear error such as sometimes occurs in the best organizations," Indian Affairs's medical director E. L. Stone wrote several months later in reviewing the case. McInnis was incensed. He wrote of his frustration to Father Mackey, saying, "The Department forgot this was…not a tuberculosis sanatorium," adding that every Maritime province was shipping "all the advanced tuberculosis cases and syphilitics" to Shubenacadie.

THE DEATH OF JOSEPHINE SMITH

In the summer of 1933 there was a long exchange between Father Mackey, Dr. McInnis, the Victoria General Hospital, and Indian Affairs over Josephine Smith. The twelve-year-old girl had been sent to hospital in March with a ruptured appendix, and died after surgery, when she was "attacked by pneumonia." Letters show animosity between Mackey and McInnis, who at times seem to have forgotten they were arguing about a dead young girl. They rightly blamed each other for various mistakes and failings, and both bore some of the blame for her unnecessary death. Mackey in particular could have done more for her by acting quickly and with greater concern. But McInnis was likely complaining less out of compassion and more out of bitterness over the loss of income he'd suffered when Indian Affairs cut the frequency of medical checkups in half. Dr. McInnis angrily accused Indian Affairs of trying to cover up the school's neglect of an obviously very sick little girl, and demanded an investigation.

Father Mackey described a long angry phone call from McInnis, accusing the principal of cheating him out of fifty dollars—the amount he was paid every six months for examining the students—until Mackey had inadvertently convinced Indian Affairs to reduce examinations to only once each year; instead, the Provincial Tuberculosis Clinic would examine the school. Mackey in turn accused McInnis of trying to compensate himself at the taxpayers' expense.

Of Josephine Smith, Mackey wrote that during a month when many children suffered from colds, "We had no reason to think that her condition was any more serious." She was vomiting and a Sister put her to bed, thinking it might be appendicitis. McInnis was due the next morning and Josephine would be his first priority. But the doctor showed up half an hour late, Mackey said. McInnis examined her and said it was indeed a bad appendix. He wanted to send her to a hospital in Truro by car, a half hour's drive, but Mackey overruled him, saying they would wait until late afternoon for the next train to Halifax. The surgery to remove the now gangrenous appendix didn't take place until midnight, and Josephine died late the next morning. "I am sure of this that were Josephine Smith my own sister I could not under the same circumstances do any more for her," Mackey wrote. He then reminded the Department of the school's excellent annual health inspection results.

Indian Affairs's director of medical services, Dr. E. L. Stone, responded to Mackey's report by requesting the clinical report on Josephine Smith from the Victoria General Hospital. The VG obliged with a letter detailing the events of her death, of post-surgical pneumonia brought on by her cold. A. S. Williams, acting deputy superintendent general at Indian Affairs, wrote to Mackey saying his investigation confirmed Mackey's version of events. "I think it only right, however," he wrote, "to say that when an Indian pupil in a residential school falls sick the principal is wise in promptly calling in medical advice if such is available." Williams wrote to Dr. McInnis the same day. "If the Department has any further observation to make in this matter," he said, "it is that it would have preferred to have been informed of the facts of the case at once rather than at some three months after the event."

Dr. McInnis fired back with an angry letter to the Department, accusing it of a cover-up and a complete disregard for the health of its wards. "The statement that [she] died of pneumonia is absolutely false," he wrote. He demanded an inquiry and threatened to take the matter to Parliament, saying that those in charge of a school where such negligence occurred weren't "fit people to be in charge..." "It is amusing to me to note," he continued, "what length a Government Department will go to cover up the Criminal Negligence of one of its employees."

Dr. Stone, director of medical services, responded to McInnis a week later. "The Department has no desire to prevent any reasonable investigation or conceal any of the facts," he wrote. He then reminded McInnis that while everyone agreed Josephine Smith had appendicitis, the hospital report was clear that the actual cause of death was peritonitis caused by pneumonia. "It is extremely regrettable that this child should have died but...it is doubtful, in the Department's opinion, if any Departmental investigation could reveal any facts not already disclosed." Stone closed the matter with an August 21 memo to his superiors: "It is not so very uncommon for a member of a private family to have appendicitis which goes on to peritonitis and death," he said, "without anyone clearly recognizing the condition."

The case was not further investigated and didn't go to Parliament, but a year later McInnis was still angry. He wrote again to Indian Affairs complaining about another child's death at the school. "It is futile to report these cases to the Department as they probably feel as [Mackey] does that they go to Heaven and that it is not worthwhile trying to keep those poor Indian children alive." He wrote another letter complaining that in general children at the school were neglected and ill treated.

WITHIN REASON

Corporal punishment was the norm in most public schools of the time, and Indian Affairs officially endorsed it at day schools and residential schools, within reason. The Department didn't clarify what "within reason" meant, however, until 1947, when it released a guide on proper strapping. Survivors recall Mackey and several of the nuns who taught there crossing the line regularly. Even when the school was open, testimony from some children to the RCMP and at a public inquiry condemned the rampant abuse at the school. Duncan Scott only said that it was his department's duty to protect its wards from being mistreated. They were not inmates of a prison, he pointed out.

Yet Scott consistently ignored reports of brutal abuse in residential schools across Canada, including the rape and impregnation of female students by priests. He would follow the same procedure with Shubenacadie, as would all of his successors at high levels in the Department. Most often, the church would be asked to investigate its own people when they were accused of abuse.

The Department preferred to keep these things private rather than inflame unpredictable public opinion. While the general public liked the idea of assimilation via residential schools, child abuse crossed the line. Moreover, Indian Affairs needed the churches to make the system work, and no one wanted to offend them. The common tactic, which Father Mackey often practiced with expertise, was to attack the character of whistle-blowers. They were either disgruntled staff persons—hysterical women usually—or typical troublemaking Indians who didn't understand what was good for them. Rarely were complaints investigated, even in the many cases when Indian Affairs staff flagged them as beyond normal discipline. Reassurances from the principals of residential schools were generally sufficient to file the matter away, or in some cases to remove the complaint from the files.

Father Mackey's discipline made the news in June 1934 after nineteen boys were beaten, shaved, and starved for stealing fifty-three dollars from a cash box in the Sister Superior's office which they spent on treats and toys before giving the rest to friends. Mackey enlisted an RCMP constable to interrogate the boys he suspected. Nobody confessed, so Mackey beat them all. He had the school handyman make him a leather strap with seven knotted tails. Mackey whipped the boys' bare backs until he was tired, then had the handyman take over. He beat them so long and hard that one of the tails fell off and two hung so loose that he pulled them off. The RCMP constable and Mackey observed. Mackey then took away the boys' eating privileges for five days.

A few of the boys managed to run away to tell the local Indian Agent, Allison MacDonald. MacDonald wrote to the Department and somehow the complaint went public. An opposition MP even questioned the superintendent general of Indian Affairs about the incident in Parliament after reading about it in the news. Indian Affairs responded by creating an inquiry on the matter, presided over by seventy-eight-year-old retired judge L. A. Audette. Isabelle Knockwood found in her archival research that Audette came onto the case with some experience with the Mi'kmaq. In 1915 he "was in charge of the Exchequer Court when it forced the Mi'kmaq off the Kings Road Reserve in Sydney…to increase the assessment value of the land." Audette had a clear perspective on the matter: "No one cares to live in the immediate vicinity of the Indians," he said, calling the reserve "a clog in the development of that part of the city."

Mi'kmaq from the Shubenacadie reserve and locals from Shubenacadie Village came out en masse to watch the inquiry, filling the local Oddfellows Hall and spilling outside. The press followed them and reported that the Indians gave the inquiry a "picturesque touch." The two Sisters of Charity nuns testifying on behalf of Father Mackey also added visual pizzazz. Despite medical experts testifying that months after the whipping seven of ten boys examined still had blue marks on their backs nearly eight centimetres wide, Audette let Mackey and the handyman off the hook in his fifty-four-thousand-word report, and the *Halifax Chronicle* cheered the judge and Mackey on in an editorial, calling the boys "mischief-makers" and mocking the idea of holding a Crown inquiry for a few malcontents. "Those administering the Dominion's school at Shubenacadie may continue their splendid work among the Indians of the Maritime Provinces," it concluded. Audette's reasoning was that corporal punishment was good for society. "Reading the biography of the big men who molded the destiny of the British nation, we invariably find a reference to these corrective punishments," he wrote. He also described Aboriginal peoples as "children having human minds just emerging from barbarism."

Several months later the Sisters and Father Mackey celebrated the "vindication of the Indian School staff." One Sister copied by hand in the Sisters of Charity Shubenacadie Indian Residential School Annals, verbatim, a story from *The Casket* newspaper in Antigonish about Mackey's exoneration. The story was unusual in that the reporter had interviewed some of the boys, describing them as "noble children of the forest." The Indian Agent, it said, "'bayed the moon' at the treatment given his innocent charges," and reporters "became more than usually incoherent as they played up the situation." But like the *Halifax Chronicle*, *The Casket* "commended and congratulated" Audette on saving an innocent man from punishment.

FATHER MACKEY'S DEPARTURE

The official records, contrary to the memories of many survivors, note sadness all around when Father Mackey left the school in 1943. The day of his departure "dawned much as the day of a funeral might dawn." It had been a tough year at the school. In the summertime, two fifteen-year-old girls from New Brunswick drowned in Snides Lake. Although many children died at Shubenacadie over the years, these deaths seemed to shake up the teachers and principal more than most.

Mary Ginnish and Doris Atquin had gone strawberry picking after lunch with a group of twenty kids, broken into smaller groups of two to four. After filling their buckets, Ginnish and Atquin found an old boat upside down by the shore. It was irresistible fun. They took off their shoes, dropped their buckets, and hauled the boat into the water—not knowing it was full of holes. They rowed out a ways before the water swamped them. They didn't know how to swim. It was near supper when the other kids headed back to the school with their own buckets full. They saw the buckets and shoes. The boat had washed back ashore into some water lilies. No one had heard or seen a thing. They ran back to tell the Sisters. Father Mackey called the police, who found the bodies four hours later. According to the RCMP report, school authorities had neglected to remove an obvious danger. The next day Mackey and the Sisters took the students to the train station with the bodies. The train took them home. "God in his mercy...overlooked their childish disobedience or forgetfulness," a Sister wrote in the school's Annals. There had also been a diphtheria epidemic that killed a boy, and three escape attempts in the extreme cold weather by poorly clothed children. "God was generous with His Graces in the form of sickness and worry," another Sister wrote in the Annals.

All these things weighed heavy on Mackey's heart. And his gut. The now forty-three-year-old became very ill with a chronic stomach condition, and possibly depressed. He spent several nights in hospital. "Finally just home from the hospital he was unfortunate enough to meet the doctor, on the doorsteps of the school," Indian Agent Rice wrote, "come out with a child on a stretcher." At that moment, Mackey decided on something he'd been considering for some time. He hurried inside to his office and wrote his resignation. "I have not been well," he wrote. "Some of my years there were really enjoyable and we had smooth sailing, and others were tough going."

Mackey expressed mixed feelings of relief and regret in taking a position with a small church in Parrsboro, doing light parish work. Agent Rice wrote in his 1943 year-end report that "this centralization project lost...a good friend and an experienced advisor...We here at the agency and all of Shubenacadie were sorry to see him go but we feel that due to his health the step he took was necessary." But there are rumours that Mackey did not leave willingly. One survivor told student researcher Kathleen Kearns in 1990, "Father Mackey was asked to resign by the Archdiocese due to reports of physical assault made by angry parents," or perhaps charges of neglect related to the drowning of the two girls. Mackey's health recovered, and in 1946 he moved on to an Amherst parish, where he was promoted to dean, an advisor to the bishop. Pope Pius XII further bestowed on him the title of Monsignor, recognizing his service to the church.

GOOD FATHER BROWN

In 1944 the children quietly celebrated the end of Father Mackey's reign of terror, when Father J. W. Brown of Cumberland County took over. "Good Father Brown...loves the Indians and is dearly loved by them," a Sister wrote in the Annals. He was familiar with the school before taking the job there, having visited in 1940. "Their great tribute is thus worded, 'Father Brown is so kind,'" the Sister continued. "This simple sentence speaks much in the Indian's way of expression." "He is a favourite of all children regardless of color or creed," added H. C. Rice, Indian Agent for the Shubenacadie reserve. "[He] will have more trouble with ration coupons and pedigrees than managing 160 children. He too is a backer of the centralization idea and will do all in his power to help and speed the project along." On the whole, survivors of the school remember Father Brown in a much more positive light than they do Father Mackey. He covered his walls with pretty, inviting pictures and was seen as a kind old man. In his letters to Indian Affairs, Brown wrote of the students as though he was fond of them.

Brown came to the school with a good reputation. He had been Agent Rice's parish priest in Kentville, and had also served in Enfield. "His knowledge of the Cambridge Indians is extensive," Rice wrote. Brown was known to like the people he often referred to collectively and individually as the "poor Indian." Brown took the job when he was sixty-three, twenty years older than Father Mackey. Immediately Indian Agents worried about his age. They wrote to the Department at various times that the Sisters were taking on a larger workload to make up for what Brown couldn't do. He had a heart condition, they noted.

Like Father Mackey before him, Brown struggled with the upkeep of the building. He too tried to solve the draft and leakage problems, and seemed to have more success spending money on these issues—possibly because several of the school's systems failed at around the same time. In February 1944 Brown wrote Indian Affairs requesting a new washing machine, repeating Mackey's request of four years earlier, a tractor—the horses being old and crippled—a new roof, and new pipes. Indian Affairs resisted the washing machine request without denying it, saying he'd waited until too late in the school year. Brown responded by mailing them wood pulp that'd once been the washing machine's slats. He got his new machine within two months.

But Brown was more worried about the fifteen-year-old pipes, which had been a problem at least since 1933 and were beyond repair. He'd dug up thirty-eight metres of them and found pea-sized holes all through them. That explained the water pressure issues. The lake water was mineral rich and ate through the cheap material. A report by the Department of Mines and Resources recommended Indian Affairs install cast iron pipes as soon as the ground thawed, at a cost of $5,000. But more than a year later Brown reminded the Department that "thousands of feet of piping through the building…is in poor condition, and should be renewed with some other more resisting pipe." There is no record of a response to this letter.

The Department took more interest in the roof, telling Brown to repair it using existing school funds rather than replace it. But Indian Affairs changed its mind by the fall, when it wrote asking him to "take an amount of $3000 from your credit balance" to replace it. Brown objected. "The cost…was to have been paid from 'House Money' the savings in seventeen years by Father Mackey and Sisters," he wrote. "May I suggest that it is a Capital expenditure…" meaning Indian Affairs should pay for it. But it would be another year before any work was done. "Our roofing repairs are being carried on as directed," he wrote in October 1945. "We hope to have a waterproof building, and can begin the interior repairs to ceilings and walls brought on by years of delay in undertaking the present repairs."

In 1945 Brown bought the school's first radio and record player for the music class. He also had all the window casings replaced, spent $15,000 to fix the plumbing and heating, put in a new boiler, and replaced the pumps. The school had to sell a war bond to cover half of these costs. "All went well for a week, and then we lost the water, and have had to draw it for every house service for nearly a month," he wrote near Christmas. The only solution was new pipes, and moving the pump down to the lake—where it should have been in the first place—instead of halfway up the hill. "May I respectfully suggest that this work of replacement may simply not be set aside, cared for in the Spring, or 'The Dept.' has not enough funds to care for such costs,'" Brown wrote with a sense of snark that Mackey wouldn't have dared. It didn't help. The new pipeline from the school to the lake was not approved until two years later.

Less than a year after the roof repairs, Agent Rice reported to Indian Affairs that the building was still leaking. Water came in through the windows and bricks. The pipes were about to burst. Rice recommended sending a qualified inspector to find a way to heat the building without destroying the pipes. The inspector came eight months later, in the dead of winter, but the inspection got things rolling. "Arrangements are being made to treat the outside walls in order to prevent further seepage of water," Indian Affairs wrote Rice. But the pipe problem inside the school proved a higher priority, and waterproofing would have to wait until the spring of 1948. In the meantime, Indian Affairs denied a seemingly more affordable request for 150 new blankets to replace the nearly twenty-year-old originals. "When Indian residential schools are first established the Department supplies blankets but it has not been our practice to supply replacements," an official wrote.

Brown struggled to keep on top of numerous smaller challenges with the school buildings and grounds. He needed a new cooling unit for the walk-in refrigerator—food was regularly spoiling—an employee's house needed $500 of urgent repair, the sinks were leaking, the root cellar needed a new roof, and the sewage was backed up from an obstruction three metres from the building. In addition to his duties, Brown found time to buy, for himself, two two-hectare plots adjoining the school property. The farmer and the older boys used these to grow produce, and Brown charged Indian Affairs $75 to use his land.

Also, at a time when Indian Affairs was becoming less interested in the schools and increasingly cost-conscious, Brown was determined to make an example out of any runaway. As he tried to bring back four boys who'd hopped a train and had been thrown off in Wolfville, the Department told him not to worry. The bureaucrats there fretted over the high cost of paying the RCMP to bring the boys back, but when Father Brown heard through the grapevine that one of the boys had moved to Portland, Maine, to work with his father at Maritime Shipyards, he made plans with Portland police to bring the boy back to New Brunswick. Brown wanted to charge the boy with stealing his school uniform and offered to pay the transportation costs, but Indian Affairs forbade it.

Despite warnings from the Department, Brown kept up his vigilance with runaways. He'd lost a boy to industry in the United States, but he was determined to make an example of the boy's fifteen-year-old sister. She ran away on a cold night in February. Four days later, when she was caught five kilometres from the school, Brown sent her to the Good Shepherd Reformatory in Saint John, New Brunswick. The next summer, when a thirteen-year-old boy ran away, Brown asked the RCMP to use a police dog—a German shepherd named Chips—to hunt him down. The dog caught the scent quickly and followed the boy until he surrendered. That fall, a ten-year-old boy reached Halifax by train on his second runaway attempt. RCMP officers found him there and turned him in to the Saint Patrick's Home. He was the last runaway on record from Shubenacadie.

In 1947 Brown had a seizure. Indian Affairs, via the Catholic Archdiocese, asked him to retire. He was saddened, but did as he was asked. He'd been hoping to stay on at the school until his seventieth birthday. Instead, he finished the 1947–48 school year.

"No one could show a more fatherly interest in the Indians," the director of Indian Affairs wrote Archbishop McNally when Father Brown retired. "He has endeared himself to these people and has always been their champion." The Sisters expressed sorrow. "A very definite feeling of sadness pervades the house as our dear Father Brown shares a hard obedience," one wrote in the Annals. He visited twice after he retired, first in October 1948; he told the Sisters "old stories oft told but never losing their interest." His last visit was in 1951, three weeks before he had a second stroke and died.

THE TEACHERS

"GOD BLESS YOU" RINGING IN THEIR EARS

Early one cold morning in late January 1930, three Sisters of Charity nuns—having already completed their 5:00 A.M. morning mass, extensive prayers, and chores—gathered their bags, and said goodbye to the other Sisters and Mother Mary Louise and all her "mellow wisdom, calm judgment, quick observation, and wide experience," her "gleam of genial humor." The Sisters were leaving behind their beloved mother house by the sparkling Bedford Basin and the most beautiful chapel in Canada, with its twelve pillars and twenty-seven windows amply lighting the stunning *Our Lady of the Immaculate Conception* painting and arched ceilings. The younger Sisters were graduating from a sheltered six years as novices at the mother house. They didn't know the real world yet.

With a "loving God Bless You ringing" in their ears, the three Sisters headed from the mother house in Rockingham to the new white limestone, high-arching-ceiling train station opposite Cornwallis Park, downtown Halifax. It was always bittersweet parting for a new assignment, leaving others behind but headed for divine fulfillment. While their backgrounds and motivations for becoming nuns varied, an educated woman at this time was unlikely to find such fulfilling work outside the church. She'd be expected to settle down with a man and keep house while he pursued more intellectual work. With the Sisters, at least she could get an education and have the chance to fulfill a calling, do a social good, without being any man's woman. She might even get a chance to work on overseas missions, see more of the world.

But these three Sisters, and another three who would meet them at the school the next week—the original six included Sisters Madeline Leo Buchanan, Mary Louisita Flynn, Mary Etienne Beaulieu, Jean Berchmans de Coste, Mary Brendan McBride, and Philomena MacEachern—were headed for a less exotic destiny. They were going to rural Nova Scotia to do "Indian work." It wasn't exciting or glorious, but it was their sacred duty and it was teaching; it was what they were trained to do. And, it was an adventure in its own way, a chance to do a social good without fighting tropical illnesses or mosquitoes or time changes. "Why long for the Foreign Missions when souls need us right here?" one Sister wrote. Mother Mary Louise chose the Sisters from whoever was available at the mother house at the time and had teaching qualifications. There was no screening beyond that, no interviews about attitudes to the assignment or toward the Mi'kmaq or indigenous cultures in general. They were not asked how well they dealt with stressful situations. No love of children was required. Indeed, the Sisters were discouraged from getting too close to the children. They were Sisters of Charity and they went where they were assigned. Cheerfully.

The first three Sisters travelled sixty-five kilometres north to join Father Mackey at the new Indian residential school. They were the first of ninety-one Sisters of Charity nuns who would work at Shubenacadie over the next thirty-seven years. Their ages varied, but most were in their late forties. The majority would work in administrative capacities, or doing cleaning and cooking. Some would be "disciplinarians," in charge of the boys' or girls' dormitory. And some would teach. Each Sister would receive $300 a year—more a stipend than a wage. The Sisters later welcomed Anita Vincent Costello, who would be Sister Superior at the school. (She was supposed to have been on the train with them but had been in a car accident. Luckily she was okay.) A week later another Sister joined them, bringing with her the unusual cargo of cows for the farm. The nuns made a game of "counting the cows as they passed the kitchen window," a Sister wrote. There were sixteen cows in all.

Whatever they thought of their assignment, the Sisters sometimes waxed poetic at the school's setting. "What a friendly river!" one Sister wrote in their school Annals, even as it flooded and threatened to put the building under water. "It kept rising and rising and rising and coming nearer and nearer and nearer on all sides, until we were surrounded with the approaching waters of the beautiful Shubenacadie...." They watched from their windows and prayed until the waters went down again. Twenty-four years later, in the final years of the school, a Sister wrote approvingly of new renovations to the building. "Some of the older children should have liked to have stayed here for the summer," she said, because the school was so much improved.

On February 5, 1930, the final two Sisters brought with them, from the Halifax orphanages also run by the Sisters of Charity, the first thirty children to attend the Shubenacadie Indian Residential School. There were ten girls from the Home of the Good Shepherd on Quinpool Road, six boys from Saint Patrick's Home on Mumford Road, and six girls and eight boys from St. Joseph's on Quinpool Road, which had recently been expanded to add an auditorium, ventilated dorm rooms, and play areas because the children and teachers had long been confined to the basement. Two "big flat sleds each drawn by two large farm horses" picked up the two nuns and thirty kids from the train station. The Sisters had no time to settle in; they had to get the children fed and in bed. Classes began the next day.

SISTERS OF SHUBENACADIE

When Nova Scotia Indian Superintendent A. J. Boyd and Department architect R. Guerney Orr met with the Catholic Archdiocese in Halifax in the summer of 1927, one open question was who would teach at the school. Monsignor MacManus, acting on behalf of Archbishop McCarthy, recommended the Sisters of Charity of Saint Vincent de Paul. They were a missionary organization and congregation whose Sisters had been teaching in Nova Scotia schools—including Indian day schools—and shaping the public education system since 1849. They also ran several orphanages. Lore has it that an orphan appeared on the Sisters' Barrington Street door the day after their arrival in Halifax from New York. They took the babe in, of course, and never looked back.

After the meeting, MacManus, Boyd, and Orr drove straight to Mount Saint Vincent on the Bedford Highway to meet Mother Mary Louise. She called together her council, the leaders of the congregation, to meet them. "Their institution and the Sisters we met made a very favourable impression and they, too, seemed quite eager to go into Indian work," Boyd wrote.

"The Mother General of the Order is at present in Western Canada and she and her staff arranged to visit the Blood Indian Residential School, to get firsthand information concerning its conduct."

The request was a formality. Mother Mary Louise knew it came with the support of Archbishop McCarthy. Whatever he asked of the Sisters, they would do. An unofficial part of a nun's duty was to hold priests in reverence—they were placeholders for God Himself. Even if she disagreed with a priest, bishop, or any other superior, a nun learned the value of suffering powerful fools quietly, acceptingly, and faithfully. An archbishop's request would never be denied. But it was a time of great expansion for the Sisters as well. The Shubenacadie Indian Residential School was just one of nineteen new endeavours for the congregation under Mary Louise's first six years of leadership, from 1926 to 1932. Fourteen of these were schools. In all, under Mother Mary Louise, the Sisters started eighty-six new missions in three decades, including another Indian residential school in Cranbrook, BC, in 1936. The Sisters sometimes called her the "Mother of Missions." Orr left his blueprints to the Sisters for review, and Mary Louise followed due process, meeting a few weeks later with her full council, which officially accepted the archbishop's request. It seemed like a good idea anyway—teaching and ministering to poor Indians was part of what they did.

THE SISTERS' BUILDING

Mother Mary Berchmans, the vicar general for the Sisters of Charity, sent the school blueprints back to the architect with comments in November 1927. The Sisters had made several recommendations, some large and some small. Having wash tables in the dorm rooms would be unsanitary, they said. They should be moved to the bathrooms, which would need to be bigger. The fire escapes should be moved from the staff rooms to the dorms, which also needed closets added. Storage room in general seemed to be lacking. The school needed a workshop and home ec room so the boys could learn trade skills—and how would the girls learn homemaking? They foresaw the need for cold storage and hot water in the upper bathrooms. And they wanted their own rooms, rather than a single communal dorm for the Sisters. Of the Sisters' many suggestions, Indian Affairs considered moving the fire escapes, adding a bathroom, and splitting the Sisters' dormitory into three separate bedrooms. Rhodes Curry estimated the changes would cost $1,580 to implement. "That is hot and cold water in seven bedrooms and a bathroom for the Sisters," the site inspector, James Crowell, wrote. The Department ignored the Sisters' suggestion to provide separate accommodation for male staff members; Father Mackey spent years rectifying the oversight.

The dozens of Sisters at the school over the following decades worked long, hard hours and rarely had days off. They had an annual retreat, but otherwise stayed put. At the school they kept the same strict routine they had as novices: up early for intensive prayer, chores and housework, a little teaching, more chores and housework, and more prayer. They had many, sometimes competing, loyalties: God, the church, the congregation, their Mother Superior, and the mother house at Mount Saint Vincent. It was a hard assignment, being sent far from the city and the libraries where they were used to studying and pursuing intellectual interests. It was far from comfort, yet seemed to lack the learning opportunities associated with work overseas. They were expected to live a pious life cheerfully, under a vow of poverty. But, while a good Sister of Charity would never complain, caring for orphaned and sometimes "delinquent Indians" at a dreary residential school was not the choicest of jobs. Daniel Paul remembers a young nun

The Sisters told children to smile for photos. SISTERS OF CHARITY, HALIFAX, CONGREGATIONAL ARCHIVES

assigned to the day school on his reserve who was so afraid of the "heathen savages" that she was sent back to the mother house. The Sisters were always on call, always available in an emergency involving a child or staff person. They disciplined, taught, and worked along with the children to keep the school clean, the meals cooked, and the residents clothed. During the Second World War, they and the children knitted for soldiers. "There seems to be no end to it," one Sister wrote in the Annals. "One supply goes over to the Red Cross branch, to be replaced with a few more bales of sock yarn, navy blue for balaclavas, and a variety for sweaters, scarfs, and mittens."

The work took its toll, largely because the Sisters were working with children they didn't understand; the culture was somehow beyond them. In 1942, when Indian Affairs bureaucrats were working hard to get as many Mi'kmaq as they could to resettle at Shubenacadie and wanted a new day school and hospital there staffed by Sisters, a Sister quipped that they'd need "special five-year courses in Indian Psychology" if only such a thing existed. But, applying their own strict routines and discipline to their wards, the Sisters consistently impressed the inspectors who made annual two-day visits. The Sisters often wrote of dreaded inspections. They and the children put enormous work into preparing: making the building gleam and the children glow, providing the best possible food and plenty of smiles. They were relieved when the visits were over "with most complimentary remarks" and "glowing reports." One inspector was "loud in his praise of the work being done." The Sisters were thankful for the cook, who "made her usual good impression with a delicious dinner." On the whole, the Sisters described inspectors as appreciative of the hard work they did, and understanding of the difficulties involved.

One consistent difficulty for the Sisters was visiting sick or dying children in hospital, one of the few occasions to leave school grounds. Some of the illnesses were mysterious. Some died unexpectedly after minor surgeries, like a boy in 1948 after a tonsillectomy, who was buried at the Shubenacadie reserve cemetery. Other times, the Sisters themselves needed hospital treatment, and they recorded some of these events with a humour the children may have never seen. A Sister who broke her arm the Saturday before Easter 1941 while waxing a floor returned from the Halifax Infirmary in an ungracious fashion and was treated to much laughter from her comrades. "Lo and behold she came back worse than she went," someone wrote in the Annals.

"Sister slipped while stepping out of the car and sprained her ankle, at the same time she hurt the knee of her other leg. It is a tragedy indeed when one cannot find something funny...."

Like those children who were able to go home for the summer, the Sisters grew excited at the end of the school year. They rarely left the school grounds from September to June and they were forever on call. The stress was immense and perhaps left them ill-tempered and mean. They couldn't wait for the decreased workload of the summer months. "It is pleasant after the year has ended, to look forward to the summer, the smaller number of children, and the relaxation permitted, when the strain and worry of one hundred sixty is lessened to seventy or eighty," one Sister wrote. But before they could take their summer break, the Sisters worked harder than ever. All the bedding and clothes had to be washed and the children going home had to have decent outfits and lunches for the train, trips that had to be arranged. Sisters had to write report cards as well. All this on top of their usual load.

The Sisters at Shubenacadie had the added challenge of turnover—not because they could quit, but because they could be reassigned at any time. The Mother Superior gave orders and they did what they were told. Every August the Sisters dreaded "those fateful envelopes, carrying God's will," that would take some of them away to new assignments. "We await the important letters that come only from Mount Saint Vincent," a Sister wrote in the Annals in 1940. "We await the slow, but steady train to pull in, then the mail carrier...who brings us the fatal envelopes. East? West? North? South? for one or two or more of us." They hated to leave one another. In some cases, they hated to leave the children. Their numbers increased over the school's first decade, from seven (including the Sister Superior) the first year to ten in the third year and twelve by 1939. From then until the fifties there were around twelve Sisters each year, but by the time the school closed in the late sixties their numbers had dwindled back down to seven.

In these later years, though, the workload seemed as great as ever. Twelve Sisters didn't seem enough to keep pace with "the constant demands in time, labour, and services" in 1958, yet two were reassigned and not replaced. "Ten Little Indian Nuns," one Sister wrote. One of whom was later called away elsewhere to be a substitute teacher.

The Sisters saw the children as God's mission for them, and the school as a place "where God's unwanted and uncared-for find shelter and loving care," as one wrote in 1947. They shared Indian Affairs's view that the children were part of a problem to be solved. "Word came today that four Sisters of St. Martha from Eskasoni were coming to visit us the weekend," a Sister wrote in 1948. "They have the Indian problem as we do, so a little discussion should be of mutual help."

The Sisters wrote mostly positive things about the children in the Annals, often praising their participation in rituals like the annual May Procession, when the children sang, danced, acted, performed recital, and presented birchbark napkin rings they'd made with "a little Indian in feathers" for white visitors. "Our Lady [Mother Mary] smiled down upon her little Indians," a Sister wrote of the procession in 1931. The Sisters' positive writings about the children in the Annals even went so far as to empathize with

their annual "mournful return to school and discipline which is so contrary to the Indian temperament." They wrote of the extreme culture shock involved: "Now one has to sit in a big room with everything so shiny—and hear a person in black speak words that are not Micmac!" one wrote in 1939. But they also expressed certainty that this condition was temporary, thanks to their own efforts. "Kindness breaks all barriers and Sister Cyprian conquered! Soon her babes strut off to class feeling proud to Say, School! Supper! Sister! Bed! All in! All out!"

Given the Sisters' religious mission, knowing how ineffective they were in improving the lives of their

(L) Guida McKenzie, (R) Elizabeth Paul, young girl in centre is unidentified, 1932.
COLLECTION OF ELSIE CHARLES BASQUE, NOVA SCOTIA MUSEUM

wards must have been difficult. During usually quiet farewells, right before the principal drove the departing children to the train station, the Sisters reflected on what lay ahead. "We hope they have profited by the years spent here," a Sister wrote at the end of the 1937–38 school year, "and will try to inculcate the virtues and habits they practiced here, into the hearts of those at home." They knew the children were excited to go home, but worried their homes were not good for them. "It is sad...[to] think of the...pangs of hunger that will be felt; the freedom, which the children consider happiness!" And they further worried for the graduates, that the outside world would be very hard on them—as it had been on most residential school graduates across Canada. "Little do they realize what is ahead of them," one Sister wrote in 1944. "They have been instructed and warned."

GOOD TIMES

Despite having received warnings about getting involved in the children's recreational time, the Sisters wrote often in their Annals about bobsledding with the children and other playful activities, like picnics, berry picking, and late summer camp-outs in the pasture near the river, singing hymns around a blazing fire. "Seventy-five dark faces smiling around it, and the old familiar songs rang out into the tranquil young night," wrote one Sister, "thus passed one of several such evenings in a summer." Throughout the year, the boys played sports, sometimes taking on boys from Shubenacadie Village.

Christmas was a favourite for the nuns, especially when the snow fell and they climbed onto the back of double-runner bobsleds the school carpenter-engineer had made by boarding two sleds together so six to nine children could go at a time: red ones for the boys and green for the girls. In January 1948, children were excused from classes one night so they could go sledding. "The youthful nuns had some thrilling rides on the 'double runners' too," a Sister wrote. Some years it got cold enough to go for a skate by November.

They held midnight Mass in the chapel every year. The children got things started, waking the Sisters with Christmas Eve singing, starting on the girls' side and going through the halls down the boys' side. "The Angels sang the carols throughout the house," as one Sister described. "What is God's is ours!" another wrote, describing the abundance of Christmas trees ripe for the chopping near the school. The Sisters had the children decorate the tree while listening to the *Santa Program* on the radio at 5:00 each evening. "All the unfortunates not favoured by a package from home were given a substantial one from Santa's donations left under the tree," a Sister wrote one Christmas. They figured only about half the kids got gifts from home in a good year, and wrote of Santa bringing the children popcorn and candy in the refectory after breakfast.

Sisters wrote fondly of tobogganing with the children.

Each month the Sisters would show the children Gene Autry Westerns or Tarzan movies. They thought Tarzan the perfect choice for the children, "letting them see in the picture their loved forests and waterways, while the characters lived again their simple woodland ways." They wrote of the boys pretending to be Tarzan for days afterward. The Sisters also showed, at least once, a home movie shot in Whycocomagh in which the children recognized relatives and friends from home.

In the spring of 1948 the Sisters held an "Indian banquet" for the graduates. "The ten old enough to leave school were all dressed up in their freedom clothes and lined up in the Reading Room," they wrote. "All the Sisters were amazed at the poise and good manners displayed." After a special dinner, the Sisters and principal let the children go to a show. By 1951 the children performed and had a valedictorian. That year, the Historical Society of Nova Scotia invited the children to sing at a ceremony at the Shubenacadie Fire Hall when it unveiled its plaque celebrating the first Mi'kmaw encampment "over three hundred years ago." The Sisters raved about the children's singing.

SISTER-TEACHER

The Sisters were better qualified as teachers than most of their counterparts in other residential schools, and were respected throughout Nova Scotia and elsewhere. As Sisters of Charity, teaching was their calling, and they'd received a year or more of training at Mount Saint Vincent University—at least as much as most Nova Scotia teachers at the time—which qualified them to teach primary to high school. The university had been founded in part to prepare young nuns to teach, and as of 1895 its training was legally recognized. It became a junior college in 1914. If they'd attended in the mid-1950s, the Sisters would have had a bachelor's degree as well. In 1934 the Sisters at Shubenacadie were invited to the nearby day school with another ninety teachers. "Great was their surprise when they were asked to give their views on the subjects discussed, as well as an account of the work they were doing at the Indian School," a Sister wrote.

However well trained they were at Mount Saint Vincent, the Catholic Church, Indian Affairs, the mother house, the school principal, and the Nova Scotia Department of Education—which provided the curriculum—also influenced how the Sisters behaved at the residential school. In the decades leading up to the establishment of the Shubenacadie school, the Catholic Church officially declared on several occasions the value of children but instructed that they be taught to obey and respect authority. Children were to listen to older children, their parents, teachers, and especially the church. They were allowed to disobey only if they had good moral reason, for the sake of their families or the Catholic faith. Love was the most important teaching tool, because children learned better from someone who cared about them, and there was no teacher as good as a parent. Pope Pius XI (1857–1939) forbid Catholic teachers from removing students from their homes without parental consent—exactly what Indian Agents and the RCMP did on behalf of Shubenacadie's Catholic teachers.

The Nova Scotia Department of Education echoed the church's sentiment on caring for students. Rather than shaming the children, it said, teachers should give constructive feedback. By the 1950s the Department of Education was instructing teachers to engage students, to get them talking rather than merely absorbing information. Teachers were to make material relevant to the life experiences of their students. But at Shubenacadie the

Sisters made little effort to understand their students. If anything, they distanced themselves for the sake of rigorous discipline. An inspector described some of the teaching he witnessed at the school as "orthodox and stereotyped." In many cases the Sisters stayed at the school for fewer years than the typical child. With such a short stay it was hard to form relationships, even for Sisters who were willing. The students' lives, it turned out, were so far removed from the curriculum that it's hard to imagine how the Sisters could have made the material relevant. The message of the texts was the opposite of everything the children knew. What the Sisters ended up teaching them was that they were flawed creatures in the eyes of Canada and of God.

A stronger influence on the Sisters' teaching style may have been Mother Mary Berchmans's 1925 *Directory for the Sisters Employed in the Charitable Institutions of the Sisters of Charity, Halifax*, in which she instructed her "darling daughters" on teaching orphans. Her view was somewhat stricter than that of the church as a whole, though Mother Berchmans warned against excessive punishments, including harsh words. Punishment was to be a last resort, never to be given gladly. And corporal punishment was forbidden, as was locking children up in a room alone. "Solitude is a bad counselor for a child who is not good," she wrote. "Discipline" was a preferable term to "punishment," and it, along with faith, was the most important thing. "Above all, strongly urge them to assist at Holy Mass and to receive Holy Communion daily. Teach them to raise their little hearts to God often during the day by the use of ejaculatory prayers."

Many of Mother Berchmans's instructions were taken to heart at Shubenacadie. She advised that students' mail should be monitored and censored, and that boys and girls be denied all communication across gender lines, both of which were common practices at Shubenacadie and other residential schools. And she said that residents should be allowed visitors only during posted hours, unless someone had travelled a great distance. For students at Shubenacadie whose homes were far away, in northern New Brunswick, Prince Edward Island, and occasionally Québec, visitors were rare. Indian Affairs would not help parents with travel costs. Berchmans wrote that children's souls are most at risk when they play, claiming, "It is generally during recreation that evil projects are formed." She forbade Sisters from playing along, or to "suffer any familiarity with them," and furthermore, "they shall not allow the children to touch them," and risk diminishing their authority over them. Children had to be taught to obey; the Sisters were to "keep them in their place." But the Sisters sometimes chose the toboggan over doctrine.

Despite the directions they received, their qualifications, and their best efforts, the Sisters didn't get good results in the classroom. When Indian Agent Harry of Annapolis County visited Shubenacadie in 1936, he was unimpressed with the academic abilities of the students. "I have met bright and sharp children of fourteen years only doing Grade 5 work," he wrote to Indian Affairs. The acting secretary of the Department took the trouble to reply, explaining that any shortcomings in the students were their own fault. In 1936 Agent Ed Harvey of Lequille, Nova Scotia, and Agent R. H. Butts of Sydney Mines wrote to Indian Affairs, criticizing the school for focusing too much on labour and not enough on the classroom. Harvey noted that he'd seen seventeen-year-old boys who'd been at the school six years and failed to advance past Grade 3. Butts added that he'd witnessed too much cruelty at the school. Their letters went unanswered. Three years later, only 2 of the 150 residents of Shubenacadie had made it to Grade 8. Yet at least 15 of the children had been there since the school opened 10 years earlier. By 1944 only 4 of 146 residents had made it to Grade 6.

RELIGIOSITY

While it urged morality as one of the primary functions of its schools, Indian Affairs forbade more than half an hour per day be spent on religious instruction. There was a contradiction here, and a loophole. For the nuns, morality was religion. They would teach both. The principal gave the Sisters a guide from Indian Affairs when they arrived. They were to instill "obedience, respect, order, neatness and cleanliness." They were to teach the difference between right and wrong. They were to take their ragged pupils and shape them into independent, industrious, honest, thrifty, patriotic Canadian citizens. Make them hard-working men and cleanly, nurturing women. And so, despite their qualifications, the Sisters did very little academic teaching at the school. They focused instead on religion, morality, and Canadian citizenship. They wrote "Idleness is the Mother of Misery" on the chalkboards, and often had children knit, sew, or repair clothing for themselves and staff and for the military during the war. This work was vocational training, and it built a sense of discipline.

In their Annals, the Sisters wrote much more about religious ceremony than class time. "We trust that Our Lady looked with pleasure on those baby hearts which became the dwelling place of her Divine Son for the first time," one Sister wrote of the children's first communion. They often spoke of prayers and visits to the chapel. "The Heart of Our Dear Lord in the Blessed Sacrament must have been delighted with the frequency and fervor of the visits made by our little children," a Sister wrote at the end of 1930. "It was not even necessary to ask them to go, they were very anxious to do so and their behaviour was most edifying."

The Sisters were perfect for this work. "Parents bring to the school spoiled children who cannot be trained at home," wrote Sister Maura in a 1956 book detailing the history of the Sisters of Charity in Halifax, about their work as teachers. The teachers would then "correct, reprimand, punish—if necessary—the delinquent, and give back to the parents a notable convert." To the Sisters, education for its own sake was a "pagan conception." One Sister wrote of "saving the children from the calamity of Indianness." It was frustrating work, as shown in their comments on discharge forms. Unlike their general comments about the children in the Annals, the Sisters' teaching notes on individuals were rarely positive. "No brains," one wrote. "No ambition whatsoever," said another. "Under-average intelligence," wrote another. Adjectives like "lazy" and "stubborn" were common, but the descriptions could be crueler. "Syliboy," one sister wrote, "well named." Another sister described a child as "mentally and morally weak."

Some of the Sisters' frustrations may have stemmed from the fact that they did not understand the cultural backgrounds of their students. As Sable and Francis point out in *The Language of This Land, Mi'kma'ki*, storytelling is one of the most important teaching methods in Mi'kmaw culture, and the story's logic is not linear. Stories are told in the present tense, making the logic of the English language—and anything taught in that language—particularly challenging. Non-Mi'kmaw teachers often criticize Mi'kmaw students on their grammar and logical sequencing in essay writing without understanding this important cultural distinction. The Catholic Diocese blamed the Mi'kmaq for being difficult to understand. "The psychology of the Indian nature is often obscure to those not of that race," it said, waxing poetic on the subject.

"Silence and impassiveness are qualities in them fostered by age-long cultivation. What thoughts lie hid beneath the opaque gleam of their eyes? What emotions rise beneath their stoic countenances? Who can tell?" But it urged patience as the quality essential to changing the Mi'kmaq, to showing them the light and lifting them from misery. "Only by patience can alien virtues be brought to flower in the Indian character, which has by nature the qualities of loyalty, courage and reverence," it reads. "Though the path to Indian souls is difficult, yet the reward is superlatively worth the trouble. To place the pearl of great price within their dusky hands, to brighten their shadowed lives with the splendor of the Gospel truth; surely this is exceeding great reward!"

THE CANADIAN WAY

With instructions from the federal government and the mother house, the Sisters taught the curriculum given to them by the Nova Scotia Department of Education. It was the same curriculum used in public schools, filled with the mythology of noble Europeans conquering the peoples and lands of the "New World." Terms like "savage," "squaw," and "buck" were used as nouns for First Nations people. As ethnologist and author Ruth Holmes Whitehead notes, when Europeans won a battle it was a "triumph." If the Mi'kmaq won, it was a "massacre." Nova Scotia curriculum had three goals: promote "our way of life," create responsible Canadian citizens, and foster a better understanding of different cultures. The actual material, however, depicted First Nations people—"Indians"—as wild, uncivilized, and ignorant. The Sisters did not teach true Mi'kmaw history or culture, and they knew nothing of it. Under the curriculum and educational culture of the era, the first objective made the third impossible.

The Sisters relied heavily on the Faith and Freedom series of textbooks. Against the directions of Indian Affairs, they used these texts along with standard provincial readers. According to Briar Dawn Ransberry, who reviewed both sets of texts for her Master's thesis, the contents of the two are "remarkably similar." Both texts promoted "our way of life," the Euro-Canadian way, as having won out over the inferior Indian culture, a singular entity. The children in the Faith and Freedom texts prayed consistently, and their prayers were always answered.

Some Sisters used *Social Studies: Primary–Grade VI, A Guide for Teachers* to teach the children about the "courage, enterprise, faith and determination of the early explorers and pioneer settlers." This text depicted "Indian medicine men" as con men who pretended they knew how to cure sickness. The Sisters taught their wards that they owed a great debt to those pioneers for, among other things, bringing them Christianity and civilization. Reservations, the text said, were created "to make the Indians self-supporting, to educate them and thus to hasten the time when, through intermarriage with other Canadians, they will perhaps cease to be a separate people." By thus civilizing the Indian, the story went, the settlers would also eliminate an outdated way of life.

The Sisters also used a Grade 4 reader that included a 1919 poem called "Indian Children" that made clear Indians were a thing of the past. "Where we walk to school each day / Indian children used to play / All about our native land / Where the shops and houses stand," the poem read. "What a different place today," it concludes, "Where we live and work and play!" Astoundingly, this text is still used in many curricula today. There are YouTube videos of young white children reciting it for their adoring white parents. A Grade 5 speller told the story of a boy who always obeyed the law and grew up to be a successful lawyer, suggesting that in exchange for their obedience, children would be protected from moral harm. Another text, *Success and Health*, Canadian Hygiene Series, was used to teach about the importance of cleanliness. It told the story of two horses: one dirty and neglected, and another named Flora, who the children washed and brushed and loved. Wash yourself and be loved, it told them, or be dirty and hated.

The Sisters, who were not directly involved in running the Shubenacadie farm, did their part to teach the superiority of farming over a hunter-gatherer way of life. The texts they used called farming the more efficient way to get food, a key historical step toward Western industrialism. The texts downplayed the ways in which North American Indigenous peoples had helped European colonialists survive. "If the Indians had not already invented [the canoe], it seems likely that the white man would have had to invent it himself!" one read.

The Sisters also relied on textbooks to teach about the proper, civilized, Canadian way to live. Readers emphasized a Canadian nuclear family as the right form of social organization. Each family member had a specific role.

Women looked after the house and two or three children. Men worked outside the home. A Grade 1 reader called *The Little White House* focused on the father of the family. The mother cooked and cleaned in the background and the children received gifts. The books rarely mentioned other family members like grandparents, aunties and uncles, let alone respected community Elders.

From the earliest grades, the Sisters taught children about respecting other people's property using *The Primary Grade: A Teaching Outline.* Some of the teachers used a guidebook called *Civics and Citizenship Grades 7, 8 and 9: A Guide for Teachers.* With this text in hand, the Sisters focused on the importance of the church and school as part of the community, and taught the children why they must respect authority and be good citizens of Canada and the British Empire.

Despite admonishing the children for their cultural background and calling them racist slurs, the Sisters tried at times to celebrate "Indian culture." They were supported in this, in theory at least, by Indian Affairs, which in 1937 reported having an objective to create "an adult Indian population proud of their racial origin and cultural heritage." The Sisters wrote of their pride in the students' natural neatness and skilled craftsmanship. The school made a great show of its children for visitors, especially on holidays. The Sisters

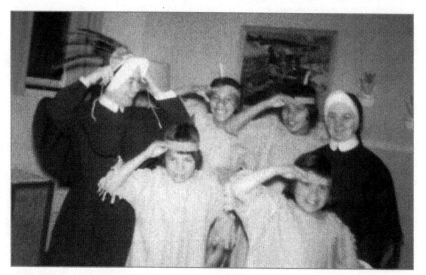

Sisters tried to incorporate Indian culture into school events. SISTERS OF CHARITY, HALIFAX, CONGREGATIONAL ARCHIVES

worked hard to make sure there was plenty of "Indian dance" and craft visible—the children made birchbark place cards and toy Indians to give school visitors—but, despite the nuns' efforts, they failed to reproduce the Mi'kmaw culture of most of the students. You can't teach what you don't know.

Given that the children had been separated from their elders and forbidden to speak their language, it's hard to know how accurate the cultural symbols created in the school were. Adult survivors of the school remember that any time they tried to show their real culture—by speaking Mi'kmaw or even of their traditions—they were beaten. The Sisters' knowledge of Mi'kmaw culture was limited and likely twisted by their own European-Canadian point of view, as it was in 1939 during a streptococcus epidemic when Sister Superior Mary Charles got all the children together to pray to Kateri Tekakwitha, the only Mohawk saint, who had died of an illness at twenty-four and who, according to a Jesuit priest, became finally pure on turning white in death. The children begged the saint for a cure and the Sisters reported that the ten sick kids were back in class the next day, healed. "Our cases all cleared up and we haven't had any since," Dr. McInnis said years later to a news service. "I have been medical attendant at the school since it was opened, and I have been in practice twenty-three years. I am a Scottish Presbyterian…I am simply stating the facts."

When the Sisters did work on the "three Rs"—reading, writing, and arithmetic—English-language lessons took most of the time. "Every effort must be made to induce pupils to speak English and to teach them to understand it," Indian Affairs's teaching guide reads. "Insist on English even during the supervised play. Failure in this means wasted efforts." The Sisters spent hours getting children to pronounce sounds that don't exist in Mi'kmaw, like "th." It took students many years to lose their Mi'kmaw accent, and some never did. Sisters also made students enunciate distinctly when they read aloud. School inspectors had complained that "Indian children either mumble inaudibly or shout their words in spasmodic fashion." Spelling was also a challenging subject. But the Sisters also had to cover math, social studies, history, and music. Hours were spent taking the children through drills on the times tables. Textbooks were usually at least a decade old, and sometimes remained in use as long as thirty years. Indian Affairs saved money that way: old ideas were cheaper. Not to mention the Sisters' own version of sex ed, in which "all bodily functions were dirty," as survivor Isabelle Knockwood puts it. A Sister of Charity once wrote in the Annals, "All well physically but the discovery of notes of a questionable nature among the girls left us all very sad. Father Brown gave the senior girls a talk on purity which should be a help with tomorrow's confession."

POTTERY

In 1940 someone discovered that the side of a ditch about a hundred metres from the school provided "unusually fine" clay in red or white, which inspired cooperation among the principal, teachers, staff, Indian Affairs, and the provincial government to raise money for the school by selling the children's pottery. Edward McLeod, the carpenter-engineer, fashioned a potter's wheel out of an old broken potato peeler. "Of course it has only the one speed, and does not run exactly true," Father Mackey wrote.

When the Nova Scotia Department of Education started a summer school to train pottery teachers, it invited the Sisters of Charity to send someone to attend. Sister Paul of the Cross took two courses. Four classes—one for boys and three for girls—ranging from Grades 3 to 8 spent half a day each

The school sold children's pottery to help cover operational expenses. SISTERS OF CHARITY, HALIFAX, CONGREGATIONAL ARCHIVES

week harvesting clay from the back of the school, sifting out rocks and dirt, moistening and drying it, cutting it into strips, and "turning out objects of art that would grace any modern home"—as one newspaper told it—making clay ashtrays, vases, bowls, pots, and model animals. "It is our intention to concentrate as much as possible on Indian designs," Mackey wrote. The children produced about fifty items a month, but until 1945 there was no kiln and they could not fire them.

E. K. Ford, Nova Scotia Technical College's inspector, visited Shubenacadie and said the children's skill as potters would give them real "economic possibilities." He wrote Indian Affairs suggesting they buy the school a kiln, and McLeod went to New Brunswick to find blueprints for an electric one. McLeod hired a Mr. Smith, from Stewiacke, Nova Scotia, a man with "no degrees from any college" but "a very definite talent for things electrical," to help him build it. It was the first electric kiln in the province.

Mackey and the Sisters quickly took to publicizing this aspect of the school. When Agent Rice made a trip to Ottawa, Mackey gave him some

"Ancient Indian Art Is Revived At Indian School," 1943. LIBRARY AND ARCHIVES CANADA/ DEPARTMENT OF INDIAN AFFAIRS AND NORTHERN DEVELOPMENT FONDS/REEL C-8160

pottery samples to show R. A. Hoey, superintendent of welfare and training at Indian Affairs. Hoey was impressed. A few newspapers took interest as well. They, in keeping with most of the press coverage of the school, heaped praise on the whole operation. "The girls are taught laundry work and sewing and the boys become proficient in their tasks on the school farm," one article said. Mackey saw market opportunities for pottery that didn't exist for handles and baskets. He also realized that the school had been open more than a decade and had done nothing to improve life on reserves in the region.

The children's work was sold at agricultural exhibitions across Nova Scotia and New Brunswick, and at a store near the school. The Nova Scotia Technical College alone sold a hundred of the children's bean crocks between Shubenacadie and Halifax. Buyers loved them and felt good supporting Indian education. The money went toward school expenses. This arrangement was not unusual in residential schools. Indian Affairs had a handicrafts section, responsible for marketing traditional products to non-Indigenous people. It shipped several thousand dollars' worth of goods across Canada each year. That year, the section invited Father Mackey to provide "one or two small articles" to include in its catalogue.

The Sisters and priests respected the children's skill as potters. SISTERS OF CHARITY, HALIFAX, CONGREGATIONAL ARCHIVES

INFLUENCING THE BOSSES

Rarely did the Sisters get involved, in any kind of official way, in running the school. Given their entries in the Annals and general practices of the day, it is likely that they took their orders with good graces from the school principal. But on a few occasions they made their needs known to Indian Affairs. In the fall of 1936, Sister Mary Charles, the Sister Superior at the school, wrote to J. D. Sutherland, assistant superintendent of education at Indian Affairs. Sutherland had visited the school the previous summer and had apparently offered to approve the purchase of a hot water sterilizer for the third floor. Sister Mary Charles noted that without this device, "care of the sick means travelling over two flights of stairs for even a cup of hot water." It had long been a challenge at the school to get hot water. "For the past two years," Mackey wrote, "[for] both the girls' and boys' baths we had to carry hot water from the laundry. While this is an improvement over what the Indian had in his own home, nevertheless with the crowd we have it makes a mess job." With her letter, Sister Mary Charles included a catalogue clipping for a $133 sterilizer. Sutherland approved the purchase a few days later and told Sister Charles of "pleasant recollections of my visit to the school last summer and of your kindness on that occasion."

A decade later, Sister Paul of the Cross was in charge of four pottery classes, in which the children used a pottery wheel made out of an old industrial potato peeler by Edward McLeod, the school's carpenter-engineer. The Sister whispered to an inspector visiting the school that she needed a proper pottery wheel—electric—and gave him a letter with catalogue clippings to give to Kathleen Moadie, who was in charge of Indian Affairs's handicraft section. Sister Paul of the Cross didn't need money. The school was already profiting from selling the children's work from pottery class, which was of a high quality. She was willing to use that money to buy the wheel, but Indian Affairs still had to approve the purchase, "the necessary priority."

Moadie went to Toronto after receiving Sister Paul of the Cross's letter and found a foot-pedal potter's wheel for only $76.50, which she could easily order. "I think you should be proud of the progress you have made in connection with the production of pottery and feel that your pupils will eventually be the nucleus of a pottery industry on the Reserve," Moadie wrote. Sister Paul of the Cross responded with a brief handwritten letter politely thanking Moadie for taking such interest in the purchase of the potter's wheel. But, she said, it really had to be electric because children as young as eight had to use it: "The one you suggested would be impossible for smaller children to use"; they wouldn't reach the foot pedal. In all, it took only six weeks, with Sister Paul of the Cross's gentle nudging, for Indian Affairs to buy the electric pottery wheel—a new Amaco Electric Potter's Wheel "No. 2" for $377 from the Denver Fire Clay Company, paid for by proceeds from selling the children's work.

SISTER SADISM

A year before Shubenacadie opened, Pope Pius XI reminded Catholic teachers about the importance of discipline. Nearly three decades later, in slightly gentler times, Pius XII warned against vindictive punishment. Neither defined clear limits on how far corporal, or physical, punishment could be taken. Indian Affairs made the same mistake, warning against excessively harsh punishments but not correcting those who made children eat their own vomit. A survivor told CBC in the 1980s that a Sister once grabbed her by the hair and force-fed her until she threw up. The young girl hadn't been able to eat because her tooth was abscessed, likely because Indian Affairs refused to pay for dentistry.

It is hard to reconcile the Sisters as they portrayed themselves in their Annals—as sweet and devoted lovers of children who bore a heavy burden—with the cruel and brutal tyrants many survivors can't forget. Survivors have often said that some nuns were kind and others cruel. Some were both—sometimes a friend and sometimes a cruel foe—and many likely followed the rules of their many masters as best they could. The nuns had agreed to take on a difficult task, to remove a child's culture and replace it with a foreign one in a remote institution. To the children's detriment, some of the nuns likely believed corporal punishment was the only way to accomplish their religious and institutional goals.

It's impossible to fully explain the extreme violence of some Sisters as reported by survivors. But regardless of the rules set out by the Catholic Church, the mother house, and Indian Affairs, the tone inside the walls of Shubenacadie was set by the school's first principal, Father Mackey, who by a great many accounts used brutal violence and psychological torture to enact his "reign of terror." He used fear to make the children obey, and several Sisters did the same. Survivors from each decade of the school remember this violence from their teachers, but it seems to have been most common in the thirties and forties, when Father Mackey was the principal and Sister Mary Leonard a disciplinarian, teacher, and secretary.

Mary Leonard isn't the only Shubenacadie Sister remembered as a sadist. Sister Paul of the Cross, the first boys' disciplinarian, is remembered for having strapped a boy's genitals among other particularly vicious acts. But she wrote fondly of the Mi'kmaw children after being transferred to the Kootenay Indian Residential School in Cranbrook, BC. "The Micmac are far superior, better workers, happier, etc," she said, than her new wards out west. Another survivor told the *Micmac News* of Sister Josephine Adrian's cruel punishments. According to this account, Sister Adrian, who was at the school from 1943 to 1953, and Sister Justinian, 1946–55, whipped a boy on his bare back with a bamboo ski pole because he'd had trouble threading a needle when Sister Adrian was teaching him to sew. "She was full of that kind of stuff," the survivor said.

But Sister Mary Leonard was by far the most frightening in her day. She was a very tall, large—about five foot ten and more than two hundred pounds—buxom, blonde, blue-eyed woman with a chubby pink face and fingers covered in freckles, Isabelle Knockwood recalls. And she was imposing physically but also in her way of talking, often monopolizing conversations even with other adults. She joined the school in 1934, replacing Sister Joseph Beatrice, and worked there for fourteen years, until being reassigned. She died in 1988.

Knockwood also remembers Sister Mary Leonard having gold-capped teeth and gold-rimmed glasses. "Her pupils contracted and dilated as she spoke," she writes in *Out of the Depths*. "The hair on her neck had been shaved...She wore a strand of large wooden beads around her waist and a wooden crucifix...bigger than the palm of my hand." (She later removed her rosary beads so the children wouldn't hear her approaching.) Other survivors told Knockwood they remembered Sister Mary Leonard—who they called *Wikew*, meaning "Fatty"—being sweet and kind on the first day of school. But she quickly turned on them, beating them regularly and seemingly arbitrarily. One survivor told the *Micmac-Maliseet News* that Mary

Leonard beat her thirty times on each end with a strap three times a day. Even the Sister's rewards felt like punishment to the children. Knockwood remembers her throwing handfuls of candy on the floor and watching the children scramble for them.

The children often wondered how so many cruel nuns had come to work with children, who they seemed to despise. They thought maybe Mary Leonard been sent there as punishment for breaking some Catholic Church rule. Rumours flew that she had chosen Shubenacadie over a leper colony as her punishment. The Sisters of Charity tell me they have no record of how or why Mary Leonard was assigned to the school or what she did before. They know very little of her. The children didn't know it, but some senior staff at Indian Affairs believed the residential schools to be a dumping ground for incompetent church staff. In 1932 one official commented that the churches seemed prone to assigning "Indian work" to priests and instructors who had failed in other fields. However she got there, some survivors remember Mary Leonard not only as a sadist, but also as a murderer of at least two children. At the Truth and Reconciliation event in Halifax in October 2011, a witness had someone read his deceased aunt's letter into the record. In it, she recounted rapes, horrible beatings, and seeing Sister Mary Leonard beat her sister's head against a concrete wall; her sister died the next day.

In the early 1940s Mary Leonard sent Nancy Lampquin to the infirmary with a vicious beating, witnessed by all the children and other Sisters in the dining hall, after the girl tried to pocket her spinach instead of eating it. Isabelle Knockwood witnessed the beating and wrote about it in *Out of the Depths*. Sister Mary Leonard grabbed Lampquin by the hair and screamed at her, then force-fed her the greens as she cried and bled from the lips from the spoon being jammed in her mouth, making the nun madder. Mary Leonard then force-fed her milk. "Nancy's eyes began to roll and she seemed to be losing consciousness," Knockwood writes. "Her mouth and cheeks were badly swollen and her lips were purple. She was sobbing and gasping for air and holding her back rigid and straight." It was the last time Knockwood saw her friend alive. "Very delicate and sick for almost a year. Died," Father Mackey wrote of her in the school's records that year. He gave tuberculosis as the cause of death. Nancy Lampquin was the first child buried from the Shubenacadie school chapel. Knockwood told her father what had really happened to Nancy, but when he raised the issue with the principal, Mackey reminded him he wasn't the girl's next of kin.

The Sisters also wrote in their Annals of Mary Agnes Ward, "a good little patient, polite and grateful, pious and obedient" who, they wrote, died a "happy, holy death" at a tuberculosis sanatorium in Bathurst, New Brunswick, in 1947. Poet and Shubenacadie survivor Rita Joe, who always tried to accentuate the positive, remembered her friend Mary Agnes Ward's death very differently. She described it in great detail to her friend and fellow survivor Isabelle Knockwood. There was some small rule infraction, she recalled, and the "fat Sister" hauled Mary Agnes over near the big boys' table and began beating her and shouting at her as another Sister watched. Mary Agnes fought back, but was outmatched. Sister Mary Leonard, Rita Joe recalled, beat Mary Agnes until she was unrecognizable, swollen and bloody. Father Brown, who the survivors remember as a much gentler man than Father Mackey, was principal at the time. But on this occasion he lost his temper and yelled loudly at the Sisters. They took Mary Agnes to the infirmary on the top floor and later to hospital, where she died. "When Sister announced that she died because her bones were too big for her heart, I didn't believe her," Rita Joe told Knockwood.

The children finally received a gift that seemed too good to be true in the fall of 1948: Sister Mary Leonard, who terrified them with her size and silent, swift violence, finally left the school. She was reassigned to the Sisters of Charity's only other residential school, in Cranbrook, British Columbia, where she took a 40 percent pay cut. The exact reasons for her transfer aren't clear, but perhaps Sister Mary Leonard got too strong a taste of the same fear she'd inflicted on the children when a knife was found in a young girl's mattress, and she its intended target. The Sisters and principal interrogated the girl and her sister until they confessed they were planning to attack the substantial Sister with it. The Sisters said the girls were annoyed "about the vacation plans." Isabelle Knockwood writes that, strangely, the girl who'd hidden the knife was not one of Wikew's usual victims; she was known as a "pet," someone who spied on the other girls and tattled on them. The police came and took the girls to the Convent of the Good Shepherd—in Halifax and Saint John, New Brunswick, respectively. The Sisters wrote that the local Indian Agent and a visitor on hand from Indian Affairs both approved of the action taken. "Our list was changed by only one name," a Sister wrote of that year's roster of nuns, "But what a big loss to the staff it meant to see Sister Mary Leonard destined for the West." Sister Francis Marian replaced Mary Leonard, "with much fear and trembling," as disciplinarian of seventy girls.

BAD APPLES IN A ROTTEN BARREL

Forty-five years after the Shubenacadie Indian Residential School closed, at the TRC in Halifax, Tony Mancini, the city's Catholic archbishop, reflected on the abhorrent actions of nuns and priests. "Unfortunately, some of us, sometimes along the line, forgot why we're here," he said. Across the residential school system, religious personnel saw themselves as martyrs. They worked hard for nothing more than the joy of offering salvation to what they considered a less developed race. Any means necessary for this salvation, even the abuse of children, was therefore just. As were any small benefits they reserved for themselves, such as hoarding the best food available in an otherwise dreary institution.

In their minds, the Sisters and priests at Shubenacadie were fighting poverty, cultural backwardness, the worst tendencies of the children, and the devil himself. They had an impossible job. They weren't allowed to get close to the children, yet they were to teach them. They had to remove their original cultures and instill another. For the most part they were unable to understand the cultural backgrounds of their wards—their traditions, or their contemporary lives on the reserves or even in foster homes. "I think they were so cruel and mean because they didn't study up on the environment or our culture," Isabelle Knockwood writes.

The residential school system, and Shubenacadie within it, was by design cruel and violent. Years after the school closed, survivor stories of severe and rampant emotional, physical, and sexual abuse emerged in the media. More than fifty years of psychological studies indicate that the innate violence of an institution will turn seemingly normal people into abusers. But at the same time, a small percentage of the general population has sociopathic characteristics, and it is possible that such individuals are drawn to positions of power over the vulnerable. Regardless, the residential school environment allowed the worst tendencies of teachers and principals to emerge. And the government did little to hold these individuals accountable for the welfare of Aboriginal children. Indian Affairs played at holding inspections at its remote facilities, warning the schools when inspectors were to arrive. The Department ignored ample evidence of abuse and neglect, making it all too easy for the worst offenders to get away with just about anything.

In 1971, four years after Shubenacadie closed, psychologist Philip Zimbardo of Stanford University conducted a controversial and influential experiment, known as the Stanford Prison Experiment. For it, Zimbardo recreated a prison environment with twenty-four psychologically healthy (although there is some controversy about his screening methods) male undergraduate students—half playing guards and half playing inmates—in the basement of a campus building. The "guards" were told not to physically harm the "prisoners," but to use whatever psychological torture they thought would give them control. In many ways, the false environment Zimbardo created was more similar to a residential school than it was to a prison. Within days, the guards were manipulating prisoners with many of the same techniques used in residential schools, including replacing names with numbers, locking prisoners in a closet they called "the hole," denying them food, dictating letters home raving of joyful times being had, putting on a good show for visiting parents, and making compliant "pet" inmates turn on those who resisted in any way.

All of these things happened at Shubenacadie. And, as happened among the adults at the school, about one-third of the guards were creatively sadistic, another third followed the rules of the game without exceeding their mandate, and the final third tried to help the inmates however much they could get away with, doing them small favours when they could. Just like at Shubenacadie, the nicer guards turned a blind eye to abuses committed by meaner guards. There was also overlap between these three categories—some of the nuns who dished out severe punishments in class were kind and patient at mealtime, in chapel, or during playtime.

Rita Joe wrote in her autobiography about the differences among the nuns. She remembered some of them fondly; these she considered friends. One worked in the laundry with Rita Joe. Every morning before they started working, Sister Justinian would reach deep into her habit pocket and pull out a little something for her—a hard candy, a notebook, a pencil, maybe even a whole box of crayons. She looked up to Sister Justinian like a mother. She never stopped loving her. But Rita Joe also remembered beatings and many, many commands, "military style." The Sisters told the children when to eat and when to pee and when to pray, even when to cough. Led in their aggression by Sister Mary Leonard, the Sisters shouted constantly. By this time Father Brown had replaced Father Mackey. Rita Joe remembered him raising his voice only once, when Sister Mary Leonard severely beat Mary Agnes.

"I treated the prisoners like they were of a[n] inferior order than myself," said the ringleader of the cruel guards in the Stanford Prison Experiment. The experiment had been called off because of escalating cruelty to its subjects. The ringleader had taken Dr. Zimbardo's instructions and creatively applied his own brand of cruelty based on the authority given him. "Once you put a uniform on and are given a role, a job...to keep these people in line, then you're certainly not that same person...it surprised me that no one said anything to stop me." Just as this guard, who returned to being a regular undergraduate student, didn't recognize himself in the role he took on during the experiment, the Sisters of Charity have had trouble reconciling their own memories of Shubenacadie with survivor testimony. "Some are certainly puzzled and saddened by some of the stories that don't fit with their own experiences," explains Ruth Jeppesen, Sisters of Charity communications director.

In 2002, academic researchers Steve Reicher and Alex Haslam recreated Zimbardo's experiment for a BBC reality show, but added more stringent ethical controls and, unlike Zimbardo, did not give the guards instructions to psychologically manipulate prisoners. The researchers also looked at how high-ranking Nazis followed orders, making the Third Reich's hatred their own. They found that people who "just follow orders" and commit crimes against humanity have to somehow identify with the mission of their bosses, who exert a strong influence.

The Sisters served many strong leaders, including the church, the mother house and Mother Superior, the Sister Superior at the school, and the priest principal, who was the highest ranking authority (excluding God) on-site. It is no coincidence that when Father Mackey, who survivors remember as a tyrant, was in charge of the school the Sisters there also acted violently. And Sister Mary Leonard could attack children so viciously because she believed the church's, government's, and Father Mackey's mission to civilize Indians was for the greater good. She identified with that mission and attached herself fully to it. The way she conducted herself was her own creative application of that belief. The behaviour of each priest and nun at the school was the result of a person reacting to a situation. Conversely, individual priests and nuns—through their creative discipline and bureaucratic finagling—shaped the situation as much as the government and church did. The school principals in particular were always responding to Indian Affairs's vague instructions, putting their own spin on government policy.

Reicher and Haslam point out that "the more extreme the actions of… institutions, the more extreme the individuals that are drawn to them." Shubenacadie may have indeed driven some of the adults in charge to be more violent than they otherwise would have been. But in the case of principals and other male staff members who had more choice in the matter, it is possible that the institution may have, by its extreme nature, attracted sadistic people who had never before had the chance to hurt people without consequence for themselves. And, as often happens in these environments, those who were gentler by nature likely felt too powerless to resist. "The nuns that were there at the time; this punishment stuff rubbed off on them [starting with Father Mackey]," a survivor told the *Micmac News* in 1978. "God was the main focus of their lives; the only way you were going to heaven is to have enough pain on this earth."

THE CHILDREN

"THE HOUSE WITH ELASTIC SIDES"

Shubenacadie was built for 125 child residents, but from the start it was overcrowded, taking 146 in its first year—70 boys and 76 girls. By far the biggest class was Grade 1, where the students ranged from 4 to 7 years old. At times, 62 of them crammed themselves into one classroom. The lower grades remained the most overcrowded through the lifespan of the school. By 1938 the number of child residents ballooned to 175, 15 more students than regulations allowed and 50 more than the school was designed to hold. But as one Sister quipped, "The house with elastic sides always has room for one more." Father Mackey knew that the more kids he had in his school, the more money he'd have to run the place. It was a bit of a Catch-22. The school was perpetually overcrowded, but if it had taken fewer children it would have been extremely difficult for it to function on such a limited budget. While Indian Affairs paid a set amount to the church for each child who went to the school, Department accountants knew it was still cheaper than paying Mi'kmaw families welfare support. And it gave them more control over how exactly the money was used.

The first children arrived from three Halifax orphanages in early February 1930, with the last of the nuns. The next afternoon they attended classes with Sister Louisita, Grades 1–3, Sister Madeleine Leo, Grades 4–5, and Sister Superior Anita Vincent, Grades 6–7. The orphanages hadn't exactly been the high life, but the school was harder. One survivor, who was sent to the Good Shepherd orphanage after four years at Shubenacadie, would describe it as "better than the Indian Residential School" because she got her own room. A week later, twin girls arrived from the Shubenacadie reserve. They were the first who hadn't come from other institutions, and by April—when the doctor finally did a tuberculosis exam of all the children and vaccinated them—it was an overfull house.

School life was chaotic from the start. That spring a girl lost a finger in the dough mixer. Twelve others had their first Communion. In the summertime, more than a hundred children stayed at the school. Forty went home for summer vacation and two didn't come back—they were tracked down and sent to a juvenile jail. In September Archbishop O'Donnell (Archbishop McCarthy had died in January) visited from Halifax to speak to the children. He congratulated them on their faith and told them to be honest and proud of their people. The children later joined others from Shubenacadie Village in decorating a new war monument and singing "O Canada." A dentist visited and filled or pulled more than 250 teeth. The Sisters of Charity's Annal entries during the first full year of operation were mostly bubbly and proud. But in the spring, Mary Gehue, a seven-year-old girl, died from an abscess of the lung. Hers was the first death recorded at the school.

TAKEN

While the school was intended to house and educate orphans, and did have a significant number of them, most of the children at Shubenacadie were taken from reserves. Indian Agents identified children they claimed needed "maintenance," who were then taken from families that Indian Agents felt were "semi-destitute"—be they foster families or parents. Other children lived where there was no day school available because Indian Affairs hadn't built one, despite its promise to provide on-reserve education. Indian Affairs, as the legal guardian of all Status Indians, didn't need to explain why it was taking the children, but a better education was usually the rationale provided.

The agents used their own discretion about who should go to the school. Collectively, they were a harrowing combination of power and unpredictability. But every agent was different. Some believed in keeping Mi'kmaw families together. Others felt the school was a better home for any Mi'kmaw child with only one parent. The rules weren't clear and were constantly changing as the government responded to shifting political pressures. Any child whose parents were receiving relief payments from Indian Affairs was a likely candidate. Agents and band chiefs consistently described conditions on the reserves as deplorable, with families living in shacks with dirt floors, dirty water, and no heat. Jobs were scarce, and few white men were willing to hire "Indians" at all.

The Government of Canada, Maritime provincial governments, and settlers in general had created this abject poverty in which the Mi'kmaq found themselves on the reserves. While Mi'kmaw children may have been aware that their families lacked money for fine things, those on reserve were likely more aware of being loved, of belonging. In traditional Mi'kmaw culture, when there isn't enough for everyone the children are often fed first. The colonialists had been so determined to win the "New World" that they'd brought newcomers by the boatload for decades and given them Mi'kmaw land, then moved the Mi'kmaq around, "centralizing" them to save money. They'd created in the Mi'kmaq a dependency on government support, and then withheld it as much as possible. As a result, almost any Mi'kmaw child at that time was poor enough to qualify for Shubenacadie.

Parents of Mi'kmaw children were supposed to sign application forms—as well as a Certificate of Health completed by a doctor—making the principal of the school the legal guardian of their children—even during the summer, whether or not they were home on the reserve. "I hereby make application for the admission of the undermentioned child into the Shubenacadie Residential School to remain therein under the guardianship of the principal, for such term as the Department of Indian Affairs deems proper," the form read. In reality, Indian Agents, backed by RCMP officers—who were made official truant officers by Indian Affairs in 1933—rarely explained what the form meant to the parents, and often took children by force. In many cases Indian Affairs told its agents not to bother getting parents' signatures on application forms. If the agent couldn't find the parents, thought they were bad parents, or that they weren't making their kids attend school regularly, no signature was needed.

In 1937 A. C. MacNeil, the Indian Agent for Glendale, Nova Scotia, was closely watching an older couple with four small children. The father wanted to leave his wife and take their kids to live with him in a shack. He asked MacNeil if the Department might pay to fix the shack up, make it livable.

But MacNeil considered the man a hopeless wanderer. Without a mother, he figured, the kids would be neglected. MacNeil responded to the man's request by bringing him forms for Shubenacadie, but the man refused to sign. MacNeil wrote his bosses in Ottawa. Indian Affairs responded by saying that one boy could be admitted without a signature, "the father not having shown very much interest in him in the past." There was no indication of how the Ottawa bureaucrats knew anything about the father-son relationship in discussion, or how they decided which of the four children would go to Shubenacadie. MacNeil hadn't mentioned anything about neglect.

Reverend Chiasson, the Pictou Indian Agent of the late 1930s, was happy to send children to Shubenacadie without a parent's signature when he felt it was in the best interest of the children. In one case, a teenaged girl was looking after her two younger brothers; their mother was dead. When the sister moved out, Chiasson felt that their father had neglected them. He was often away working and no one cooked for them, he said. The older boy drank and had gotten in trouble with the law. The police threatened reform school if he kept it up. Both boys skipped school often. Chiasson suggested that the father send them to Shubenacadie. The father said no, "believing, wrongly of course, that children there are not well cared for," Chiasson wrote; he sent the boys to Shubenacadie without the signature.

Even seventeen years into Shubenacadie's institutional life, agents were sending unsigned application forms to Ottawa. People on reserves never knew what to expect. In many cases Indian Agents did advocate on behalf of parents, if they figured a home was clean and cozy enough. "I would think it reasonable to let this girl remain with her father," the Richibucto, New Brunswick, agent wrote Indian Affairs in 1937. "He has a good comfortable home but no one to take care of it as his wife is dead." The agent found the girl big and strong and a good housekeeper.

A visit from the Indian Agent could mean anything, from new supplies to the disappearance of your child forever. Despite agents sometimes trying to keep families together, the residential school system was committing its first act of violence in taking the children en masse, by train or on the back of a truck, away from home. Uniformed RCMP officers ripped some children from their parents' arms. They cried and clutched and grabbed desperately for the protection and love they'd known. They were supposed to be at least seven years old, unless they were orphans, or poor, or neglected.

Agents took children as young as four. They cited all kinds of different reasons for taking kids to Shubenacadie. It might be a dead parent or one "of little consequence" or "low mentality." Some parents were, in the opinion of the agent, "of such a character…entirely unfit to bring up a child." Others were in jail or a mental hospital. Often the parents had a serious illness like tuberculosis. Sometimes the children were described as "illegitimate." Or, the agents said, the parents had a "roaming nature." And while it was common in reserve life, as in ancient Mi'kmaw tradition, for children to treat numerous houses as their own, "wandering about the reserve" was also reason to send children to residential school.

In other cases, children were taken to Shubenacadie not because of their parents but because they themselves were seen as delinquents, "of an unruly disposition…a difficult pupil in the day school," "rather uncontrollable at home," "saucy with the teacher." One agent wrote, regarding a teenage boy he took to Shubenacadie, "It was reported to me that he was intoxicated." Agents knew the students would be severely punished for such antics at Shubenacadie. Children and parents saw it as a reform school. Parents sometimes chose to send their children there. Many who signed application forms used an "X" because they could not write. They had no idea that a primary goal of the school was to assimilate children into mainstream Canadian culture, or that the children would be forbidden from speaking their mother tongues. Some parents didn't have enough money to take care of their children. Others wanted to make sure they got the best education possible, hoping that by learning to write and speak good English they'd escape poverty. At least at the school they would have enough food. Most didn't know they were surrendering their role and rights as parents, or that constant hunger would become one of the survivors' most lasting memories of the school.

SUDDENLY ALONE

Mi'kmaw children stood on the platform at every stop, alone and crying. "There were no families, no relatives, no uncles, grandfathers, nobody to say goodbye to them," one survivor told the Halifax Media Co-op in 2011. Most had no clue where they were going or why they had been taken from their families, homes, and communities. They often wondered what they had done wrong. Some believed lies they'd been told. "We were there on the understanding that we were going to spend one night there, and leave the next day for home," a survivor told the *Micmac News* in 1978. Some survivors remember their parents lying to them, saying they were just going for a walk or to see a sibling at the school. They just knew they were suddenly alone. Some children were haunted throughout their time at the school by the parting image of a mother or father, waving goodbye. The train ride was a long and frightening journey—leaving a small hometown in the morning, arriving in Halifax in the evening, and taking a second train to Shubenacadie, arriving late at night—longer if they came from New Brunswick or Prince Edward Island. Some carried written instructions from an Indian Agent. The principal or a Sister met them at the station.

The Shubenacadie school building was imposing to those who had spent their lives on humble reserves—tall, red brick against the skyline. It "looked like a castle: the ornamented door, the shiny waxed floors, the pictures on the walls and curtains on the windows," survivor and poet Rita Joe would one day write of the school. First they had to climb "thirteen high cement steps," writes Isabelle Knockwood, to two heavy wooden doors with glass panels. A priest in black stood just inside, his pale hand extended from under his robe. The children were shuffled in. The Sister Superior led them down a gleaming hallway. In her book, Knockwood describes the appearance of the school in detail. She remembers a picture on the wall of a guardian angel sheltering two small children, and standing in the chapel pews before a "small white altar with a gold cross painted on the front and mounted on a platform." It was covered in white linen with embroidered flowers, fruit, and crosses. Everything ornate. A red candle was always lit. The Sister told them the chapel was a sacred place. There were pictures of Jesus hauling his cross as the soldiers watched. And there was a parlour across from the priest's suite, which Knockwood describes as having a blue-patterned rug, lace curtains, and a bookcase filled with leather-bound books.

Older children stood eyeing new arrivals in front of the chapel. They looked a scary bunch, pale, hair cut short or shaved. They wore uniforms that were either black-and-white stripes or colourless. If the new ones were lucky, they'd find some children from their own reserve to commiserate with, kids who already knew their names. Those children who came with their parents inevitably had to say goodbye. First there was paperwork, then usually more tears and last words of wisdom. The older ones often heard something like, "Look after your little brothers and sisters here." As the parents left, sometimes a Sister would give a crying child a candy. Although they were officially Catholic, many of the children had never been to school or seen a white person, let alone a nun. The white women, dressed all in black and white with veils covering their hair, were frightening for some—a ghostlike image.

Next the children shuffled up two sets of cement stairs with steel rails to the recreation hall, where there was a radio hanging from the ceiling. The floor was red cement and there were two large pillars. The Sisters stripped them down, marked their clothes, and put them into tubs. Some survivors remember the Sisters burning their clothes. They scrubbed them hard, as if "trying to take the Indian away," as one survivor put it to the TRC session in Eskasoni. The children dried off and got their two new khaki outfits with vertical stripes—one for weekdays and a nicer one for weekends and outings. The uniforms looked like prison clothes. They rarely fit properly, and felt like rough, heavy canvas. The boys had a red tie—to match "their dark colouring" as the Sisters put it. The girls got plain wool skirts that blew up atop the windy hill. They were given hand-me-down shoes. The shoes fit some, but others got blisters. After years at the school, some children's feet became disfigured from always wearing too-tight shoes. Many saved the shoeboxes to hold the trinkets they found like treasure. (Every now and then Sister Mary Leonard would dump these on the floor and have her favourites throw out the contents.) The Sisters cut the children's hair short, gave each of them a number, and in many cases an English name, or sometimes arbitrarily changed their name—such as from Margaret to Marjorie or Peggy—to identify them by. "You have no parents or grandparents to help you," one survivor recalled a Sister saying.

Quickly the loneliness and claustrophobia set in. Children used to freedom on the reserves, being able to play in the woods and learn directly from Elders, were suddenly stuck inside a cold, bland institutional building. In the evenings they watched jealously as the school's farmer, assistant farmer, carpenter-engineer, and other staff members went home for the evening. The students could always see the school, even when a nun took the class for a walk; it was never far enough.

The school was divided by gender. Brothers couldn't talk to their sisters. For some, this separation was the hardest thing. Siblings saw each other on occasion if they were lucky enough that their parents could visit. Boys and girls had separate sleeping quarters and playgrounds—both at opposite ends of the building—sections of the dining hall, chapel, and classrooms. This was standard practice in public schools as well, but the concept of separating boys and girls so completely was new to Mi'kmaw children.

Many of the children were strangers to each other. They had not yet figured out their own social order. Who would be the favourites and who would be the bullies? Who would be the protectors? In time the children did establish a hierarchy, as well as many close friendships. As journalist Conrad W. Paul wrote in 1978, they established "a mini-government, with its own laws and monetary system." Survivors remember the Sisters having favourite students, whom the others called the "pets" or "squealers." They kept their eyes on the other children and reported back any misbehaviour or rule breaking to a Sister. Sometimes they would be enforcers; the youngest children had to watch their backs. Some older kids were friends and protectors; others were dangerous. Survivors have haunting memories of abuse, the threat of which hung from many directions—the priest, the nuns, the older students. One survivor who was raped in the shower by boys who'd threatened him with a homemade knife kept it a secret until 1978, when he

Interactions with the opposite sex were strictly controlled. SISTERS OF CHARITY, HALIFAX, CONGREGATIONAL ARCHIVES.

unburdened himself to the *Micmac News*. "You sorta had to take your showers with your own group for protection," he said. If you wanted to avoid beatings you could pay for security with food, a scarce commodity. Some small children paid the older ones to beat up their enemies.

Decades later, at TRC events throughout Atlantic Canada, Shubenacadie survivors described a robotic numbness that set in and lasted several years—feelings buried as deeply as possible to preserve their sanity. This repression prevented the creation of memories, of conversations, of emotion or personal growth. For some, it took many more years to recover, to feel again, and to understand what had happened. Some families had as many as nine children taken away to Shubenacadie.

RIGOUR

Survivors have described being treated like a "herd of animals," shuffled from one place to the next on the hour. They experienced a level of regulation they'd never known before, an hourly schedule and rules for how to sit, speak, and eat, regulated by a series of nine ringing bells throughout the day, beginning in the very early morning. The first bell called the Sisters to prayer and roused the children from bed. Sisters came into the dorm at 6:00 A.M., clapping their hands loudly to make sure everyone was awake. The children would then kneel down on the cold floor to pray. They prayed till their knees hurt, and longer. After morning prayers they marched downstairs to use the bathroom. Thirty sinks and fourteen stalls for each sex: lots of lining up and waiting your turn, fighting to get a look in the mirror.

Then came another lineup and another march, this time to mass, which started at 7:00 A.M. More prayer. Everyone attended mass, even if very sick. Then another lineup for breakfast in the dining hall in the basement before wolfing down some porridge fast so the nuns wouldn't get mad. The boys did the dishes in the scullery behind the refectory and reset the tables for lunch. Another bell started morning classes at 9:00 A.M. The next bell signalled a fifteen-minute recess, a precious slice from the two hours of playtime each day. The games the children played then were a refuge from the strict discipline of the nuns and priest; it was their time to create their own rules within their own games. They had snowball fights, built forts, skated on the frozen marsh, jumped rope, and played basketball, baseball, marbles, hopscotch, checkers, and cards. The skipping rope, toboggans, and cards were all homemade. The skates were in hot demand, and the "pets" got first dibs.

At noon the lunch bell rang. At 12:30 the girls did the lunch dishes and set the table for supper. There was half an hour to play outside before the 1:00 P.M. bell, which brought the younger ones—under ten—back to class. For the older ones, it was time to do chores in the kitchen, laundry, or on the farm. Another bell granted a fifteen-minute recess at 3:30, giving the children an hour to play before the supper bell. After supper they knit for an hour, making and mending clothing for themselves, the Sisters, and the male staff members. At 7:00 P.M. they reported for benediction. The older children closed the day with an hour of study time.

Additional prayers were thrown in throughout the day—while children waited in line for food, when they lined up for class, when class started, after first period. Before they slept, they knelt by their beds and prayed again, saying the rosary, once again long after their knees were sore. Prayer suffused quotidian life. "All we did was pray," a survivor told Isabelle Knockwood.

The Mi'kmaq had adapted the Catholic faith to their traditions and culture, for example singing traditional songs as well as Catholic hymns translated into Mi'kmaw and believing in a single Creator while maintaining a belief that all things, animate or inanimate, have that Creator's spirit within them. Traditionally, God was a process, an act of creation and care, a relationship. But the God that Father Mackey presented in the chapel, the God the Sisters prayed to, was a different thing. Though most of the children were Catholic, many were used to praying in Mi'kmaw. And all things Mi'kmaw were frowned on.

Playtime. Sisters of Charity, Halifax, Congregational Archives

Many, perhaps one-third of the children, spoke little if any English. But anyone who spoke Mi'kmaw—"gibberish" or "mumbo jumbo," as the Sisters often called it—in any circumstance was severely punished. One survivor recalls witnessing a girl receive a vicious strapping by a Sister who screamed, "Speak English!" with every blow. The girl refused, no matter how long it went on. Older students translated this danger to new ones who did not yet speak English. Until they learned the language, they had a choice between being beaten and being mute. They could not safely ask to use the washroom. Many graduated still unable to read or write in English. Those who went on to public high school found themselves far behind their classmates.

The children at Shubenacadie learned that their own culture was inferior. Sisters and the principal used terms like "dirty savage" and "heathen." They told the students they would "never amount to anything," that they were stupid and no good, and repeated a popular refrain of the times: *The only good Indian is a dead Indian*. Their people were uncivilized. They were godless pagans. Isabelle Knockwood wrote of how the children resisted the strangely garbed women who imposed these rituals on them. The boys made up their own names for the nuns using obscene Mi'kmaw puns. They called one sister *Bujigm*. It was nonsense, but implied that she was sexually loose. Knockwood also wrote of the boys peeing into the teachers' and principal's milk while working in the barn. During a hymn, a young girl changed the Latin words *resurrecsit sicut dixit*, or "he said he would rise again," to *resurrecsit kisiku iktit*, Mi'kmaw for "when the old man got up he farted." According to Knockwood, the Sister patiently stopped the song to correct the girl's pronunciation, much to the delight of the rest of the children.

After a day of lineups, prayer, and labour, each child changed into flannel nightclothes and returned to a white iron bed with cartoon characters on the bedspread, in one of four long rows in a dormitory with several dozen other children. There were large statues of the Virgin Mary on the walls. When the lights went out, the boys could look out the window of their dorm and see the girls' window, and vice versa. They kneeled again on the polished, cold hardwood floors for bedtime prayers. Some survivors remember being made to bend over and pull down their pants to be strapped on an almost nightly basis. They then crawled under blankets that had long ago worn thin—Indian Affairs refused to replace them—and shivered through the night. Finally, they were locked into their dorms. "There was a fire escape," survivor Rita Joe wrote in her autobiography, "but I often wondered what would have happened if there was a fire."

The children were supposed to remain in their beds. Many could not stop crying for weeks or even months, despite the consequences. Others listened to their crying through the night. The disciplinarians turned off the tap water each night. Survivors remember drinking from the toilets when they were thirsty. They were made to use the bathroom before bed and never during the night, so bedwetting was common. Some snuck to the toilets at bedtime and tried to sleep on one so they wouldn't pee in bed. Sometimes a bully would pee on someone else's bed to get them in trouble. The children tried to hide or dry it with their blankets. In the morning the disciplinarian Sister inspected the crotches of their underwear for stains. If she found anything suspicious, she would push the suspect's face into the stains, strap him, or send him on a "pee parade" through the cafeteria in front of everyone, wearing wet, stained underwear or bedsheets as a hat.

Despite the risk involved, there was also a fair bit of sneaking around at night, especially among the older kids. Sometimes the boys would climb from fire escape to fire escape and into the girls' dorm after the Sisters were asleep. But other times it was more innocent than that, just siblings seeking each other out to snuggle and whisper and check in on one another. Many children snuck out during the evenings to go to town, sometimes to take in a movie but mostly just for the sake of adventure and a little variety, risking severe punishment for the thrill.

STUDY AND WORK

In class the children knit, mended clothing, and studied—spending most of their time on English. But according to Knockwood, "The attempts at English-language teaching were quite rudimentary." Their texts were religious and the stories they read had morals about being good Canadian citizens. They learned that their own culture was backwards, uncivilized, and that it was dying. It was not the way forward. The children could not identify themselves as good citizens, given that their own lives were nothing like the stories they were reading about white nuclear families. They had grown up among extended families and tight-knit communities.

Their parents often travelled to find work and food. Many of the children had no parents at all. With their parents dead or away, uncles, aunts, cousins, siblings, and family friends took care of them. This way of living, they were taught, was wrong.

And now they lived in a residential school. There was nothing in the stories about residential schools. As the textbooks explained it, all human progress came from Europe, especially Britain. The most intelligent and noble people all had their origins there. Europeans, finding the rest of the world uncivilized, had improved things everywhere. The children learned—in story, song, verse, and image—how Britain had come to a wild, savage Mi'kma'ki and civilized it. "*Rule Britannia! / Britannia rule the waves / Britons never, never, never shall be slaves,*" the Mi'kmaw children sang. Christopher Columbus was also honoured. He "*sailed across the sea and found this land for you and me,*" they sang. Curriculum included a song called "The Canadian Way": "*We work together / we learn together / the good Canadian way.*" From another songbook they sang all praises to the brave, strong white men who had discovered and conquered an unfriendly landscape. "*This land was built by pioneers,*" they sang.

The texts showed First Nations people, too: the province provided texts with pictures of Hurons scalping missionaries. It wasn't discussed, just shown as if it spoke for itself. The children learned of the inferiority of their cultures' ancient political systems. "We must not suppose…that the Indians all had strong governments like those of the French and English," one textbook read. They learned of a few ill-advised, weak attempts by their people to resist progress. "Indians found it difficult to learn the white man's ways," the students read in a textbook called *The Story of Canada*, which went on to say that the Indians would trade anything for liquor and behaved badly when they got drunk. "Not all the white men…were willing to let the Indians carry on so foolishly," it assured them. The children learned that their people were still in a prehistoric state, that they needed to learn farming as well as proper dress and behaviour, to become more like Euro-Canadians, the more advanced race. It started with small groups organized by family and moved into tribes. Eventually the tribes formed a nation with a royal family. Ultimately, the nations get together and form a commonwealth.

The study of the White Man's hard-working habits was supplemented with actual labour. The gleaming walls and floors of Shubenacadie always impressed visitors. This was the work of the children. They had "chores," jobs that took most of their time. On Saturdays, older kids supervised while younger ones cleaned. They swept and mopped and waxed the floors until they could see their faces in them. Some knelt, scrubbing so long they suffered painful inflammation in the knees. This is how they learned to be properly "civilized" homemakers and farmers. Every afternoon the children—boys and girls—made socks, mittens, blouses, skirts, and pants, repaired shoes, did hemming, patchwork, mat-hooking, and quilting. During the war years they "knit for Britain," making socks for soldiers. Each child made a pair a week. "The children are usually deft with their fingers," the Catholic Diocese wrote. The younger girls did laundry. Every weekday morning and afternoon, except Tuesdays, they washed school uniforms, sheets, blankets, towels, and the Sisters' and principal's clothes, often by hand. They ironed and dried them using the mangle, which Isabelle Knockwood described as a one-by-two-metre "red monstrosity of a machine" with three long rollers, ten centimetres in diameter, surrounding a larger central roller.

Knockwood remembers witnessing a young girl nearly lose her hand in a gruesome encounter with the mangle. The girls tried to turn it off but the propeller broke and the emergency switch was too high to reach. The girl screamed for several minutes until the Sister in charge came running in from her tea break. The girl's hand was missing a layer of skin. She was pale, her lips purple. She fainted, and was rushed to hospital where she stayed

Older girls worked the kitchen, where survivors remember many accidents.
Sisters of Charity, Halifax, Congregational Archives

several months. Her fingers never totally healed, but crochet work helped bring back some dexterity. When Father Mackey reported the accident, he said the girl had found she could warm her hands on the mangle. She'd already done it once, Mackey said, almost getting her hands caught the first time. "No one questioned how her hands could be cold working on a steaming machine in a hot laundry," Knockwood notes. No safety device was ever installed and no safety training ever given. Knockwood remembers five girls who were maimed by the mangle or dough mixer in her eleven years at the school. The girls worked unsupervised.

The older girls got kitchen duty. Four at a time worked with two Sisters and a famously cranky, and sometimes cruel, cook in the kitchen. They got up at 4:00 or 5:00 A.M. to get the coal fires going and put on two giant aluminum pots of porridge. They each sliced and buttered a few dozen loaves of bread, boiled a couple hundred eggs, and made soup. They worked until 6:30 P.M., a fourteen-hour day. It required lugging ten-gallon milk pails around. Some of the girls weren't tall enough to reach the stovetops and had to stand on stools. When they started they were partnered with another girl who'd been at it awhile, and the Sister might show them how to clean the fireplace and light the fire. It was children training children to use knives and machinery, including an industrial milk-and-cream separator, and a dough mixer. The kitchen-girls spent about an hour a day in class.

Three months after the first children arrived at Shubenacadie, two girls got their hands caught in the dough mixer. The first had been cleaning the mixer; the second, not noticing where her friend's hand was, turned the machine on. She reached in to help the first girl. A Sister heard their screams, turned off the machine, and took them to the Victoria General Hospital in Halifax, forty minutes away. The second girl lost most of a finger. "They were warned many times about tinkering with the machines," Mackey wrote.

Each girl worked four weeks at a time in the kitchen, twice each term, in rotation so that a new girl was added each week. During preserving season, two more girls were brought in. Survivors remember being severely punished for mistakes. "Sister Maria Adrian has beaten me many times over the head and pulled my hair and struck me on the back of the neck with a ruler," one fifteen-year-old girl told RCMP officers and the Indian Agent at Shubenacadie in 1936. She said the Sister also beat her on the back with her fists. She had run away after five years at the school. Eleven weeks in the kitchen had been her breaking point. Another Sister made her clean windows by tying one end of a rope around her waist, with a little girl holding the other end, and having her climb out the top-floor window. She chose this task over a beating. The girl told the police this treatment was common. "After we get a beating we are asked what we get the beating for and if we tell them we do not know we get another beating," she explained. The Indian Agent reported the incidents to J. D. Sutherland, acting superintendent at Indian Affairs. Sutherland passed the complaints on to Mackey, who took them to Sister Maria Adrian, who denied the incidents. Nevertheless, the girl was discharged and went to day school.

The kitchen work was meant to groom the girls to be housewives, with a focus on cooking. They made basic Canadian food: bread and buns, meat and vegetables, pies and cakes. Survivors recall that the food was often rancid, and always scarce. But the Sister in charge of the kitchen made a special breakfast for the principal and teachers. The children learned how to set a proper table and serve a three-course meal on china in the principal's dining room, which had a mahogany dining set and high-backed chairs under a crystal chandelier, and lace curtains.

The boys didn't have much time for class either. As Mackey said in a letter to Indian Affairs, they were too busy with "work other than reading, writing, and arithmetic...By the time we have ball playing, coasting, skating, and keeping the house clean, the day is pretty well used up." Mackey

Unknown male student, 1932. Collection of Elsie Charles Basque, Nova Scotia Museum

started each year by making a list of twenty to thirty boys, fourteen and older, of a certain size to do the hardest work. He divided these up into five or six teams, each with a few experienced farm and carpentry workers. He posted the lists in his office, the dairy barn, and the recreation room. Any boy from Grade 5 up worked half of each day on the farm or else stoking the furnace. The furnace boys shovelled 200 tons of coal every year and cleaned out the ashes daily. They worked from 4:00 A.M., relieving the night watchman, until 7:00 P.M., a fifteen-hour day. The farm boys planted and tended the fields, producing 15 tons of turnips and 25 tons of potatoes each year, as well as other fresh produce. They fed and later slaughtered the hens, cows, and pigs. There were also fifty head of Ayrshire cattle on the farm, producing 142 litres of milk each day.

The idea of the farm was to sell the vegetables, dairy, and meat, but some of it was eaten at the school. The boys rose even before the nuns to get the milking done by 5:15 each morning, and milked again in the evening. They also had to feed the animals, keep the barns clean, fertilize, hay, plant, harvest, and plow the fields. Each boy put in about ten weeks of work with the cows per term. A hired farmer and his assistant supervised when they were available, but sometimes the boys were on their own with the cows. And like the girls, the boys sometimes got seriously injured. One fell from the loft while pitching hay and broke his neck. He had to wear a brace for several months.

Some boys rotated between farm work and furnace work. "I was as black as coal one day and stinking to high heaven the next," one survivor recalled.

Older boys with a farm horse. SISTERS OF CHARITY, HALIFAX, CONGREGATIONAL ARCHIVES

These same boys also helped construct new buildings. Father Mackey stressed this in his letters to Indian Affairs, claiming that the lack of school funds for skilled labour created "a good opportunity [for the children] to learn carpentry work." Mackey said the older boys preferred the labour to being in class. The smaller-sized teenage boys did other work: taking meals to sick kids confined to their beds, washing dishes, and cleaning common areas like the washrooms and refectory.

Superintendent General of Indian Affairs M. Christianson, however, was not impressed with the children's labours. After visiting Shubenacadie one afternoon in the spring of 1937, he predicted that the graduates would soon join a lineup of "Indians depending, for a livelihood, on what relief they get from the Department and the sale of Indian handicraft." He felt that the children should learn to make baskets and handles to sell for a living. If anything, Shubenacadie was *too* focused on book-learning. Mackey disagreed. He replied that the girls would only end up competing with their own people making baskets on the reserves: "The market for these things in this locality is over supplied." If he had the money, Mackey said, he'd hire a domestic-science teacher. The girls would be more useful as proper homemakers, European style. It wasn't the school's job to teach about baskets and axe handles. It never occurred to either man that the students could learn to make handles and baskets, or how to keep a house clean, at home.

HUNGER AND ILLUSTRIOUS VISITORS

At breakfast time the children ate a morning dose of cod liver oil. It was no worse than the food. Some remember a predictable diet of bread, potatoes, turnips, carrots, beef, and milk. Many remember the awful "porridge-like substance" that made them feel ill. But survivors have most often talked of a hunger that never went away. There just wasn't enough food. At their most resourceful, the children ate meat off the bones they'd find in the principal's garbage can. "There used to be a special garbage can called the river can," one survivor told the *Micmac News*. It was the principal's. "There would be very select pieces of roast pork or beef in this thing." Some hunted pigeons or fished for eel in the lake. They used butter knives stolen from the kitchen to clean the fish, and hooked them with safety pins and string. They lit fires in eel barrels and boiled the fish in used cans. Boys on farm duty were hungry enough to slice up cattle feed and raw turnips and mix them into a chow. They also stole whatever milk they could drink and as many raw potatoes as they could eat.

Yet as the children starved, Indian Affairs turned a blind eye. The director of medical services, Dr. E. L. Stone, inspected Nova Scotia's reserves and residential school in 1935 and found that the children at Shubenacadie were in better physical condition after a year at the school. Stone didn't mention that two months earlier Indian Affairs had cut back on relief payments for the reserves. An agent had recommended they do so to motivate the Mi'kmaq to work harder at fishing and farming. Stone's report was typical. Various visitors to the school, including H. W. McGill, deputy superintendent of Indian Affairs, had reported witnessing shiny, happy students, clean and healthy. The Sisters led out the darkest students they could find, who were considered more representative of the charitable work being done there. Shubenacadie's survivors remember being scrubbed and told to wear their cleanest clothes, and warned to be on their best behaviour for visitors. And to smile, masking any problems that might lie beneath the surface.

Indian Affairs sent inspectors, with plenty of advanced notice, every February and May. The cook always made a special meal for them. Survivor Isabelle Knockwood wrote that before an inspector's arrival the priest gathered up the straps from the Sisters and had a student burn them in the furnace. The children were told to say they were well fed or else keep their mouths shut completely. And whenever newspaper reporters or members of the public visited, the children were to change from their everyday prison-style garb into their special-occasion formal wear.

In the spring of 1936, Dr. Thomas Robertson visited the school with a mission from Indian Affairs to report on the health and nutrition levels of the children. It was part of his overall objective of "investigating conditions among the Indians in the Maritime Provinces." Like other visitors, he noted that the children were "neat and clean in dress and appearance. Apparently happy and well nourished." The school itself was "scrupulously clean and orderly." The staff was "doing everything for the betterment of the children." It was noted that the children were weighed every month and that a doctor visited the school every other week to see sick children. Yet Robertson also wrote of his concerns with residential schools. He didn't like that they broke up families, taking children away from good homes where they belonged with their loving parents. He admitted he hadn't studied the impacts of the schools on the children (though others had found that residential school graduates were worse off than their counterparts on the reserves), but he suggested Indian Affairs consider looking into it. His report had no impact.

Despite the rave reviews of the health of the children, Indian Affairs was well aware of the constant hunger at this and other residential schools. Parents had been demanding solutions for hunger at the schools for decades. In the 1940s Indian Affairs used this widespread hunger as a chance to conduct experiments on the residents of Shubenacadie and five other residential schools without telling them about it. Dr. Lionel Bradley Pett, who was in charge of Indian Affairs's new nutrition division, was the man behind the experiments. He would eventually use the results to start the Indian Health Services Branch of the Department of National Health and Welfare (now the First Nations and Inuit Health Branch of Health Canada). Pett saw the widespread malnutrition in residential schools as a chance to see if vitamin pills alone could improve health, independent of a good diet.

First, Pett needed a sense of just how bad nutrition was at residential schools. He sent dieticians into six schools for several hours or a full day. As always, Indian Affairs warned the schools in advance. The dieticians would interview staff members and children and review menus, grocery purchases, kitchen and storage facilities, the dining halls, and farmlands. The dieticians had a meal—bulked up with extra butter and meat for the visitors' sake—with the children. They ultimately found that conditions at the schools were "overwhelmingly poor." The students were underfed, sometimes to the point of sickness. Indian Affairs wasn't meeting its own basic nutritional requirements. It was spending about half of what was needed to provide those basic needs. At Shubenacadie, they noted, "The school has a larger number of small pupils than is usually the case."

In 1946 Pett hired nutritionist Alice McCready to do a follow-up study. She was "utterly disgusted" by the lack of progress from the Department's new food-training program for cooks and the children who helped in the kitchen. She concluded that the training was wasted on kitchen staff who were paid so poorly by the Department that they never stuck around long. Conditions were perfect for Pett's five-year experiment, which he started two years later with the help of Indian Affairs. It's unknown how much Indian Affairs spent on the experiment, but the Department that was chronically underspending hired a large team of nutritionists, doctors, psychologists, nurses, dentists, photographers, and lab technicians to travel across the country conducting intelligence tests, blood work, and physicals on a thousand children. Pett chose Shubenacadie because the conditions were particularly poor there: the children's diets were, even by residential school standards, deficient in vitamins A, B, C, iron, and iodine, the children had low levels of ascorbic acid in their blood during winter, and there were high rates of gingivitis, which was believed to be linked to diet.

At Shubenacadie and the other experimental schools, the team of professionals descended on the children, telling them they were "carrying on what we call a nutrition study...to help you and the school." The government told researchers what to say to the children in its *Outline of Talk to Children in Indian Schools Prior to Taking Dietary Records.* As government wards and children, they weren't asked for their consent. The experimenters divided the children into two groups. The first ate vitamin C pills and other supplements every day, and the second ate sugar pills they thought were medicine. The experimenters then tested the blood and checked the teeth of both groups to see if the vitamin C had had any impact. The five years of ongoing physical exams were intensive, exhausting, and sometimes painful. Researchers took dozens of photos, and the teachers had the children write thank-you notes afterward, in which they wrote things like, "The pokes that I got didn't hurt me very much."

To ensure that any change in dental health was really because of the vitamins, Pett told Indian Affairs, "No specialized, over-all type of dental service should be provided, such as the use of sodium fluoride, dental prophylaxis or even urea compounds." Once again children at Shubenacadie were denied dental treatments, even while children at other residential schools received them. When he spoke of the work, Pett talked about students at "boarding schools." According to Ian Mosby, the University of Guelph food historian who uncovered information about the study in a 2013 paper, human research was common at the time, but researchers were smart enough to be discreet about it—the general public was squeamish about the idea. It was easier to get away with if your research subjects were considered public burdens.

In the end Pett found "no beneficial effect" to the supplements, and the research did little if anything to change the food situation at Shubenacadie or any other residential school. "Their findings were not important," Mosby tells me. "They were rarely cited. They were not addressing the root causes of the malnutrition they saw." Undaunted, Pett planned a second experiment at Shubenacadie using enriched flour, the same kind that had been found to potentially cause anemia. But the experiment never happened and the team of researchers and their food supplements disappeared from the children's lives, leaving them to their hunger.

DISCIPLINE, PUNISH, AND ABUSE

Survivors remember a dizzying, wickedly creative array of punishments, physical and otherwise. There were too many rules to remember, and the punishments seemed arbitrary anyway. They came between bouts of gentleness, out of the blue, swift and hard and often vicious. The children lived in fear, never knowing when it was coming or what exactly "it" would be and who would deliver it. They felt the sting of a harness-leather strap—or a steel ruler, wire pointer, bamboo ski pole, long-handled shoehorn, chalkboard eraser, fist, open palm, or else they'd be shaken or feel their ear pinched—if they snuggled with a sibling, ran in the halls, spoke too loudly, avoided eye contact with an adult (which they had learned in Mi'kmaw culture was the respectful thing to do), or didn't pray properly. Yelled insults accompanied the physical punishments. Besides beatings, Sisters would make boys wear dresses or would rub medicine on their genitals. Children were denied food or made to do the worst chores or given extra work, locked in the "dungeon" or "the hole," had their mouths washed with salt or soap or lye, their heads shaved, or were made to go barefoot in the winter.

Some survivors recall that darker-skinned children, those without parents or with disabilities received more beatings. Disciplinarians also targeted children whose parents lived far away and couldn't visit, and told those with parents nearby that it was wrong to say what went on at the school, that to do so would be a betrayal. Some pundits have pointed out that corporal punishment was the norm at all schools during this time. But survivor testimony—to community Elders, police, and Indian Affairs while the school was open, and publicly after its closure—shows that even by the standards of the day, some of the nuns and priests crossed way over the line between corporal punishment and abuse. Children were whipped and beaten bloody, and many survivors still have scars. One boy couldn't feed himself after his hands had been sliced bloody by the edge of a ruler.

Many survivors recall being force-fed rancid or wilted food, having their faces shoved into it when they refused, and being made to eat their own vomit. There was a great deal of sickness at the school in general, paired with another commonly reported form of abuse, neglect. Sick children were often ignored and sent outside during playtime even on the coldest winter days. Some survivors remember receiving serious beatings for complaining of stomach pains or diarrhea. Others remember the Sisters and priests humiliating, belittling, and shaming them. And a great many remember being sexually abused by a nun or priest or both.

One survivor told Isabelle Knockwood, when she was researching for *Out of the Depths*, that Father Mackey demanded oral sex from him as a boy. When he refused the priest gave him the strap. Some remember the physical and sexual abuse as separate things, but sometimes they were related. One man told the TRC in Halifax about falling sick at the age of seven. A Sister gave him a sponge bath and "took liberties." When he resisted, she had older boys come and beat him, leaving permanent scars. Another former resident told the TRC that a Sister gave him candy hoping he would give her oral sex. His brother told him the same Sister had given him oral sex many times, until he urinated in her mouth.

Women also remember sexual abuse at the school. Several survivors have memories of a Sister who liked to watch the girls take their underwear off and then would go look inside them. "We were all sexually abused by the priests and the nuns," another survivor told the Commission of her and her siblings' experience at Shubenacadie. "[The Sisters] told us the more pain we had, the closer to heaven."

ACHING FOR HOME

The children did their best to let their parents and other elders in on the abuse and neglect they experienced at the school. But the Sisters told them not to tell. They said that good children were loyal to their school. Letters home were screened and censored, as was any mail children received. Other times, a Sister would dictate a letter home, or write it on the chalkboard, and the children would write it down. Every parent received the same happy message. Sisters also monitored parental visits, which happened on Sundays in the visiting parlour on the second floor. The room had a piano and several books the children weren't allowed to touch. Some survivors remember toys being put there for visits and then mysteriously disappearing soon after the parents left. The visits were stale, uncomfortable events for the children. They could only speak English, a difficult language for many of the parents. But it was better than nothing, which is what children whose parents lived far away got. Until the mid-1940s, Indian Affairs didn't allow these children to go home in the summer. "If the children from New Brunswick who are attending Shubenacadie Residential School were allowed home for holidays there would be, in many cases, considerable difficulty in having them returned," wrote J. D. Sutherland, acting superintendent of Indian education, in June 1936. "At the same time, it is doubtful if the parents would provide the cost of their transportation, and, as our funds are limited, the Department is not in a position to incur the expenditure...." Some parents offered to pay for a return train ticket. Indian Affairs ignored them or told them it wasn't possible.

Parents wrote letters saying they missed their children. They asked to have them home for the summer. "We know the worry, the emptiness and the desolation of our homes because as parents our hearts are with our little children who are away at school," one parent told *Micmac News* years after the school had closed. Indian Affairs or the school principal told the parents not to worry because the school was so much fun during the summer months, and besides it was too expensive to send everyone home. (One elder in Burnt Church had a stroke waiting for the Department to change its mind, after years of asking for his sons back. After the stroke, they sent home the eldest of the man's two boys.)

The Department also denied vacations to some children who came from the nearby Shubenacadie reserve. If the principal thought a child's family was a bad influence—or on welfare—that child could not go home. Indian Affairs wanted to avoid paying out extra relief so families could take care of their children over the summer. "The Department will expect the expenses to be kept as low as possible," Sutherland wrote. For those few who qualified for summer vacations, parents had to pay half the rail fare. But Sutherland reassured an Indian Agent that the children enjoyed the school during summer because chores were lightened and they "are taken on picnics and... other entertainment is provided for them." When children did come home for summer, some parents tried to keep them there come fall. For the school principal, September was about making lists of absent children. He'd then give these lists to Indian Affairs, who sent Indian Agents looking for the children, taking RCMP officers with them if need be.

Some survivors remember the summer being a better time than usual. "The nuns tried to treat us a little better," Rita Joe wrote in her autobiography. She recalled eating cornflakes and juice every day for breakfast. The Sisters piled them into a pickup truck and drove down to the lake for a swim. There were more toys available, and no one felt like they had to fight over them. They even got to sleep in sometimes. The praying and church services were less frequent. Others remember it differently: they were forced to pick berries in the heat all day, and if the Sisters found any berry stains on their tongues they were beaten.

No child was allowed home for Christmas or other holidays, a policy that lasted until the 1950s. Indian Affairs told agents to reassure parents that Christmas at the school was a fun time, full of celebration and festivities. The children decorated the school with tied fir boughs. They were given special presents by the principal and teachers, as well as whatever their families sent. Many survivors remember the gifts bitterly; they received them only to have the nuns take them away again on January 6, locking them away, hanging them on the walls where they could be seen but not touched, or giving them to more favoured children. For some children it didn't matter; it was more important that they got to spend a few precious hours with a sibling during the holiday. Others treasured the oranges they received so highly they put them away to look at rather than eat. They would have to throw away the fruit's shrivelled remains in March. During Christmas 1939, parents from Cambridge reserve showed up at the school demanding their children. The children watched from inside as Father Mackey threatened their parents and ultimately sent them away empty-handed. Eight years later, on Christmas Eve, "Two inebriated Indian parents marred the quiet and peace of the house for some hours," according to the Sisters' Annals. The parents left, when the RCMP came, to avoid spending Christmas in jail.

Even when an agent took a family's side, it was not a guarantee they would see their children. In Bear River, Indian Agent S. E. Darris requested that one family's five children be allowed to go home for the summer of 1937. The Department denied the request and chastised Darris for being too soft. That same summer, Charles Hudson, Indian Agent in Restigouche, New Brunswick, argued that if parents could pay for travel the children should be allowed home. A father in Hudson's jurisdiction wrote directly to Indian Affairs. "They never came home since they left," he wrote of his three boys, who he hadn't seen in six years. They were teenagers now but he remembered them as small children. "They wrote to us and they said that they were lonesome," he pleaded. But here the Department policy was firm: no vacations except for those living very close to the school. Three years later, Indian Affairs changed its mind. It would pay train fare home for children from Restigouche; parents could pay for the return trip. This time Hudson kiboshed the idea, telling the Department, "In all cases home conditions are unsuitable."

Many children decided not to wait for approval to go home. Several ran away from the Shubenacadie residential school nearly every year. In one three-year period, from 1939 to 1942, there were thirty-three reported escape attempts. Four were successful. The children couldn't have known that hundreds of others like them were fleeing residential schools across the country. Escapees usually went straight to the reserve, but they didn't always make it. Some froze to death, starved, or were attacked by animals or vigilantes. Suicides were also common in the residential schools. Indian Affairs responded by providing survival courses. If a body didn't show up, the RCMP knew to look on the reserve. Some children simply walked away from the playground. Others went to more dangerous lengths, jumping out of windows to get away or tying sheets together and climbing down. Some got away "using a fire hose to climb down from the dormitory to the ground, using fire escapes, crawling out of basement windows, and in one case filing down a skeleton key to fit all the doors and leaving via the stairway in the middle of the night," Isabelle Knockwood writes.

"No matter how far he may roam, I want him brought back here," Mackey told the RCMP of the first runaway of 1937. Officers found the boy working on a farm two weeks later. They put him in jail for a few nights and then returned him to the school. In July another boy ran away for eleven days. He made good distance before the RCMP tracked him down and called Mackey, who drove more than four hundred kilometres to pick him up. Three more boys ran away the next year. The RCMP had no trouble finding them. The runaways were trying on Father Mackey, who spent much time dealing with the RCMP tracking them down. Sometimes locals tipped Mackey off about a runner's whereabouts—he was known to pay bounties for successful tips. "This is the fifth time during the past two years," he wrote of one boy's escape attempts. "I feel that Saint Patrick's Home is the only place for that imbecile."

The runaways became so frequent that in the spring of 1938, RCMP officers visited Shubenacadie to warn the boys about a new specialist in finding runaways and lost persons. The specialist was named Perky. He was a young Doberman Pinscher with eighteen months training. He could track runaways down by their scent. The general public didn't yet know of the dog. The RCMP's first use of their new dog was to find two Shubenacadie runaways—twelve and thirteen years old—a year later. The dog found the boys within an hour of their 6 A.M. disappearance, eleven kilometres from the school and deep in the woods. A newspaper article praising the dog said he'd tracked them across a frozen lake. Children ran away much less often after Perky joined the police force.

The runaways, who were mostly boys, were captured and punished severely, brought before the principal to be whipped on the bare buttocks, screaming as the other students were made to watch. One survivor told the CBC of a student who had run away in the winter, was caught, and spent several days in the dungeon living on bread and water before a Sister realized he had severe frostbite on his feet. When she yanked his socks off the skin came with it. They rushed him to hospital, where part of his foot had to be amputated. Other children pleaded with the authorities for their freedom. Few were successful. In 1936 a girl at Shubenacadie wrote to her sister asking for help getting discharged. The sister wrote to their agent, Dr. B. W. Skinner, but he was not supportive or helpful. The sister then wrote to Indian Affairs, mentioning that she also hoped to have her own children home for summer vacation. J. D. Sutherland, acting superintendent of Indian education, received her letter. He replied that the children would have a good time at school during the summer.

GOOD MEMORIES

Since the 1970s, some survivors have defended the school, or at least pointed out that it wasn't an entirely bad experience. Some told *Micmac News* in 1978 that they were glad to have learned English, or practical skills like sewing and knitting, even though they weren't given a choice. Others recalled friendships that developed at the school. "It taught me how to look after myself," another told the CBC in the 1980s. "A child needs discipline," one survivor told the *Halifax Daily News* in the 1990s. "I don't call it abuse. If we were punished we brought it on ourselves." In her autobiography, Rita Joe wrote about the bad and good of the school. Despite its hardships, Shubenacadie gave her strength, she said. And she learned pottery, sewing, knitting—useful things. And occasionally fun things, like skating or the forbidden sweetness of passing "I love you" notes to boys—risky behaviour under the sharp watch of the Sisters. She made sure she got some book-learning too. If she finished her chores by 2:00 P.M., the teacher would unlock the reading room for her. The first time she entered she grabbed the first book she saw. Astronomy. She was astounded. She worked extra hard after that. There were other worlds locked in that room, and she wanted to go there. She managed it about once a week.

A woman who lived at the school from 1955 to 1962 wrote an article for the *Micmac-Maliseet Nations News* in 1992, saying she was well cared for at Shubenacadie, and that it was an improvement over the poverty she'd known living in Eskasoni. She recalled her summers at the school being "peaceful and tranquil," some of the best times of her life. She said she'd been free to speak Mi'kmaw and that older girls had even translated between her and the Sisters. She learned to play several instruments there, including the flute, piano, and organ. She also learned "love, care, responsibility, good manners, politeness, respect for others and how to pray and give thanks to God for what we had." Any punishments, she said, were reasonable, and not physical. She remembered children being denied privileges like playtime and television if they disobeyed, and nothing worse.

Sister Donna Geernaert, who is now the chancellor of Mount Saint Vincent University and congregational leader of the Sisters of Charity, says that survivors sometimes approach her to confide having had positive experiences at the school. One student told her that she remembers Sister Gilberta very fondly. Sister Gilberta worked at the school from 1956 until it closed in 1967, filling roles as a teacher, sewing instructor, disciplinarian, and choir leader. She made a special effort to get gingham aprons for the girls so that they could make them into special clothing—something other than their uniforms. She was a talented musician and seamstress. When the school closed, she was transferred to the Academy of the Assumption in Wellesley Hills, Massachusetts. The woman told Sister Donna that as a little girl she would lie awake in bed at night, afraid. She would go looking for Sister Gilberta, seeing if there was light coming from under her door at the end of the dorm. She'd knock gently and beg the Sister to come into bed with her. Sister Gilberta would not do that, but she took the girl gently back to her own bed with soothing words. However, not every student remembers Sister Gilberta so well. Others told Isabelle Knockwood that Sister Gilberta was one of the most vicious of the nuns during the last years of the institution. One recalled her strapping each of his hands ninety times every day for speaking Mi'kmaw.

COMMUNITY RESPONSES

From the beginning, the Shubenacadie Indian Residential School had a poor reputation when it came to learning. A letter from a Mi'kmaw man in a 1931 issue of *Truro Daily News* described it as a place "Where everything 'Indian' is to be forever obliterated or cast into the Bottomless Pit." The results of the "millions and millions of dollars" spent on the residential school and the day schools in the province, the letter argued, were that, "We have not one single Injin who can earn his bread and butter, through or by the use of his pen."

The general population of Nova Scotia had some idea that all was not right at the school, though the worst of it was usually ignored, if not whitewashed by the media. The 1934 public inquiry into abusive punishments presided over by Judge Audette (who sympathized with white people who didn't want to live near Indians) in which the staff members of the school were exonerated, resulted in jubilant media coverage that sometimes mocked the children's complaints. The *Halifax Herald* depicted the boys who testified to having been severely physically abused by the principal as disgruntled whiners lacking ethics and sincerity.

Many complaints had reached Indian Affairs. The police knew of the violence at the school—some elders have since reported that RCMP officers once intervened to stop the beating of a child there but ignored many other testimonies of abuse. If the police responded at all, it was to tell a family to stop making up lies just to get its children back. After the first school year, Chief Dan Francis of the Cambridge reserve in Nova Scotia wrote to Indian Affairs. He was disgusted by the violence the children reported when they returned home for the summer. "I thought that the school was built for Indian children to learn to read and write," he wrote. "Not for slaves and prisoners like jail…one Indian boy of this reserve was so beaten by Father Mackey he was laid out for seven days." Indian Affairs forwarded the letter to Mackey, but explained that the Department "did not place much reliance in [Francis's] charges." Francis's complaints were the first in a twice annual—spring and fall—cat-and-mouse tangle between Maritime First Nations communities, Indian Affairs, the principal of Shubenacadie, and the RCMP.

In 1932 Chief Ben Christmas of Membertou wrote to Mackey on behalf of a parent who didn't want to send her child back to the school. She was concerned that after two years he hadn't learned anything; he'd only lost his "own graceful tongue." She was upset that he could no longer pray in Mi'kmaw. She promised to enroll him in a mission church Sunday school and to pay back the cost of a return ticket that Indian Affairs had paid for. The results of her petition are unclear.

Some parents went to their Indian Agents, but rarely found a sympathetic ear. Others, lacking confidence in the agents, wrote to Indian Affairs in Ottawa. These letters were often forwarded to the school principal. Other parents wrote to the principal only to be passed back to the Indian Agent. This bureaucratic dance was further complicated by the church's involvement. Some parents enlisted white lawyers. A former resident at the school hired attorney R. H. Butts in 1936 to keep Mackey from taking his younger sister and brother. He claimed he was abused and overworked when he was at the school, that he received no real education. He didn't want his siblings to go through the same. Mackey dismissed the man's claims: "To keep them from spreading falsehoods," he wrote to the Indian Agent who relayed Butts's message, "about those who try to do something for them, seems hopeless. And why white people fall for such stories is hard to explain…I never hope to catch up with the Indian and his lies." Mackey went on to attack the complainant, calling him a "big body in the mind of a ten-year-old child," and defended the school vigorously: "Each child spends far more time in the classroom than the regulations call for," he wrote. "To make an Indian work is the unpardonable sin among them...I am getting a bit tired of playing square with the Indian and in turn have him cut my throat."

Lawyers weren't the only white experts parents sought for help. In the fall of 1937, after Mackey threatened a man with sending "the RCMP [to] take [your twelve-year-old son] back to the school and he will remain until sixteen years of age and have no further vacations," the man took a tremendous risk. He ignored Mackey's threat and took his son to see a Fredericton doctor. The boy had received such severe beatings he was scared to return to the school. "We have a nice little home and there is nothing to hinder me from keeping my family together from now on which they haven't had for some time," the father wrote. "They think a lot of one another and there will not be any need of separating them anymore." The man brought Mackey's threatening response with him to Dr. H. S. Everett, who in turn wrote to the local Indian Agent, stressing that the father was not reliant on welfare. "[He] has a home in Rollingdam right across the road from a rural school which [the boy] can attend...I think he would be OK at home," he wrote. "[The father] hasn't had any help from the Department for some years and is self supporting." The man's Indian Agent, R. Lee McCutcheon, then wrote to Mackey questioning the use of threats: "Is this a bluff?" he asked. Mackey denied the boy had been beaten. "That is the usual line of the Indian," he wrote. "It should be impressed upon the Indian that he cannot have his own way in matters concerning which the Department has set regulations." But in this case, Indian Affairs decided to discharge the boy from Shubenacadie. It happened sometimes. Two years later, in 1939, nine students who didn't return after summer vacation were discharged.

Other times, parents were hindered more than helped by the white men they enlisted. In 1941 a Cape Breton Mi'kmaw mother asked a lawyer, F. C. Cotton, to help her keep her child at home. She'd told Mackey the child was staying home after summer vacation, and Mackey had told the local agent to retrieve the child or have the RCMP do it. Cotton wrote the agent and reminded him the woman's husband was sick, that she needed her children to help out at home. There was a day school in their community and she swore to send them there. "She says that she 'loves' her children," Cotton wrote. But by putting the word "love" in quotation marks, he completely discredited her. The child was brought back to the school.

Parents also weren't clear on how long their children would be gone. In some cases, once their children were taken they didn't see them again for as many as twelve years. By the time some children returned home, their parents had forgotten their age. Other parents lied and said their kids were too sick to return to school, or that they were more than sixteen years old even if they weren't. But the principal could retain students who were more than sixteen if he felt the youth had nowhere else to go, if he or she was too small, "simple-minded," or otherwise "deficient."

Parents tried to get their kids back in many different ways. Some encouraged escape. Others showed up at the school demanding their children back. Some issued legal challenges. But most followed the rules and wrote letters to agents, the principal, and to Ottawa bureaucrats. The federal government had long been too powerful and too ruthless a foe for most Mi'kmaw individuals or families to risk defying.

FREEDOM DAY

Usually, students "graduated" from Shubenacadie at the age of sixteen, though the school principal could keep them longer if he felt they needed it. Some stayed there until they were twenty. Few graduates got past Grade 8, and almost none went on to other schooling. Some students were discharged before they were sixteen. Some went to on-reserve day schools. Others were deemed mentally incapable of handling school. Some were too sick to attend. Some died at school or at home during the summer.

The children called the day they left Shubenacadie "Freedom Day," and sometimes the Sisters did too. In the early decades of the school, the children received no certificates or diplomas, no official indication that they'd been there or graduated but a new (second-hand) ill-fitting outfit for the outside world. School principals would often put the children on a train to the wrong reserve. The children, now young men and women, would arrive at a station with no one there to meet them, lost and alone. Sometimes Elders from another First Nation would take them home.

When the first Shubenacadie residents came home, many on the reserves were shocked. The children had so quickly become like strangers. They could no longer speak the language. They no longer understood tradition and culture. They acted like outsiders; not like whites exactly, but different. Some were timid and nervous, and so quiet. Something was wrong with them—"not right in the head," as some put it. Some told horrifying stories. Word quickly got around. Many Elders who hadn't attended the residential school remember, as children, how their parents would threaten them, using the school as a kind of bogeyman. "If you don't behave, I'll put you in the residential school!" a mother might shout. It was an effective warning.

Life after Shubenacadie could be a traumatic experience. For many years residential school was all they'd known. In prison terms, residents had been "institutionalized." But unlike inmates leaving prison, the children leaving Shubenacadie were given no help transitioning to the outside world—be it on a reserve or in a city. Survivor Rita Joe recalled sitting on the train and crying as she left the school for good. She was leaving home. But she was also relieved. Her soul was free of the nuns. "If I was going to commit a sin, I would commit it with my own free will," she wrote.

Some had been at the school more than a decade. Whatever family they'd come from had changed. Parents had often died, or moved. "I didn't remember my mother," one survivor recalls. "Coming back into my community I felt as if I didn't belong," said another, "we no longer had that connection with family." Like the children leaving schools in Sussex, New Brunswick, and Port-Royal, hundreds of years earlier, they found themselves stuck between a white world that would never accept them and a First Nations world they could no longer understand. Some found acceptance for a time in the army—especially during the Second World War—but struggled as veterans. Others entered public school and found they were far behind their peers. Even those who had been the best students at Shubenacadie often had to repeat grades in public school. But some persevered and went on to university or community college.

In many cases, Indian Agents took over for the school principal and teachers when children left the school. The agents would place a child in a suitable home back on the reserve—either with the family or elsewhere, sometimes finding them work and accommodation in white households as servants, an ideal situation from Indian Affairs's perspective, which remained intent on assimilating Aboriginal children into white Canadian culture. "I have placed in the last four years some thirty girls in white homes as domestics," Agent McCutcheon bragged in a report to his superiors in 1939. The arrangement did not always work out, he said, "But I am more than satisfied with the average."

Many of the boys who graduated got work as farmhands. As with the girls, it often didn't work out. Their education was poor, and it had failed to make them white. The children's time at Shubenacadie also had no impact on white people's ability to understand them, work well with them, or treat them respectfully. Many former residents quit their jobs to return home. Others, like Rita Joe, found work in the city. She was sixteen years old, and the Sisters of Charity had hooked her up with a job at the Halifax Infirmary, which they'd founded in 1886 and relocated to Queen Street in 1933. Others quickly "reverted to type," as Indian Affairs put it. Having been "no trouble" at residential school, these youth became listless, wandering, often destitute, homeless, and suffering addictions. Many never returned to the reserve, shunning their own people and way of life. Some died this way.

Most, however, eventually returned to embrace their heritage and culture with the passion of the newly converted, eager to relearn the language, music, customs, and ways of living in community. In decades to come, some of these young graduates would grow into the most successful advocates on behalf of their people. Others became great leaders in the ongoing struggle for healing and justice. Rita Joe became a revered poet, never afraid to educate about the lasting pain of colonialism and the strength of Mi'kmaw culture. In taking a job at the Halifax Infirmary she had turned down the Sisters' other offer, which was to study to become a nun. In fact, Rita Joe didn't set foot in a church again for a year. "I was venting my anger at religion as I had experienced it in the school," she wrote. When she returned to church, she said, it was on her own terms. As a parent, she taught her children "about religion but also about our Creator and Native spirituality." The journey to reclaim such cultural confidence often took survivors decades. Today, many respected Elders are also survivors of the Shubenacadie Indian Residential School, and some have been outspoken about those experiences, patiently teaching their stories, lest they be forgotten.

III

ONE YEAR
FROM ANOTHER

PUSH FOR CHANGE

INCREASED SCRUTINY

In many ways, one year at the Shubenacadie residential school was inde-cipherable from another. The Sisters taught a curriculum designed for white children, the students walked a careful path amidst numerous threats to their health and safety, and the principal ran the show. But each decade there were several key shifts in how the school functioned, which had impacts on its hundreds of residents.

In the mid- to late 1940s, there was a societal shift to increased sympa-thy for poor people and children. Canada was laying the groundwork for a welfare system, and the residential schools were part of this system—they would continue to house the "neglected Indians." The Family Allowance Act of 1944 required all families to send their children to school if they wanted to receive the "baby bonus," a monthly allowance to help with childcare costs. For families on reserve who had few employment opportunities, this money was a powerful incentive when an Indian Agent came around talking residential school.

After the Second World War, the global human rights movement was born, and with it the concept of respecting all cultures found legs in the mainstream. Some Canadians grew to dislike the idea of kids being beaten in schools. More believed that to do well, students needed to feel respected and safe. The colonial idea of assimilating "lesser" cultures became disturb-ing to some. Aboriginal leaders and activists, many of whom had survived residential school and were aware of the changing sentiments of European-Canadians, pushed the federal government for change.

In part due to its gratitude to Aboriginal war vets, the Canadian government held a joint parliamentary committee of the Senate and House of Commons. Starting in 1946, it reviewed the administration of Indian Affairs. Missionaries, teachers, federal government bureaucrats, and Aboriginal leaders and Elders gave statements. It was one of the first times politicians heard directly from Aboriginal peoples, without Indian Affairs intermediaries. Aboriginal people lined up to make statements, criticizing, among other things, residential schools as a misguided attempt to assimilate their cultures with disastrous consequences. There were now generations of broken residential school graduates who had returned home to communities with high rates of sickness, alcoholism, suicide, and child abuse. They had learned from the adults who ruled their residential school lives that to raise a child was to beat a child. The abuse became cyclical. After graduation, Indian Affairs sent its agents in once again to scoop out the children, sending them away, often to receive beatings from someone else.

In the meantime, some within Indian Affairs would have been happy to shut down the residential school system completely. The schools were expensive, complex, increasingly controversial, and ultimately useless. The graduates were mostly returning to their reserves no better off. In 1945 only one hundred of the more than nine thousand residential school students had made it to Grade 8. No one had advanced past Grade 9. Even the highest-level bureaucrats had tired of watching children languish and suffer in the schools. Laval Fortier, the deputy minister, wrote in a 1951 letter about the dangers of sexual predators in residential schools. Fortier also worried of the ongoing spread of infectious diseases, especially tuberculosis. Decades after Peter Bryce's warnings, the schools remained dens of sickness and death. "If I were appointed by the Dominion Government for the express purpose of spreading tuberculosis, there is nothing finer in existence than the average Indian Residential School," one Indian Agent wrote in 1948. The conditions of the schools were so bad that if they hadn't been federally owned, local municipalities would have condemned them. Many of the schools burned down. But Indian Affairs was unable to shut down seventy-two schools with ten thousand students overnight. That would take it almost fifty years, as it turned out. Instead the Department focused on improving academic standards, better funding the schools, improving nutrition, and "integration"—moving as many students into provincial public schools as possible.

For decades, children in residential schools across Canada had participated in the "half-day system"—a half-day in class and a half-day doing farm or domestic chores, so they could learn "civilized" ways and provide food and clothing for the school. Indian Affairs had never provided enough money to properly feed and clothe the children, so in reality the principals and teachers worked them much harder than half of each day. In response to the pressures Aboriginal leadership placed on the special joint committee in 1946, Indian Affairs soon made changes, requiring that residential school students spend as many hours in the classroom as their public school counterparts. In effect, it abolished the half-day system. The changes were also meant to improve the quality of education at residential schools. Teachers would need to be better qualified, with teaching degrees. By this time, about 40 percent of the nearly two hundred teachers in Catholic-run residential schools had no professional certification. At Shubenacadie, the academic standards were higher. The Sisters of Charity had always prided themselves on teaching. From the fifties onward, all the teachers there had the same qualifications as required in public schools.

The Sisters did, however, take advantage of some opportunities arising from the new emphasis on education. They received a subscription to the *Journal of Education*, the *Education Office Gazette*, and regular bulletins, and could attend in-service training and conventions for "Indian school" teachers. For the particularly keen, the University of New Brunswick offered coursework on teaching at federal Indian schools. Just before graduation time in 1956, several Sisters drove over to the nearby Shubenacadie reserve for a teachers' conference. "We enjoyed a very profitable day," one wrote in the Annals, "discussing our problems with teachers from other Indian schools." In the fall, they were at it again, with three Sisters attending a convention for Indian school teachers in Eskasoni. "After settling all the problems behind the Buckskin Curtain for another year, they returned to Shubenacadie," a Sister wrote in the Annals.

But the Sisters also found themselves on the defensive as public attitudes toward their work changed. In November 1958, a busload of mostly Mi'kmaw social workers arrived to see, according to the Annals, "whether or not it was worthwhile sending children here." The writer felt she and the rest of the staff did the best they could with what they were given. "We get only the problem children," she wrote, "whose parents cannot possibly manage them; also, an occasional orphan case."

The Sisters, under increased scrutiny from Indian Affairs, struggled to teach and manage overcrowded classrooms, especially in the younger grades. In the late fifties, Indian Affairs ordered the schools to keep class sizes under 30 students, basing this number on the standards of the day in most provincial public schools. But at Shubenacadie the smallest class had 34 students. The largest, Grade 2–3, had more than 50. There was no way around it. In any given year the school had about 4 teachers and 4 classrooms, but

The school grounds were notorious for biting winter winds. COLLECTION OF ELSIE CHARLES BASQUE, NOVA SCOTIA MUSEUM

160 children lived at the school in a typical year. The inspectors weren't impressed. Unlike their predecessors in the thirties and forties, cleanliness was insufficient. "The type of child coming to the residential school requires much more individual attention," an inspector wrote in his 1957 report.

A new teacher and classroom were added that year, but it wasn't nearly enough. The principal proposed a new outbuilding with five classrooms, workshops, and a gym. The children would still live in the same dormitories in the old building. The new structure would cost $175,000, slightly more than the estimate for the original school building in 1926. Not surprisingly, the new addition was never built: budget constraints. While Indian Affairs was trumpeting its new focus on healthy learners, it still lacked the basic funds necessary to run a school system.

School curriculum was also evolving in the aftermath of the Second World War, Nazism, and the birth of the human rights movement. While Nova Scotia had a tendency to use texts for decades, there was a shift even here. Ironically, in a school designed to assimilate, new social studies texts urged "friendly fellowship [toward] people who live otherwise than we do and thus to counteract the tendency, natural to all children, to consider such peoples queer, strange, or inferior." The new rules also allowed for more time spent outside playing, and limited religious instruction to half an hour per day. Indian Affairs also expected more reporting from teachers and principals on the academic progress of students. Like other residential schools, Shubenacadie's academic success record was poor. Only 20 to 40 percent of its students got past Grade 3. Nearly half never got past Grade 2. The students consistently failed, despite a later policy not to hold students back. "Many pupils will need more than two years to be ready for Grade 2," one inspector wrote. The agents now had to report monthly—instead of annually—on students' well-being. The Department sent suggestions to principals based on these reports, but the Sisters, serving a higher authority than Indian Affairs, continued using religious texts as part of the curriculum.

By this time, some of the Sisters were lingering far past retirement age. This wouldn't have mattered except that their teaching methods had also gotten old. "Were she replaced by a younger teacher who would introduce more activity and project work the learning situation would be considerably improved," an inspector wrote in 1957 of seventy-year-old Sister Maria Ursula, a teacher for Grades 6 to 9. She had come to the school from St. Paul's Convent in Herring Cove, Nova Scotia, six years earlier. She was indeed replaced at the start of the next school year. Another inspector described one Sister's methods as "orthodox and stereotyped," but regardless of the age of the teachers, the morality lessons continued. Survivors recall that even halfway through the twentieth century, the nun in charge of the girls' dorm forbid pubescent girls from using feminine hygiene products at night. Yet if they bled on their sheets they were beaten.

Back into this picture stepped the now grown-up Rita Joe. The Sisters invited her to come back and talk to the older students about life on the outside. Rita Joe didn't answer. She showed up on her own, wearing bright red shoes, a fancy dress, heavy-duty lipstick, hair flowing long—her body a message to the kids and the nuns: she would not be controlled. She spoke to the students—in Mi'kmaw. She told them about the racism she encountered in the city, that white people wouldn't give them a chance. A Shubenacadie education wouldn't be much help. They had to go further, it was the only way to find good work. Better to go back to their reserves, she told them, if they could. Safer, more family. They applauded and thanked her. She left and didn't come back until long after the place had been shuttered. The bad memories were too strong.

MORE MONEY

Teachers at Shubenacadie started the 1950–51 school year making double their previous salary. They would now be paid almost as much as public schoolteachers in Nova Scotia. Some secular teachers were also employed at Shubenacadie, but they didn't tend to last. Teaching in a remote residential school wasn't something a young white teacher wanted to do for long. Mackey, the farm instructor, and the carpenter-engineer got significantly larger raises than the teachers.

Two fundamental problems with the schools were the overall insufficient funding and the per capita system—the government paying the schools a set amount each year per student—that rewarded churches for taking in more children than they had space for. In response to the special joint committee, the Department experimented with that funding formula. Some schools got a higher per capita rate. Others got the same rate, but the Department took on the burden of paying staff directly instead of through the churches. And it gave raises. It was a pilot project to see if paying salaries directly would increase the number of well-qualified teachers. Shubenacadie was one of the first schools Indian Affairs approached to test this new system. It would get the same per capita rate, but increased salaries and funds for other needs Mackey identified. The change caused some confusion when Mackey asked for an annual increase in the per capita amount, as he'd seen other schools receive. "Such adjustments were not made for schools in which the Department is experimenting with the payment of teachers," the Department reminded him. Two months later Indian Affairs changed its mind and increased its per capita rate for Shubenacadie, from forty-five dollars per child to sixty-six, retroactive to 1948, giving the school a windfall for repairs and new buildings. But we don't know how exactly this money was spent. After 1950 there are no publicly accessible records on maintenance at the Shubenacadie Indian Residential School.

Ultimately, Indian Affairs ditched the per capita grant system. From 1957 on, all school principals were to submit requests for real expenses. Daily necessities like food now had to be accounted for. The principals and teachers of all schools were to report directly to Indian Affairs, further reducing the role of the church. As part of its increasing oversight of the school, Indian Affairs audited Shubenacadie's books in 1959. It found a $4,000 surplus. The new principal, Father Collins, reimbursed the full amount. However, he reimbursed the church, not Indian Affairs. He wrote the cheque to Gerald Berry, archbishop of Halifax. Despite the new reporting arrangement, per capita payments to Shubenacadie continued at least as late as 1961.

INTEGRATION

By the early 1950s, bolstered by the human rights movement, integration was all the rage in Canadian education. White academics and activists began questioning the concept of race, and of dividing classrooms and schools based on this flawed concept. The change in public sentiment provided the perfect chance for Indian Affairs to move day and residential school students to provincial schools, where provincial governments could ultimately pay the cost of education. But the aim—assimilating Indians into white society—was the same. Indian Affairs's 1959 annual report made this goal crystal clear: "The task of education is to assist acculturation."

Six years later, a book written by various Indian Affairs bureaucrats showed a belief that Indians were finally ready for the "acceptance of responsibility on the part of Indian parents for the education of their children." Ellen Fairclough, the minister of Citizenship and Integration, where Indian Affairs now lived, echoed that ideal in a speech to the Canadian Association of School Administrators. Fairclough was Canada's first female cabinet minister, had made great gains in reducing racial discrimination in the immigration system, and was a champion of women's rights. "The fundamental aim of the government's policy toward Indians is the gradual integration of our country's fastest-growing ethnic group into the Canadian community," she said. By moving Indian Affairs into the immigration department, Canada sent a clear message: "Indians" were no longer a resource, and they were no longer "natives," either. They were outsiders. The job of government was to integrate them into the role of Canadian citizen.

To the mainstream, integration was all about equality: give everybody the same opportunity, in the same institutions, together. As a concept it was flawed. It failed to account for the different places from which varied groups of people were coming. Young people leaving the Shubenacadie residential school were forced to compete with hostile white peers and judged by hostile white teachers and administrators in public schools. In practice, integration was never fully implemented. Half of the Mi'kmaw students in the Maritimes attended all-Mi'kmaq day schools after Shubenacadie closed.

The churches lobbied hard against integration. They had long battled over the souls of Aboriginal people, and they weren't prepared to let the provinces have them. Religious education was too important, they said. The Catholic Church was particularly adamant. It fought to keep the residential school system alive with whatever political leverage it still had. The Canadian Catholic Conference warned that public school teachers were too ignorant of "Indian" culture to handle an influx of residential school survivors. Teachers at schools like Shubenacadie, it argued, were more likely to get to know "Indian culture and mentality." Catholic residential school principals concluded that Indian education must be based on "respect for [the Indian's] ethnic and cultural background and a desire to meet his special needs." The "special needs" were those of children who had lived difficult lives, often bouncing from foster homes to orphanages to juvenile prisons to the residential school.

At Shubenacadie, the orphaned and delinquent children kept arriving by train, new ones every year. The application forms from this time show a litany of crises—impoverished children and families with mental and physical health issues, addictions, parents in jail or who couldn't afford to care for their kids. The residential system as a whole had become more like Shubenacadie over the years—housing Aboriginal children who had fallen through the cracks. By the early fifties, Indian Affairs considered more than 40 percent of residential school children to be "neglected." As always, Indian Agents took them from home at their own discretion. The Catholic Church correctly predicted that such children would get little respect in public schools. It also foresaw that because the children of Shubenacadie were from poor families, they would hit class barriers in public schools. White children would not accept Mi'kmaw peers. Mi'kmaw children would feel squeezed out from the privileges and wealth enjoyed by their white peers. The Catholic Church wanted to rid the residential system of the provincial curriculum that had always been used.

In a reversal of roles, the Catholics, who feared losing control of the schools—and the souls therein—to the government, cautioned the government about wasting money. The new system of integration would cost 50 percent more than the old one, they argued. The principals felt that before integration could take place, the children of Shubenacadie would need to learn more about life with the White Man, a "frank, pleasant, gradual and methodical initiation to the uses and customs." Otherwise Mi'kmaw learners would become bitter. Rather than integrate into white society, they would feel more separated than ever. Indians had to be recognized as a distinct learning community, the principals argued.

In many ways, the provinces weren't able to take on the now more than eleven thousand children in residential schools—a number that was still on the rise. It was not just a matter of education. Who would care for these children? Who would love them? Who would teach them values? It wasn't just ideas about education that were changing, the childcare model had changed too. "It was considered better psychology to give these [orphan] children a normal home environment or what approximated it," Sister Maura writes in her account of the Sisters of Charity's first hundred years in Halifax. The Sisters' own orphanages were, like the residential school system, slowly winding down. That left Indian Affairs in a pickle: what could it do with all these "delinquent" Indians? To ease itself of its burden, the Department simply revised the Indian Act in 1951, extending legislation in the provinces to protect those very children. The welfare part of the "Indian Problem," at least, was to become a provincial matter.

THE LAST DECADE

FATHER COLLINS

Monsignor Mackey died in the spring of 1957, at the age of sixty. Though he had been seriously ill for two years—Father Myles Power took over as principal in 1955—he'd remained at the school until the end. Mackey's body was "laid out in an expensive coffin in the main parlour," Knockwood writes. Survivors of that time remember having to line up to pay last respects to their tormentor, then kneeling and praying for him. "It was especially gratifying for the Sisters to see the many Indians from Shubenacadie and the former students," a Sister wrote in the Annals that year. "Monsignor dearly loved the Indian children, and the tears and wet cheeks testified to all that the feeling was mutual. The visits to the parlor were almost constant and the Hail Marys were surely heard in Heaven…his little Indian charges will never forget him." "I didn't pray," a survivor told Knockwood. "I just knelt there and I was sort of happy." Mackey's funeral was held in Springhill, his hometown, which was an hour from the school. "No one except the Chief, John Bernard, attended the funeral," writes Knockwood.

In 1956 Father Paddy Collins took over from Father Myles Power, who'd been assigned to temporarily replace the ailing Father Mackey. Power had already agreed to take a post as a pastor in Flin Flon, Manitoba, after a year at the school. Originally from Ottawa, he'd spent a few years as an assistant priest at St. Patrick's Parish in Digby. Father Collins, an Irish-Scottish immigrant, had spent his entire twenty-four-year career doing "Indian work" in British Columbia, and his uncle (after whom he was named) had a seventy-year career doing the same. Collins would remain the principal of Shubenacadie for a decade. He had "a lot of compassion for his students," wrote Ernest Skinner, assistant Indian Agent of Eskasoni. "He was a fairly good man," a survivor told *Micmac News* in 1978. After Monsignor Mackey died, Collins looked through the third-floor storage rooms and found a wealth of new shoes, stockings, and linens. But they were moth-eaten and fell apart. It seemed they had been there since the school opened in 1930.

Collins worked to make the children more comfortable and better prepared for life after residential school. He let them leave the school more freely to visit the nearby village of Shubenacadie, or the reserve. He brought in the Boy Scouts and Girl Scouts and encouraged the children to join. They learned drills and did relay races for an audience at graduation. More significantly, after thirty years of priests and nuns forcibly separating siblings, Father Collins let brothers and sisters visit with each other in the parlour and sometimes even play together during recreation time.

The rules segregating the sexes were relaxed some in the later years.
SISTERS OF CHARITY, HALIFAX, CONGREGATIONAL ARCHIVES

Collins also let female students perm their hair and allowed monthly birthday parties. He added colourful touches to the building, had the dorms painted and tiled, and hung pictures on the walls. He added sofas and a fish tank to the common room. He bought bicycles and even a television set. He wrote that he wanted the children to feel "wanted and loved." He used the increased funding from Indian Affairs to buy new textbooks and recreation equipment. He told the Sisters to stop punishing students for speaking Mi'kmaw, to remind them to use English instead. Several of the older Sisters who'd served under Father Mackey left the school. Younger, more qualified nuns replaced them. Indian Affairs, in its continued efforts to improve the residential school system it was slowly shutting down, assigned a dietician to visit the school twice a year. The food improved. The cook and older girls made bread daily. The Sisters served milk and fruit three times a day.

The Department had changed its policy on summer vacations five years before Collins became principal, but Mackey hadn't asked for summer travel funds for the children because he hadn't thought their homes were suitable. Collins was the first to take advantage of the new policy and funds, in 1957. He wanted the children to go home for Easter and Christmas, too. Collins and Sister Roberta, who played piano, started a new music program as well. Father Collins bought a guitar for a gifted older student; Roberta led the choir at daily chapel and holiday programs. "Sister Roberta wanted

Music became a prominent activity in the 1960s. SISTERS OF CHARITY, HALIFAX, CONGREGATIONAL ARCHIVES

her students to have as normal a life as possible," one survivor told student researcher Kathleen Kearns in 1990.

The most significant change Collins implemented—though it happened eleven years after the special joint committee released its report on Indian Affairs, recommending a more academic focus at residential schools—was the shutting down of the school's farming and labour operations. Collins leased the land to a local farmer and had the barns converted to a gym and houses for kitchen and laundry staffers.

Collins also hired women—many of them Mi'kmaw—to do the cleaning, laundry, and cooking the older girls had always done. Until 1955 Saturday had been cleaning day for every child at Shubenacadie, the older ones supervising the little ones as they scrubbed the school clean, top to bottom. Indian Affairs had finally put out the official word that Indians be hired whenever possible at the residential schools. Mi'kmaw men on the other hand still had trouble finding work at Shubenacadie. The white male bosses of the school—in the church and government—still saw them as lazy Indians.

There was a greater focus on learning during the later years. SISTERS OF CHARITY, HALIFAX, CONGREGATIONAL ARCHIVES.

Collins did, however, bring in white men, unordained Brothers, to supervise the boys' dormitory. Alex Sampson held that role in 1960 and wrote one of the few first-hand accounts of what it was like working at the school. "It meant being with the 75 kids 24 hours a day except when they were in school," he wrote. "Get them up in the mornings, showered and dressed, to Mass, to breakfast and get them ready for school. It meant you chased after runaways or sat up all night with a young fellow who wanted to jump out the third storey window to go home." He wrote of organizing games for the younger children to play while the older ones went fishing, skating, or swimming. It was exhausting work. "I used to be so tired, if I sat down for a few minutes, I'd just fall asleep. I could sleep through the noise, they could tear the place apart, but let one child cry, and I'd hear it."

Father Collins was the second-longest serving principal of the school. After a decade there, he left in 1966. Father Michael Kearney took over for the final year before Indian Affairs finally closed the school and sold the property.

THINGS CHANGE; THINGS STAY THE SAME

The counterculture decade of the 1960s, which brought the North American mainstream a paradoxical mix of heightened individual freedom and Cold War fear, also gave Canadian Aboriginal peoples the legal right to vote for the first time. The civil rights movement had caught on, and white Canadians were becoming more interested in Aboriginal issues. Many were writing letters to Indian Affairs demanding a better education system. The Department responded with a memo to its senior staff responsible for residential and day schools: "Your personal involvement in this sphere...is most essential because it is your attitude to public inquiry which will create in the minds of the people the image of Canada's concern for the Indian problem," it said. Bureaucrats were urged to reply to all inquiries—to non-Aboriginal and Aboriginal Canadians. In the past, many such letters had simply been filed away.

At Shubenacadie, for the first time in the school's history, enrollment was at, rather than over, its capacity of 125 children. Yearly attendance had averaged 123 students over the last seven years. While the integration of day and residential school students into public schools was never complete, dozens of Shubenacadie children did end up in public schools. The first agreement with a Mi'kmaq First Nation—Eskasoni—had been struck, allowing its children to attend public high schools, and soon Mi'kmaw students across the province were attending schools including Shubenacadie Public School, Mount Saint Vincent Academy in Halifax, and the Agricultural College in Truro.

A quarter of Nova Scotia Mi'kmaw students were in public schools early in the decade, including 80 in high school, 9 in vocational school, and 7 in university—2 on Indian Affairs scholarships. They were part of the national integration effort. Across Canada, the number of Aboriginal students at public schools jumped from 600 in 1948 to 6,000 in 1966. In that time, Indian Affairs closed more than a dozen residential schools. Another sixty-six stayed open. At Shubenacadie residential school, despite the new focus on teaching and academics, in 1964 only 9 of 110 students had made it to Grade 8. Some of the teachers were certified only at the lowest allowable level, and throughout the fifties and sixties the average teacher stayed at Shubenacadie only two or three years. Indian Affairs noted the school's high turnover rate—almost 30 percent a year—in its 1965 annual report. Some of the nuns were retiring or requesting reassignment to more comfortable environments. The Sisters of Charity still supplied most of the teachers at the school. The new policy said that Indian Affairs was to hire and manage teachers, but in reality they mostly continued to leave those decisions to Mother Superior Stella Marie, in the mother house at Mount Saint Vincent. Mother Stella Marie would write to the district superintendent each year to let him know of any staffing changes. They would write back and thank her.

The Sisters continued to project a happy image of the school in their Annals and in photos of children skating and tobogganing, kneeling in prayer beside their beds—each of which had a doll on it—and doing an "Indian dance" at a concert. They "established a precedent" by eating with the children for the first time. "It was hard to decide which table to occupy because the children were all so anxious that we sit at all the tables," one wrote in the Annals. When Sister Gilberta became mistress of the girls' choir in 1960, singing became a popular activity. Her Christmas concert in the school's final year was a massive hit and the children were invited to perform shows at the East Hants-Windsor Music Festival, East Hants High School, and on CBC television's *Firehouse Frolics*. Shubenacadie's flute band also took first prize at the Halifax Music Festival.

Indian Agents and the RCMP were much less likely at this point to force children to attend residential school. Indian Affairs cracked down on its own rule that parents had to sign consent forms, and the word was out on the educational shortcomings of the school—it was seen more and more as a form of punishment. In the early 1960s a Richibucto judge sentenced a First Nations juvenile delinquent to a year at the school, which was still a strictly regimented existence with harsh punishments.

Despite there being fewer children in residential school, the funding continued to increase a little each year as Indian Affairs continued pushing for better academic outcomes—with a focus on English language and math. In 1961 it dropped industrial arts and home economics for children below Grade 7 so that they could focus on reading, writing, and arithmetic (the three Rs). But not everyone agreed with the changes. Murray Campbell, a school inspector with the Nova Scotia Department of Education, visited Shubenacadie in 1964 and found the attitudes and habits of the children, and of the parents on the reserve, lacking. He did not think the Mi'kmaq were ready to integrate at an academic level and was baffled that practical training in industrial arts and home ec had been cut. Those classes "would better meet the potential needs of these students," he said.

Wondering if Indian Affairs could perhaps improve both literacy and the employment prospects for its young wards at the same time, the Atlantic regional supervisor for Indian Affairs, Frank McKinnon, held a series of meetings that year with teachers from Maritime day schools and Shubenacadie. They were not enthusiastic about the Department's new policy of preparing Indians to get by on their brains. They told McKinnon to bring back the half-day system, at least for the older male students who lacked "the mental capacity to go on to high school." They could spend half a day in class and the other half in the industrial arts workshop. A language arts specialist brought in to test the kids and figure out who might qualify for such a program found forty-five children—including some in Grades 5 and 6 the teachers had given up on—who fit the bill. Most were in Shubenacadie, and were removed from regular classes to take industrial arts instead, with McKinnon's approval.

"Vocational fitness" was now the thing, but the Department didn't look too carefully into why Aboriginal graduates couldn't find work. The poor education they received in residential and day schools was only part of the problem. There was also the racism of employers to contend with. As an unnamed Cape Breton Mi'kmaq was quoted in the *Chronicle Herald*, "Education without opportunity is no good, and there are no opportunities." The half-day system had been abolished for several years, but Indian Affairs was having trouble getting the message across to principals and teachers. In 1962 the Department circulated a memo, clarifying that attending class was what mattered most for students. Principals were not to make the students do any other work that would prevent attendance. But some Shubenacadie survivors of this era remember being forced to labour well into the sixties. Boys still stoked the furnace, for example. Clothing still had to be made and repaired. The school was better funded, but it had lost its source of produce and free farm labour. It still needed the sweat equity of its wards.

The Sisters continued making students repeat grades—even against Indian Affairs policy—holding back more than 10 percent of Grade 1 and one-third of Grade 2 students for poor academic performance. Higher-grade failure rates ranged from 15 to 19 percent. In the early years, when the school was still a labour camp, Sisters had failed many students based only on their size. Chores were divvied up by grade, with higher grades using heavy machinery—you needed a certain size for that. To comply with new maximum class size rules, Father Collins had a sixth classroom added in the main building, for which Indian Affairs approved adding a new teacher. But class sizes remained well above provincial standards: forty-four students sat together in the Grade 4–5 class.

Outside of Shubenacadie, Mi'kmaw student performance was reportedly improving post integration. A 1965 *Chronicle Herald* article reported some curious figures. It said that the average education level among Nova Scotia Mi'kmaq was Grade 8—up from Grade 5 just a few years earlier—but that less than 2 percent of Mi'kmaq went beyond Grade 8. Those numbers would indicate that almost every single Mi'kmaw student got as far as Grade 8 and went no further. The *Herald* didn't ponder why that might have been.

THE END

In its final year, registrations at Shubenacadie were limited to about sixty children, half of the previous year's enrollment and not enough for Indian Affairs to justify keeping the school open. The Indian Agent at Eskasoni, Ernest Skinner, purposely kept about sixty children out of the school, which he saw as a place for parents to dump unwanted kids, and sent many of them into foster homes instead. Nationally, more Aboriginal children were now attending public school than residential school. Fewer than 20 percent of school-aged Aboriginal children attended the sixty remaining residential schools. But by this point, pressure from Mi'kmaw communities had already ensured the Shubenacadie school would close. If Indian Affairs was pulling back from its commitment to the residential school business, Mi'kmaw leadership was happy to push them out the door.

Around 1966 two prominent Mi'kmaw Chiefs, Ben Christmas of Eskasoni and Noel Doucette of Chapel Island/Potlotek, paid a visit to the regional Indian Affairs office and complained about the Shubenacadie school. Doucette, who was only twenty-nine years old at the time, was a survivor of the school, having lived there from 1946 to 1951, and would go on to found the Union of Nova Scotia Indians. (Five of the seven founders were Shubenacadie survivors.) Doucette was also instrumental in preparing the National Indian Brotherhood's 1972 Red Paper, or *Indian Control Over Indian Education*—which would change education for the better for millions of children. Ben Christmas had long been a champion of Mi'kmaw rights, having been at the forefront among objectors to the centralization scheme in Nova Scotia. Indian Affairs saw him as a radical, but was willing to listen to him now: Canada had signed on to the *Universal Declaration of Human Rights*, and the Shubenacadie school was a black mark on Nova Scotia. The United Nations was now watching. According to Daniel Paul, Christmas and Doucette told Indian Affairs officials that too many complaints about the school had mounted over the decades, particularly from the 1930s and 1940s. It was outdated. It was a symbol of oppression. Its time had come.

The 1966 visit from Christmas and Doucette represented the highest level of Mi'kmaw resistance against the school in its history. Paul points out that Indian Affairs had all the power. Resistance could, and often did, result in the loss of one's children. Meanwhile, most Mi'kmaq had only a Grade 4 or 5 education. "Most didn't want to rock the boat," Paul explains. "It took a few brave individuals to demand that the school be closed." Only Shubenacadie (Indian Brook) First Nation voted to keep the school open—possibly because some parents relied on the handy seasonal childcare while they worked in the United States during the winter. Every other band favoured closing it. "As a member of the [Maritime] Indian Advisory Council in 1967, [Noel Doucette] led the way in insisting that the Shubenacadie Indian Residential School be shut down," wrote Daniel Paul in a 1996 column for the *Halifax Herald*. In February of that year, it was Doucette who successfully motioned, at the Grand Council of Nova Scotia Indian Chiefs meeting, that the school be closed.

Indian Affairs agreed with the idea of closing the school, but for different reasons. To the Department, the school had done its job but was now obsolete. Department staff members had been complaining about it. "Practically all the children now in residence have been placed there mainly for reasons other than to facilitate school attendance," wrote F. B. McKinnon, Maritime director of Indian Affairs. Cecil Thompson, assistant superintendent of the Shubenacadie reserve, added that he felt parents were only sending children they didn't want to the school. Eskasoni Indian Agent Ernest Skinner wrote of children "crying for affections and attention as they huddled around the priest and teachers at the school." He felt the school had become a welfare institution for children whose parents had grown tired of raising them.

In 1990 Skinner told student researcher Kathleen Kearns that it was he who suggested Indian Affairs close the school. He'd been uncomfortable taking children to live there and often took them to foster homes instead. G. Watts, a senior local official with Indian Affairs, said the Shubenacadie school was a "convenient dumping ground" for Mi'kmaw children the Department didn't know what else to do with. He pointed out that no effort had ever been made to find a better option for the children. Unlike halfway houses or other institutions for poor children, there were no social workers at Shubenacadie. The children, McKinnon said, showed "serious psychosocial problems which require treatment." The school wasn't up to it. In truth, it never had been. Foster care was the only answer, McKinnon felt. The Maritime Regional Advisory Council on Indian Affairs passed a resolution on February 1, 1967, to close the Shubenacadie Indian Residential School at the end of the school year.

McKinnon and Director of Indian Education Charles Gorman visited the Sisters of Charity Mother Superior and her committee at the mother house in July 1966 to let her know they were shutting down the residential school. The Sisters' main concern was that the children get a Catholic education, and so they suggested sending them to the public school in Enfield where they taught. "Although [government officials] were satisfied that many students from the residential school had made satisfactory adjustments to society, they noted that the general attitude to the school in Shubenacadie was not good," Mary Olga McKenna writes in her 1998 history of the Sisters of Charity. "There was a feeling that the children were being driven, not taught to make decisions." But the government still had faith in the Sisters as teachers, and asked if four nuns could be supplied for the school in Enfield and two for a preschool on the Shubenacadie reserve. McKinnon and Gorman were also working to find places for the rest of the children—those without families they considered stable—to live. They figured it would take about three years to put them into foster homes. They would work with the Indian Advisory Board to place them.

In its final months, the school attracted more visitors than it had for some time. Gorman visited several times and, despite his criticisms of the school, praised the Sisters in their work. Sister Mary Matilda, the Sisters' director of education for the Shubenacadie area, came by to make plans for the education of the children after the residential school closed. Government consultants did the same. The building was filled with things Indian Affairs no longer needed, including expensive equipment like industrial sewing machines. Isabelle Knockwood describes the furnace man paddling these out to the middle of the Shubenacadie River in a canoe and dumping them there. "A few people from the Reserves asked for beds and got them," she writes, adding that staff members burned whatever school records remained on-site at this time. In March the remaining Sisters joined chiefs, band councillors, and Indian Affairs bureaucrats at a two-day conference on Indian Education. The Sisters were impressed by the "sincerity and eagerness of the various Indians who spoke about the necessity of a good education and character formation for their children," one wrote in the Annals. In April, Chief Simon Nevin, an Indian Affairs official, and a Sister who taught at the school, participated in a panel discussion on "Indian education and the Closing of the Residential School."

In May the Sisters had their farewell supper. Really it was for Sister Helen Patrick, who had been reassigned to an orphanage. But they knew their "own time for final departure" was just weeks away. They got their obediences on June 10. Two weeks later they would board trains to Halifax, some of them eventually bound to work at orphanages, schools, and hospitals in Québec and Massachusetts. But in the meantime they prepared the children for the closing of the school. The Grade 6 class wrote essays about their sadness at the school's closing. One June 13 they held a goodbye picnic near Enfield.

On June 22, 1967, the school's last principal, Father Michael Kearney, dismissed the students. They left as they'd come: taken away by white men. They were boarded on to trains that took them to reserves across the Maritimes. The first thing to do was figure which of the children would go home, and which would go to childcare agencies or foster homes. With the closing of the school, there was a massive spike in the number of Mi'kmaw children in these situations. Dalhousie University social work researchers trace the roots of this change back to 1951. This was when Canada added Section 88 to the Indian Act, giving provincial child-protection departments authority to expand their

The blinds are all closed in this June 1967 photo of the school.

services onto reserves. It was the first time provincial social workers could go onto reserves and take children away from homes. But the federal government failed to pick up the costs. Since then, provinces and Aboriginal Affairs have fought over whose job it is to protect Aboriginal children.

In 1964, three years before Shubenacadie closed, Nova Scotia and Canada signed a new agreement that the feds would pay the costs for care and custody of Mi'kmaw children taken from reserves into care, plus salaries for child-protection workers. With the school's closure, the shift toward Aboriginal education in provincial schools, and the involvement of the provinces in child protection, the number of Mi'kmaw children in protective government care spiked dramatically over the next two decades. Most children were fostered or adopted into white families, often in the United States. Their Aboriginal status was usually not recorded, so many disappeared without a trace. Some were placed locally in foster care. "It often left them in situations far worse than the residential school environment," says Daniel Paul. Aboriginal Affairs tells it differently. "I'm told that the kids returned home and just went to local schools," says Steve Young, a spokesperson at the Aboriginal Affairs office in Amherst. "There was no placement, so to speak." Calls made to the Ottawa office of Aboriginal Affairs were not returned.

Some survivors remember feeling great sorrow at leaving the school for the last time. For some, whatever its dangers and flaws, the school had been the closest thing they'd known to a home. Those without families didn't know what lay ahead. Indian Affairs scrambled to place them, sometimes splitting up siblings. A brother might be in Nova Scotia and a sister in Alberta with another in the States. Often that was the last they would see of one another.

PUBLIC SCHOOL

In the final years of the Shubenacadie residential school, the media hailed an age of change and trumpeted Indian Affairs's efforts to "educate-and-elevate the Indian from poverty and isolation to a proper place in the Canadian sun," as a 1965 *Chronicle Herald* article put it. The story spoke of government and industry preaching these ideals to the Mi'kmaq. But the students who went on to provincial schools found new challenges. They had become used to the Sisters lecturing in English, a language some of them still struggled with. The Sisters had paid little individual attention to their actual learning needs. Many had failed the same grade numerous times. In public school, they became the oldest students in their class. They were used to curricula that taught them of the inferiority of their own people, and now encountered white peers who had learned only that version of history. Most of the white students had never before seen a Mi'kmaq or Wolastoqiyik (Maliseet) person.

When Shubenacadie closed, the anthropologist Harry B. Hawthorn published the second volume of his massive three-year research report on the conditions of Status Indians across Canada, which echoed American work from forty years earlier. Hawthorn noted that the curriculum on "Indians" was "inaccurate, over-generalized, and even insulting." He urged schools to drop it, focus on giving Aboriginal children a sense of self-worth. He said that Indian Affairs should work to provide updated content on Aboriginal history and culture. Unfortunately for the children coming from Shubenacadie and into Atlantic Canadian public schools, Indian Affairs ignored Hawthorn's recommendation. The responsibility for curriculum was with provincial education employees, who likely never saw the report to begin with.

Besides obvious racialized and cultural differences, most former Shubenacadie students were poor. At least at residential school their clothing and some food had been provided. To the white kids they looked dirty, shabby. They were insulted and bullied and often dropped out as soon as they were old enough. Meanwhile, Indian Affairs was trying to wash its hands of education. Shubenacadie was just one domino in a rapid-fire closure of residential schools. Two years after its closure in 1967, there were fewer than eight thousand students attending fifty-two remaining residential schools. A decade later, fewer than two thousand residents lived at only a dozen schools.

HUSK

The Nova Scotia Department of Welfare considered buying the old school building from the federal government, via its Central Mortgage and Housing department, in January of 1968. "We are impressed with the quality of it and the location," the department's deputy minister told the *Chronicle Herald*.

The *Herald* reported that the building had been well maintained, and that the Province thought the facility might be a good home for "the mentally disabled." In the meantime, with the Sisters, carpenter-engineer, janitor, cook, and children all gone, a few priests lingered on in the building—Father Kearney and his juniors cooking lonely meals on hot plates, as Isabelle Knockwood described it. But a Halifax businessman beat the Province to the punch and bought the building in August for storage. He told the priests to leave. They stayed with the parish priest at the nearby reserve.

Knockwood describes a sad last mass held, based on an account from an anonymous source in attendance. A small procession of white Catholics and a few Mi'kmaq walked reverently down the front steps. "The older priest seemed distracted at first. He turned back toward the school with tears in his eyes," Knockwood writes. "He took a black prayer book out of his pocket and began hitting the palm of his other hand gently with the book and crying." Then, according to Knockwood's witness, the priest looked up at the building. "I don't know if this building was cursed before but no matter what we tried to do, it never turned out right...I hope to the Holy Mother of God in heaven that this building is never used for anything else," he called. The priests placed their things into two cars and drove away slowly. The businessman sold the school again less than a year later—to someone who wanted those Bluenose facing bricks, until he realized how easily they crumbled in his hands. For the next couple of decades the building sat vacant, decaying as local teens had parties there.

Rita Joe and her husband visited the building then. The windows were smashed out. Her husband, also a survivor, couldn't bring himself to go in. Something told him not to. "Maybe the spirits of the children who have died here are trying to warn us not to go in there," she told him. But she forced herself. Inside, she saw plaster and pipes falling down. She left in a hurry. Later, at the end of the summer of 1986, Isabelle Knockwood also felt compelled to return to the building that had been such a source of pain for her. That once imposing institutional tower was crumbling, a broken-down shell of itself. Its graffiti, dated August 20, 1986, said it all: *This was Prison for Indians. The Brave Die...Burnt in Hell*. "The front door was hanging on one set of hinges and the front of the building had pock marks on its face, where people used to take rifle shots at it," she writes. "The chapel windows had been nailed over with some kind of tin sheeting [with] gaping holes in it."

The roof was gone too. Knockwood found her way inside and was struck by the garbage and rotting pigeon feces strewn across the swollen, uneven floors. The same floors that boys and girls had once scrubbed on hands and knees so they would gleam for visiting inspectors.

The property changed hands again in the mid-1980s and the new owner hired a man to rid his new land of the eyesore. A slow, controlled fire was the mode of demolition on September 4, 1986. It burned all day and all seemed well when the crew left the site in the early evening. Ninety minutes later, there was a steel-beam-bending explosion lighting the sky. The controlled fire was out of control. People from the village and reserve quickly gathered, sitting in their cars to watch. "It appeared as if spirits were dancing inside the tar and brick," Knockwood recalls. The media reported the fire as suspicious and there were rumours that maybe a former resident had turned the controlled blaze into a farewell blast. According to Knockwood, no one called the RCMP or the owner to the site. The rapid spread of the fire through a building without much wood was confusing. There was fire-proofing around the kitchen, where the controlled fire burned, and forty-six-centimetre brick-and-cement walls separating four different sections of the building.

The morning after the fire, September 6, 1986.

Two days later, crews bulldozed the charred remains, at one point hitting a live wire that should have been shut off, sending sparks flying and forcing the municipality to cut power to the whole town. A crowd of Mi'kmaq cheered when the bricks finally came down. Some hadn't come near the site in years, and doing so was still difficult. It brought back the memories they'd

TOP *The site is a plastics factory now.*
BOTTOM *The pump house never worked very well but it still stands.* CHRIS BENJAMIN

Looking across the river at the site of the school. CHRIS BENJAMIN

tried hard to destroy. As much as the school had been an evil presence, it was part of their lives. "Part of me has gone," one survivor told CBC. "It has burnt. But the wounds are still there."

The land is now owned by ScotiaPlastics, the site of its bright blue factory on Indian School Road. The old pump house that never worked so well is still there, between the lake and where the school used to be, its roof dilapidated, door and window long gone. The site is still surrounded by farmland. The hill doesn't look like much, but the wind still whips around atop it with no trees or shrubs to stop it. When I visited the site on a mild December morning, it wasn't hard to imagine the school's residents shivering under threadbare, decades-old blankets. At the bottom of the hill are three boarded up wooden houses, the original farm buildings. One is still inhabited by the school's last caretaker, an old man now, his memory failing. In front is a tall, dead, barkless tree, with an image of the school painted on the front and the words *WE WILL NEVER FORGET* over a set of claws. *MI'KMAQ*, it says at the base of the tree.

A simple memorial. CHRIS BENJAMIN

IV

AFTER SHUBENACADIE

CHILDREN IN CARE

SIXTIES SCOOP

The slow shutdown of the residential school system across Canada fed directly into what has been called the "sixties scoop"—a process of fostering and adopting Aboriginal children into white homes. It actually started in the early fifties when Indian Affairs empowered the provinces, via Section 88 of the Indian Act, to take children from homes on reserves. Indian Agents and provincial child-protection workers took twenty thousand Aboriginal children from their homes, or as they left closing residential schools. Nearly 80 percent were placed in non-Aboriginal homes.

This "scoop" lasted for decades, and is, in a sense, ongoing. Across Canada, there are more Aboriginal youth in foster care than there were at any time during the residential school days. Child-protection workers today take three times the number of children as did Indian Agents at the peak of the residential system. According to the latest Statistics Canada data, nearly half of Canadian children under age fourteen and in foster care are First Nations, Inuit, or Métis, even though children in these groups represent only 5 percent of Canada's child population. That's 15,000 Aboriginal children in foster care. In all, about 27,000 Aboriginal children are in the national child welfare system. The problem seems to be getting worse, not better. From 1995 to 2001, child-protection workers increased the number of Aboriginal children placed outside their homes by 71.5 percent.

"The Sixties Scoop was not coincidental," Patrick Johnston, who coined the term, wrote in 1983. "It was a consequence of fewer Indian children being sent to residential schools and of the child welfare system emerging as the new method of colonization." Without the residential schools, many Aboriginal children had no place left to go. Their parents were either dead or considered—by Indian Affairs employees who acted on the children's behalf—incompetent. The agents and provincial child-protection workers assessed competence on their own impressions, which could be influenced by anything from a cluttered house, to parents who moved around for work, to neglect and abuse. American agencies sometimes took $20,000 fees to place Canadian Aboriginal children with white American families. From the late fifties to the late sixties, the percentage of Aboriginal children in care went from just 1 percent all the way up to 40 percent—kicking off yet another national crisis.

At the TRC sessions held in Atlantic Canada, Shubenacadie survivors from the school's latter years spoke of having their families split up by the scoop. Even in those years many kids had been sent straight to foster care or adoptive homes, with barely a trace. Indian Affairs withheld birth information from the children, believing that the knowledge of who they were and where they came from would somehow prevent them from "integrating" into their new family. The children were often told that everyone in their family had died, whether it was true or not. Siblings were split among different families. They ended up living in Maine, Ontario, Alberta, Atlantic Canada—all over. And they lost each other. Some tracked each other down decades later. Others have family reunions in the works. But ties were severed and the damage is not easily undone.

Placing Aboriginal children in non-Aboriginal families was another attack on culture. Even the most "culturally competent" white families—to use the phrase of Nova Scotia's Department of Community Services—simply cannot raise a Mi'kmaq as a Mi'kmaq. To adopt a culture as your own, you must be immersed in it. Reading books and attending the occasional pow-wow is insufficient. First Nations and Métis people who had been adopted to white families spoke out in the 2010 book, *Aski Awasis/Children of the Earth: First Peoples Speaking on Adoption*, edited by Jeannine Carrière. In several cases, these children had grown up and reached out to their biological relations and found profound relief, a sense of belonging they'd always lacked. Until then, their entire sense of their cultural background had been defined by their white adoptive families and communities—people with different histories and traditions, people who didn't know what it was like to experience racism and who could not explain or put it in context when their adoptive children went through it.

Instead, white parents often encouraged adoptive Aboriginal children to try to pass as white, in order to avoid racism altogether—a loving and unintended assault on their true culture. Their adoptive families took them to powwows as cultural tourists, not as insiders. One person interviewed had been told she was Cree, but it turned out she was actually Ojibwe. She had been learning about the wrong traditions. Not all adoptive families made the effort to connect their new children to their heritage. Some, despite adopting a First Nations child, were quick to remind the child how lucky he or she was to have escaped the drunk, lazy Indians. Often they changed the child's name and his or her birth name was forgotten. Dr. Simon Nuttgens, in his research with the Graduate Centre for Applied Psychology at Athabasca University in Alberta, found that people of one culture who are adopted by people of another culture often experience a sense of disconnection—exclusion, rejection, and alienation. Based on her research with First Nations and Métis people adopted into white families, Carrière found that, "even adoptees who reported they had received good parenting, love and stability did not successfully negotiate their adolescent years in the adoptive homes. Most…left home by the age of fifteen or sixteen years."

First Nations pushed back against these latest attacks on their children and cultures. By 1982 there was a ban in all Canadian jurisdictions on sending the children to live with families in the US. Provinces and territories began amending their adoption laws to prioritize placing Aboriginal children with extended family or other families in their communities. In Nova Scotia, Mi'kmaw leaders advocated until they were able to sign an agreement with the Government of Canada and the Nova Scotia Department of Community Services in 1985. They created a new body called Mi'kmaw Family and Children's Services (MFCS), which took over the administration of child and family services from the Province. MFCS was now responsible for investigating reports of abuse and neglect of children under sixteen on reserves, and taking the lead on the placement of Mi'kmaw children into foster care or adoption.

Around the same time, four small, federally funded New Brunswick First Nations child-welfare agencies were formed. Generally, these agencies deal with communities whose populations include fewer than 250 children.

In all, there are thirteen First Nations child-welfare agencies in Atlantic Canada, the mandates of which present a seemingly impossible paradox: following provincial child-protection rules that view the child's needs separately from culture and community while focusing on healthy, safe families and children using a First Nations community-based perspective, determined in consultation with chiefs. They work to prevent neglect, abuse, and addiction, rather than only reacting to these problems once they occur. But the task is monumental, and staff members frequently burn out and move on. These organizations inherited the ongoing ravage of colonialist education and control as well as disputes between provinces and the federal government over who pays for what.

CONTEMPORARY CHALLENGES

According to the Department of Community Services in Nova Scotia, of 1,315 children in all forms of government-administered care, 282 are with Mi'kmaq Family and Children's Services (MFCS). That's 21.4 percent, compared to 4 percent of all children in the province who identify as First Nations. As recently as 2010, there were 396 children with MFCS. As in every other part of the country, there are a disproportionate number of Aboriginal children in care in Nova Scotia. But according to the Nova Scotia Department of Community Services (DCS), these statistics can be interpreted differently. "Because there are more Mi'kmaw children available for adoption than there are Mi'kmaw families available," says Elizabeth MacDonald, spokesperson for DCS, "Mi'kmaw children often remain in foster or kinship care longer—while awaiting adoption by an available Mi'kmaw family—than children of other ethnic origins." Still, hundreds of Mi'kmaw children have been taken from their homes into government care.

In 2005 the First Nations Child & Family Caring Society of Canada brought together experts from across the country in First Nations child welfare, community development, economics, information technology, law, and social work, to attack this national crisis from every angle. They surveyed workers at First Nations child-welfare agencies, including those in Nova Scotia, New Brunswick, and Newfoundland. In these three provinces, more than 10 percent of First Nations children were in child-welfare care, compared to less than 1 percent of non-Aboriginal children, and were 15 times more likely to end up there. As a result of these numbers, Mi'kmaw families report being hesitant to go to MFCS or the justice system in cases of domestic abuse, for fear of losing their children. When St. Francis Xavier's Canada Research Chair on Indigenous Peoples and Sustainable Communities, Jane MacMillan, did a study on Mi'kmaw family violence, Mi'kmaw participants told her that violence is common in their communities, is rarely reported, is getting worse, and is driven by addiction, loss of culture, and poverty. Poverty on the reserve, even now, is often used as justification for removing children from homes. Many blamed these things on the Shubenacadie Indian Residential School. "People don't know how to parent," participants said. And as a result, neglect is the main reason MFCS removes children from homes.

Pre-colonialism, family violence was extremely rare in Mi'kma'ki, and when it happened the whole community got involved to help the children and sort out any conflicts, usually with a talking circle where everyone had a chance to speak. But now, even violence-prevention and other community-building programs offered by MFCS are sometimes avoided because of the organization's association with taking children from homes. These community programs are the very things that can keep families together. Besides taking children into protective care, MFCS provides support programs for youth leaving foster care, summer camps for kids in care, and family healing centres providing shelter for abused women and their children.

Compounding these challenges is the fact that First Nations child-welfare agencies in Atlantic Canada are chronically short of cash and overworked. The funding formula from Aboriginal Affairs allows a cost-of-living increase in funding, but there hasn't been one in nearly twenty years. In that time, prices have increased more than 20 percent, which amounts to a $10 million loss to these agencies in Atlantic Canada. Meanwhile, the workload keeps increasing. It's not just the number of kids in care, it's also the number of reports of abuse and neglect that must be investigated by these small agencies. Nationally, there are more than twice as many investigations involving Aboriginal kids as non-Aboriginals.

And yet, First Nations child-welfare organizations receive 22 percent less money per child than their non-Aboriginal counterparts. Contrary to popular belief, this lower rate of government support is the case for all services.

According to the First Nations Child & Family Caring Society of Canada, "The average Canadian gets services from federal, provincial and municipal governments at an amount that is almost two-and-a-half times greater than that received by First Nations citizens." Federal funding is given the same way residential school funding once was—on a per child basis. Agencies get money for each child in care, which leaves very little to focus on keeping kids out of care—that is, with their families. In some cases, children are temporarily placed by agencies into group or foster homes in order to get funding. Too often, these children go back and forth between foster care and home.

To complicate matters, the provinces and federal government continue to argue over who pays for what, and too often children wait in dangerous situations for the red tape to get sorted. Aboriginal Affairs claims that under the constitution the provinces are responsible for child and family services. The feds fund the basics, and the amount is their choice to make, but the provinces should cover the rest. "Provinces delegate authority to agencies and are thus responsible to ensure that the agency operates pursuant to the established standards," the Department has stated. The Province counters that Aboriginal peoples are the federal government's responsibility. Period.

WHOLE FAMILIES

Despite enormous challenges, agency workers have had success placing Mi'kmaw children within their own culture, in kinship care with extended family. In Nova Scotia, workers are required to do so whenever possible. "We make every effort to place Mi'kmaw children for adoption with families where at least one parent is Mi'kmaw, and that happens for over 78 percent of Mi'kmaw children in care," says Elizabeth MacDonald, a spokesperson for the Nova Scotia Department of Community Services. And when workers remove a child who speaks Mi'kmaw from the home, they must place him or her where the language is at least understood. However, foster parents receive provincial government money to help take care of foster children, but when Mi'kmaw children are placed with kin, those extended family members do not receive the same funding. In many cases, these families are already struggling to pay the bills, and another mouth to feed with no financial help is a huge burden. Neither the federal government nor the provinces have stepped up to address this challenge.

Even when placed with Mi'kmaw families, children in care are more likely to abuse drugs, become tangled up in the criminal justice system, and have health problems. But with insufficient funding, it's difficult for overwhelmed workers at First Nations child-welfare agencies to address the root causes of neglect and family violence. In response to these criticisms, Aboriginal Affairs changed the way it funds MFCS in 2008 to allocate funds for prevention work in Aboriginal communities. As a result, MFCS got a $1.9 million increase in funding that year. But in determining the amount of annual funding, Aboriginal Affairs guesses how many children will be pulled from their homes based on the previous year. In reality, the numbers change each year, and there's no reason not to fund the work based on actual costs. MFCS continues to evolve in an effort to be more community and culturally based, using time-tested customs to resolve conflicts and build healthier families and communities. Workers visit people's homes to support them there, providing parenting and life-skills training.

For a time, the MFCS Family Group Conferencing program, based on traditional healing and talking circles, effectively addressed and curtailed family violence at an early stage. In this program, counsellors sit with immediate and extended families to work out a plan to protect and care for the children. But according to a former staff person, Nova Scotia's Department of Community Services audited and took over every private children's services society in the province except MFCS. It then cancelled the Family Group Conferencing program and tightened rules on kinship—or extended family—fostering, making it even harder for these arrangements to work.

The First Nations Child & Family Caring Society notes that much more preventative work could be done to keep families together and safe. With full funding, workers might—possibly in collaboration with respected Elders—do outreach on fetal alcohol syndrome for pregnant teens, give parenting lessons incorporating traditional parenting styles, facilitate marriage-preparation workshops, provide daycare services and babysitting courses, give cooking classes using traditional foods, teach Mi'kmaw language classes and addictions counselling. Unfortunately, judging by ongoing jurisdictional struggles between Aboriginal Affairs and the provinces over who pays for services for First Nations peoples, and also by the fact that on a dollars-per-person basis no group in Canada is less well served by government programs, governments still tend to see First Nations as a liability, an expense to be minimized.

LASTING HURT

"I'm not a survivor. I didn't survive. What you see is what's left."
—Testimony at the Truth and Reconciliation
Commission, Halifax, 2011

SEX ABUSE REVELATIONS

Although some within the churches and at Indian Affairs had always known of sexual abuse at residential schools, they managed to keep the public in the dark until 1990. An earlier light had fallen on rampant abuse of Catholic Church wards in 1988, when an east end St. John's orphanage for boys made national headlines. Several men who had attended the school as young boys alleged that nine Catholic Brothers physically and sexually abused them. It would prove to be the first domino in a long and protracted series of abuse scandals involving the Catholic Church and its congregations in Canada.

The next several dominos involved residential schools, including Shubenacadie. In 1990 Phil Fontaine went public about having been physically and sexually abused—along with all of his male classmates—at Fort Alexander Indian Residential School in Pine Falls, Manitoba. He said he later learned that girls also experienced horrific abuse. As it turned out, Fontaine's experience was a common one. In a 1995 study, nine former Indian Agents said they'd known of physical abuse at the schools. Two knew of sexual abuse. Those who'd reported the abuses to Indian Affairs received no responses. Some had gone so far as to meet with church officials, but the churches would either do nothing or simply move the offending priest to a new assignment.

As the head of the Assembly of Manitoba Chiefs, Fontaine was an influential and high-profile person with much to lose. Yet he took the risk of being the first to openly and publicly discuss abuse at residential schools. He called for a national inquiry on the issue. Within a year, two former priests at a British Columbia residential school were convicted and sentenced for the sexual abuse of four boys during the 1960s. The principal at the school was also charged with assaulting five former residents, and raping one of them. He claimed there was consent. He had fathered the girl's child. The charges were eventually dropped after he apologized in a healing circle. With charges being laid in British Columbia and the Yukon, police investigations were triggered across Canada. In 1993 the RCMP created a Native Residential School Task Force. Survivors filed more than 3,000 complaints against 170 priests and nuns. But only 5 were ever charged. In many cases, the accused were dead.

When researcher Kathleen Kearns spoke to Father Paddy Collins in 1990, he denied any sexual abuse at the Shubenacadie school. Nothing that horrible could have happened there, he told her. A survivor told Kearns that Collins himself gave quarters to girls who lifted their skirts for him.

DISLOCATION

Leading addiction researchers have found that people who lose connections to family, clan, community, nation, and custom often create a "substitute lifestyle." They fill the hole created by loss of connection—often called "dislocation"—with excessive work, drugs, food, sex, pornography, video games, television, crime, religion. All to forget the loss or replace what has been taken. Given this phenomenon, the fact that the Canadian government took 150,000 Aboriginal children away from their families, communities, nations, and cultures, and the self-destructive and illegal natures of many of the survivors' resulting addictions, the incarceration rate of Aboriginal peoples is no surprise.

The hurt of the Shubenacadie Indian Residential School resonates today not only with survivors but also their descendants, and other members of the community who suffered through losing the children. Every child who went to Shubenacadie represents a family torn apart. Some managed to reconnect, but many never did. After residential school, many survivors found themselves adrift, still unacceptable to the white majority but no longer able to speak their mother tongue or understand their own cultures.

The loss of language has been one of the most painful impacts of the school. "A culture without language is a culture without a soul," says Mike Isaac, a student services consultant with the Mi'kmaq Liaison Office of Nova Scotia's Department of Education. Bureaucrats, politicians, and women and men of the cloth systematically attacked the soul of Mi'kmaw and Wolastoqiyik culture for decades while the Nova Scotia media cheered them on. In *The Language of this Land, Mi'kma'ki*, Trudy Sable and Bernie Francis note that many of the terms that once richly described the land of Mi'kma'ki have been forgotten.

Among the two thousand souls who went through Shubenacadie, dislocation has taken myriad shapes. Survivors have testified—in media coverage since the late 1970s, during a class-action suit against the federal government in the 1990s and 2000s, and later at the TRC in 2011—of the lingering hardships encountered since they were taken from their communities and homes. While each individual's experience is unique, several of the impacts were common to many survivors.

ISOLATION

In her account of life at the school and its impact on survivors, Isabelle Knockwood writes that, for many years, those who had been at the school avoided each other. The subject of Shubenacadie became taboo, something people didn't want to think or talk about. Better to suffer in silence than to pick at scabs. Dredging up old ghosts was so frightening that when Knockwood started writing her book in the early 1990s, she was threatened with lawsuits and violence.

Shubenacadie's spectre was so powerful that even siblings who had been there together, who had bonded tight in surviving the experience, did not speak of it. Brothers and sisters who were residents at the school simultaneously but could not interact with each other sometimes heard about each other's experiences for the first time at the TRC. When they had their own children, some survivors would not talk to them about Shubenacadie. Some didn't want to be negative. Others simply weren't able to speak of it. Fear was the teaching tool at Shubenacadie, and as it turned out, fear was the lesson learned. Children did not learn of love there. If they were touched it was to further instill fear. They hadn't received love and they didn't know how to give it either. Many survivors have spoken publicly of a fear of touch, and of being too close to others—common among people who have experienced physical and sexual abuse as children. A simple hug could instill panic: "I would freeze up," one survivor said at the TRC.

CULTURAL SHAME

Years of psychological abuse left survivors with invisible scars. The children at the school heard the same thing every day: "You will never amount to anything." In many cases, the message hit its mark. Former residents had learned to be ashamed of themselves, to hang their heads. "I've failed in everything," one survivor told the TRC. Others reported being unable to hold a job or finish further attempts at education.

Children also learned that their language was simplistic and out of date, something to be punished for. Some who returned to Mi'kmaw communities refused to teach their children or grandchildren Mi'kmaw. The fear of punishment for speaking the language, once instilled, became permanent for some, as if the strap hung forever over their heads, ready to drop with the slightest misplacement of the tongue.

Survivors often speak of seeing, at Shubenacadie and in the years after leaving the school, cowboy and Indian movies, and cheering for the cowboys. It was what you were supposed to do. But worse, they had been taught to be ashamed of who they were. "Brainwashing," is what one survivor called his experience at Shubenacadie. It was the worst thing about it for him.

Mental Health

Some survivors have testified that the school drove them to suffer severe mental anguish—including being hospitalized repeatedly over decades. Adding to the horror of that experience, one survivor observed, was the fact that the mental hospital looked identical to the residential school: gleaming and institutional, as if regularly scrubbed clean of damning evidence.

Hour after hour of lectures on Catholic morality were undone by sexual, physical, and psychological abuse by priests and nuns. Some survivors were left without a clear sense of right and wrong, and in turn hurt their own loved ones. They were consumed by unquenchable rage. Years of living in survival mode—trying to fly under the radars of school authorities, taking careful note of everything in order to anticipate and avoid danger, manipulating the right allies to avoid punishment—had taken away their ability to trust. They lived the same way outside the school, carefully and with skilful manipulation. "I learned crazy mental games," one survivor said.

Several people who went through Shubenacadie have also reported memory loss or blackout—knowing they went to the school but not realizing they were there for several years. One survival technique, common among abuse victims, was for residents to visualize another place, to imagine they weren't there experiencing a personal hell. It's possible this technique contributed to lost years. One survivor testified at the TRC that she had an emotional breakdown every decade—always on the anniversary of her admittance to the school.

Drugs

Alcohol, and sometimes other drugs, is perhaps the most commonly cited escape from residential school memories. Even survivors who had never been exposed to alcohol before residential school have talked of struggling with alcoholism. For some it was a self-induced blackout, driving the experience out of mind, numbing the pain and anger. Many have overdosed or ended up in detox. Sometimes the children and grandchildren of residential school survivors inherited the addiction. Already vulnerable families were driven further apart. But many also kicked their habit, and apologized to their loved ones for what they had done, for the affliction they'd given their children, adding profound guilt to their list of ghosts.

DOMESTIC PROBLEMS

About 80 percent of survivors who testified at the TRC spoke of hurting their own families, taking their guilt and shame out on them. Shubenacadie denied its residents the chance to *learn* how to parent—something usually passed down from parents or guardians. Instead, children at Shubenacadie did hard labour and learned a certain world view: that success in life could only be attained through cold, hard discipline, a strict schedule, and punishments for noncompliance. They were not hugged, cuddled, or mentored. Nor did they learn about dating or falling in love. For the most part, those lessons were repressed. They were not allowed to interact with the opposite sex. "I became a willing partner in what I thought were expressions of love," Rita Joe wrote in her autobiography of her years immediately after Shubenacadie. But she was yet to learn what love really was. Her experience was not unique. Many fell quickly into family situations—often with many children, in the Catholic way—but had only learned how to cook, clean, and sew, not how to be in a loving partnership with a spouse or raise a family. Some went through multiple marriages like this. What they had learned, as children in residential schools across the country had learned, was how to discipline with violence. Many more survivors lost their children, who were either taken away by child protection or estranged.

Sparked by the residential school experience, but extending beyond just survivors and into the general community, physical and sexual abuse reached crisis levels in Aboriginal communities across Canada from the 1980s onward. For example, researchers of one 1989 study sponsored by the Native Women's Association of the Northwest Territories found that eight of every ten girls and five of every ten boys under eight were sexually assaulted in Aboriginal communities. Survivors often pass their pain—what they call "Shubie rage"—on to their children. For children of survivors, part of that rage is the result of trying fruitlessly to figure out why their parents are so angry. Some survivors took their anger out on their children until Children's Aid took them away, only to then be denied access to their grandchildren.

SUICIDE

It is difficult to know how many people have committed suicide in order to end their struggles with Shubenacadie demons. Survivors have testified that many former residents have died at their own hands. But many more have driven themselves to slower deaths by abusing alcohol and other drugs. "Most of the people who came out of that school had real problems and are dead today from suicide and alcoholism," one survivor said.

Many survivors testified at the TRC that they have struggled for years with suicidal thoughts. Some had thought of it every day since leaving the school. And one woman explicitly linked high suicide rates on her reserve with the residential school experience. "I had no life," another man said. There seemed to be no point to surviving any longer. Those who considered or attempted suicide had been lucky enough to find the support they needed—people who understood them, loved them, and could help them during their most vulnerable moments. Many had come through years or decades of struggle. They had kicked their addictions, learned to love again, reconciled with their families, or found work. The journey back was the hardest road imaginable. But most often, the cure was simply the opposite of the cause. The cause was an attempt at cultural genocide. The cure was reconnecting with that culture.

RECONCILIATION

SURVIVOR STORIES

The more than two thousand survivors of the Shubenacadie Indian Residential School—about seven hundred of whom are believed to be still living—have proven that the way mainstream society, the government, and church saw Mi'kmaw culture was wrong. Even the name, Mi'kmaq, or MicMac back then, was rarely used. Settler Canadians called them "Indians" and saw them as part of a massive homogenous, and backwards, culture. In reality, the Mi'kmaq were of course distinct from other First Nations. And amongst themselves, they were diverse. Therefore, their reactions to the school were diverse. Some lived recklessly within the school, thumbing their noses at authority, consequences be damned. Most went into some sort of survival mode, but the tactics varied a great deal. Some stayed quiet as mice, hoping not to be noticed. Others became "pets," cozying to the teachers so punishment would fall on others. Some were bullies, making themselves powerful in an otherwise powerless situation. Others tried to escape. Some, when they got big enough, fought back against the Sisters and principal, and they usually ended up in juvenile detention or an orphanage.

The experiences of survivors have been equally diverse. At the Maritime TRC events, the theme of "getting revenge" by living a good life—proving the Sisters had been wrong when they said the children would amount to nothing—was prevalent. But many went through hell to get to the good stuff. And others are still going through hell. Of those who became parents, many survivors reproduced the violence they had learned in school on their own children. Too many became addicted to alcohol or other drugs. Some ended up in jail. As was written in the TRC interim report, "The prospect of going to jail had been of little consequence to them because they had already been through hard times at residential school and were familiar with the feeling of being locked up and isolated." One of the legacies of residential schools is that nearly a quarter of all Canadian prisoners are Aboriginal, compared with only 4.3 percent of Canadians.

Many survivors resented the Catholic Church after Shubenacadie, and never set foot in any church again. Some became immersed in Mi'kmaw spiritual traditions and found healing there. But many have remained devout Catholics, blaming individual priests and nuns rather than the institution as a whole. As one survivor sang at a TRC event, "*God was just a victim as well as I was. He was used to take me there. And to brutally treat me.*" Some have gone on to preach the "Micmac religion [as practiced] before it was sullied by Christian missionaries' narrow view," as the *Micmac News* put it in 1978. But some, a small number, became nuns.

Several survivors took whatever they had managed to learn from the experience and went on to high school and university. Some have written about their experiences. Many have become activists, warriors for Mi'kmaw language and culture. Others have ended up working in education, with a Mi'kmaw lens.

CHILD OF CHANGE

Wayne Nicholas of Tobique First Nation in New Brunswick arrived at the Shubenacadie residential school in 1955 and lived there until 1962. Despite the improvements, it was no picnic. Like most kids at the school, Nicholas's family was poor. His mother had contracted tuberculosis and his father, brother, and sister had to move to find work. The first thing he remembers is being called a "dirty Indian" and hit with a strap and a metal ladle, having his cheeks pinched and ears yanked. "The nuns had hands like vice grips," he recalls. Contrary to Father Paddy Collins's letters, Nicholas remembers being punished for "talking Indian." If he behaved well, the Sisters gave him candy.

In his first few years Nicholas spent much of his time doing chores, from cleaning toilets to shovelling manure. But that all changed during the

1958–59 school year, when the barn was converted to a gym and the cows and pigs were slaughtered or sold. It was a relief to no longer labour so hard, but class time wasn't exactly a thrill. Forbidden from speaking his own living language, Nicholas had to learn Latin instead. Even the teacher had trouble staying awake. Collins had hired Mr. Hugh MacLean, from New Glasgow, to teach Grades 5 and 6. He was one of the few teachers who wasn't a Sister—a hire made possible by the recently increased teacher salaries at Shubenacadie—but the quality of instruction wasn't an improvement. "He slept almost every afternoon," Nicholas recalls.

He remembers the nuns as people he avoided. "There was Sister Mary Raven, Sister Gilberta, Sister Ursula—but I never established any kind of relationship with them." Nicholas remembers them trying to comfort the children at times. He cried a lot, being far from home. He couldn't wave to his sister on the girls' side. But he did find some comfort from the other boys; at first, an older one took care of him and helped him speak English. He did the same for the young ones when he got older.

They couldn't drink water after suppertime, so they designated a toilet they would all drink from. And Nicholas remembers nonstop prayers. "We had morning prayer, wash-up, pray in the breakfast line, grace, line up for school and pray, pray in class, benediction, mass, rosary, night prayers. I decided I would never say another goddamn prayer when I got out." The routine, the prayer, the punishments, and the boredom hit Nicholas hard as he recovered in a Truro hospital after breaking his collarbone while skating at the pond. The hospital, for Nicholas, "was like heaven." He got three solid meals a day. Despite improvements over the years in the quality of food at Shubenacadie, many residents still found it inferior to what they ate at home. Nicholas felt like the nurses actually cared about him. He so dreaded going back to school he faked a high fever on the day he was to leave the hospital. That bought him three more days. Back at the school, Nicholas lost it. Overcome with rage, he hurled a chair at the wall and threw tables over until a priest wrestled him to the ground and threatened to send him to a mental institution. "After being so well cared for at the hospital, I had to accept going back," he says.

Things improved in the years he was there. The praying became less frequent in his last three years, and he remembers two young men, Boy Scouts named Gerry and Carl, who spent time with the boys. "They were a real blessing," he says. "If we misbehaved, they talked to us sternly instead of hitting us." After Shubenacadie, Nicholas tried going to public school but found himself too far behind. He quit high school, and it was many years before he experienced enough healing to finish his diploma. He's now part of the Tobique Band Council, and helps other survivors find healing.

SURVIVORS FIGHT BACK

In 1995 hundreds of Shubenacadie survivors formed the Association for the Survivors of the Shubenacadie Indian Residential School. It had started with Nora Bernard. In 1945 an Indian Agent came to Millbrook, Nova Scotia, and gave Bernard's mother, Mary, an impossible choice: send her nine-year-old daughter to residential school or into protective custody. And so Nora ended up at Shubenacadie for the next five years. In the late 1980s, Nora Bernard put out the word that she was looking for other Shubenacadie survivors. The newspapers covered her story and soon she found a handful of people on the step of her little house. She travelled across the province—often paying her own expenses from pension money—giving talks to other survivors. Bernard, a Catholic, also contributed to the United Church of Canada's reconciliation program and did counselling work for the Native Alcohol and Drug Abuse Counselling Association.

It took her several years, but Bernard eventually found more than nine hundred survivors—only about five hundred are alive today— to create an association. It was more than a support group. She wanted it to sue the government and Catholic Church. She contacted numerous lawyers, including Halifax-based John McKiggan, a personal injury lawyer. "Nora told me what she wanted to do was to bring forward a claim on behalf of every single residential school survivor who had ever attended the Shubenacadie Indian Residential School," McKiggan told the TRC in Halifax. "She had this tremendous warmth and this tremendous smile but...this strength." Bernard's faith, which was both Catholic and traditional Mi'kmaw, was part of what made her strong.

And it was the strength that pulled Nora Bernard and other survivors through. And it pushed McKiggan into action. The Association for the Survivors of the Shubenacadie Indian Residential School filed a lawsuit in 1997 against the federal government and Catholic Church for allowing children to suffer "physical, sexual and racial" abuse by priests and nuns. The lawsuit was unprecedented. The government and church fought hard, knowing millions if not billions of dollars were at stake. The charges could not be fully denied as they had been for so many years while the schools were still running. But despite its earlier apology at two Nova Scotia reserve parishes, the Halifax Diocese wanted to protect its image. "Even though we recognize that there are some people who seem to have had very negative experiences in the school system...and that is not to be ignored or pushed aside," said John O'Donnell, the Diocese director of administration at the time, in an interview with the Halifax *Mail-Star*, "we're very proud of the people who ministered on behalf of the church in the Shubenacadie school system, and...we want to protect their memory."

But the survivors' case was strong. The Catholic Church was careful to point out that it had not acted alone, that it had simply enacted federal government policies. It wanted the public to know that the government was at least *as* responsible for the impacts of the schools—the loss of language, culture, and tradition, parenting skills, and cultural pride. O'Donnell stressed the historical context for the schools. "I don't think there was the sensitivity back then that there is now of the innate dignity of the Mi'kmaq people," he said, "and the fact they have a history and they have traditions and an identity that should have been recognized as being more valuable."

The suit snowballed as other survivors' associations across the country filed their own suits. In time, the associations got together and turned their efforts into one massive lawsuit—fighting the loss of Aboriginal languages and cultures. And as the battle raged on in the courts, more and more survivors came forward with their stories, and more organizations were founded to help the healing. On Prince Edward Island, survivors founded Aboriginal Survivors for Healing in 2000. The organization hosts regular healing circles and provides counselling, safe spaces where survivors and their families support each other. Survivors like Wayne Nicholas have helped other survivors. Since 2005 he's been deeply involved with the Aboriginal Healing Foundation's work in New Brunswick.

The federal government was overwhelmed by the lawsuits. It created a new department, Indian Residential Schools Resolution Canada (IRSRC), in 2001 to handle the tens of thousands of claims. A year later, it created its National Resolution Framework to resolve the sexual and physical abuse claims using an Alternative Dispute Resolution process, whereby an adjudicator would hear claims and award compensation if abuse could be proven. But the survivors were critical of this process. It was another case of the government designing and imposing its systems on First Nations peoples without even consulting them. It focused only on abuse claims, without recognizing that forcing people to attend residential schools—and attempting to destroy their languages and cultures—was itself a horrific abuse. IRSRC pushed for a restorative justice model, focusing on the needs of survivors, abusers, and communities, instead of using rigid, individualized European-Canadian legal proof. The Assembly of First Nations (AFN) said that everybody who attended residential school, whether or not they were physically or sexually abused, deserved compensation. AFN also called for a national truth and reconciliation process, a chance to get the full truth about the schools out to the public and for the Government of Canada to formally apologize.

In 2005 a House of Commons Standing Committee on Aboriginal Affairs and Northern Development (ANNO) recommended scrapping the Alternative Dispute Resolution process, which was satisfying no one. Instead, it recommended court-supervised negotiations to decide on fair compensation, and supported the call for a truth and reconciliation process. The following year, the government announced a $1.9 billion compensation package for seventy- to eighty-thousand survivors, approved by the churches, Aboriginal leadership, and the survivors' lawyers. The agreement included a Common Experience Payment for anyone who could prove having attended an Indian residential school, as well as an Independent Assessment Process, whereby individuals would have to testify regarding any abuse they experienced. And there would be a truth and reconciliation process and healing programs for survivors.

The courts approved the deal in 2007. The Indian Residential Schools Settlement Agreement, the largest class-action settlement in Canadian history and the largest historical redress settlement in the world, would be Nora Bernard's legacy. "She had a mission and she wasn't going to stop until it was over," McKiggan said. Bernard received some compensation—$14,000—two years later. But she died very soon after at the hands of her grandson, James Douglas Gloade, who had taken $500 worth of crack, Valium, and OxyContin, and come to Bernard for money. She was named to the Order of Nova Scotia posthumously, less than a year after her death.

CHURCHES APOLOGIZING

Even when Shubenacadie was still open, its former residents often led the way for the rights and well-being of the Mi'kmaq. Many found healing in reconnecting with traditional Mi'kmaw culture. And they could read and write in the dominant language. Some used that skill to advocate for their own children to stay home from the school. They could learn what they needed at day schools, but be protected from colonial ideology by staying within their communities.

And it was residential school survivors across Canada who led the effort to close the schools. They were effective political leaders and spokespeople. In Nova Scotia, Mi'kmaw leaders pushed the provincial government to finally protect the Mi'kmaq under the provincial Human Rights Act in 1991. It was the same year that the Roman Catholic Church and the Missionary Oblates of Mary Immaculate issued official apologies for the harm caused by residential schools. They did not, however, support Phil Fontaine's call for a formal inquiry into the system.

Within a year, most of the churches in Canada had issued apologies for their roles in the residential schools. Austin Burke, archbishop of Halifax, visited St. Catherines Church at Indian Brook First Nation a few weeks before Christmas 1992 and apologized to the congregation for the "suffering caused in the Indian Residential School." Burke gave a homily about the role of Catholics in making a straight path for the Lord. "We have not always understood the difference between gospel and culture," he preached. "We have confused language and faith. This happened with all groups. It is part of the pain of the history we share." Burke pointed out that, as an Acadian, his people also had their language repressed by the church. "The straight path is not about correct language or perfect posture or special music," he acknowledged. "The good news is about the God who created us in infinite variety." He then offered the Archdiocese's apology. "I apologize for whatever pain the church itself may have been responsible for causing in the residential school. The church is not meant to hurt, but to heal—and I must say that I am truly sorry if people caused some lingering hurts in the name of the church."

Burke called for reconciliation. "The Church of Halifax and the Mi'kmaq people are a part of each other," he said. "We have been bonded to each other for many years. Our partnership has weathered many storms. We rejoice with you in the publication of the *Book of Mi'kmaq Prayers*. The Archdiocese and the Sisters of Charity were pleased to contribute to the costs of preparing this material for publication and distribution." Burke did the same at Sacred Heart Church in Millbrook in 1993. This time he stressed reconciliation throughout his homily—using the word nine times in a three-page address. He outlined the historical context of injustice and heralded the dawn of a new day. "Much that happened in the past was wrong," he observed. "In North America white European settlers brought the gospel of Jesus Christ. That gospel was presented in their language, filtered through their traditions and culture. The governments they established supported all of that. This has led to injustice for many people."

And he repeated the official apology.

Government Apologizing

In 1990 parliamentarians took up Phil Fontaine's call for a public inquiry. But Indian Affairs had to figure out how it could make amends without exposing itself to liability. The whole residential school system was run on a shoestring budget and the last thing Indian Affairs needed was an expensive lawsuit. It would be several years before the federal government experimented with its first official apology to residential school survivors. This statement, which honed in on abuse at the schools, was issued on January 7, 1998, under the authority of the minister of Indian Affairs and Northern Development. It was part of a new government plan, *Gathering Strength: Canada's Aboriginal Action Plan*, "an action plan designed to renew the relationship with the Aboriginal people of Canada."

The plan contained a section called "Statement of Reconciliation: Learning from the Past," which the minster read out at a lunchtime ceremony in a Parliament Hill meeting room. "To those individuals who experienced the tragedy of sexual and physical abuse at residential schools, and who have carried this burden believing that in some way they must be responsible, we wish to emphasize that what you experienced was not your fault and should never have happened," it read. "To those of you who suffered this tragedy at residential schools, we are deeply sorry….The Government of Canada acknowledges the role it played in the development and administration of these schools." With this new plan, Canada established the $350 million Aboriginal Healing Foundation (AHF), which for eleven years funded more than a hundred community-based support groups and initiatives for survivors across the country.

In 2010 much of the fund was cut, and the rest was channelled through Health Canada. The cuts left these groups scrambling for new funding, which only some have been able to find. The official apology itself failed to address the fact that the residential school system was a violent attempt to destroy cultures and peoples. And it was half-hearted, coming from a minister with little fanfare. Prime Minister Jean Chrétien was in Ottawa but didn't attend the ceremony. And the money for the AHF was nowhere near enough to meet the needs of survivors, tens of thousands of whom struggled with residential school ghosts.

On June 11, 2008, nearly a decade after this initial apology, Prime Minister Stephen Harper stood in the House of Commons and gave a formal apology for the residential school system. Having already been forced to pay out billions of dollars in compensation to survivors, there was nothing left for the government to lose in admitting responsibility. The leaders of each opposition party followed and did the same. Aboriginal leaders looked on, in a circle on the House of Commons floor. Hundreds of survivors stood above in the gallery and listened. "There is no place in Canada for the attitudes that inspired the Indian Residential Schools system to ever prevail again," Harper said. He also announced the establishment of the Truth and Reconciliation Commission, a series of hearings to be held across the country in 2011. "This commission presents a unique opportunity to educate all Canadians of the Indian Residential Schools system," he said. "It will be a positive step in forging a new relationship between Aboriginal peoples and other Canadians, a relationship based on the knowledge of our shared history, a respect for each other, and a desire to move forward together with a renewed understanding that strong families, strong communities, and vibrant cultures and traditions will contribute to a stronger Canada for all of us."

For many survivors, their families, and communities, it was a momentous day. But the jury is still out on the apology, the settlement, and the truth and reconciliation process. "It made no real difference that government officials and some representatives of the Catholic Church apologized to Native people for the schools," Isabelle Knockwood writes. "Those individuals who directly caused our suffering never admitted their wrongdoing and were never called to account for their actions." But another survivor told Knockwood that she accepted the apology and would "forgive everything." Doing so relieved her of the burden of what had been done to her.

CULTURAL GENOCIDE

"We have never admitted to ourselves that we were, and still are, a colonial power."
–Paul Martin, 21st prime minister of Canada

In terms of acknowledging past mistakes and learning from them, the Government of Canada has gone no further than apologizing, and has gone so far as to contradict its own apology by denying its history as a colonial state. Prime Minister Stephen Harper, who delivered the government apology, told a crowd in Pittsburgh in September 2009 that Canada had "no history of colonialism [and] all the things that many people admire about the great powers, but none of the things that threaten or bother them." Canada's Aboriginal leaders, including the high-profile Assembly of First Nations, repeatedly use the term "cultural genocide" to describe Canada's centuries-long efforts to assimilate Aboriginal peoples. Yet the Canadian government has repeatedly denied the truth of the term, and has yet to acknowledge its attempt at cultural genocide despite the immense and clear documentation of Canada's intent to assimilate First Nations, Métis, and Inuit cultures and people.

In 2011, soon after the TRC's East Coast swing, Aboriginal Affairs Minister John Duncan joined the long list of residential school deniers. Specifically, he called the system an "education policy gone wrong." In doing so, he denied the reams of archival evidence showing that education was never the intent of the schools. They were to cut children off from the "influence of the wigwam," as Nicholas Flood Davin advocated in 1879. Duncan's statement also denies his prime minister's apology of 2008, which stated, "Two primary objectives of the residential school system were to remove and isolate children from their homes, families, traditions, and cultures, and to assimilate them into the dominant culture." When John Duncan's comments went viral and livid emails swamped his offices, officials at Aboriginal Affairs made plans to shut down and avoid any further questions and comments about the matter, according to emails obtained by APTN *National News.* "There will be no messaging prepared to address this issue," the director of communications for Aboriginal Affairs wrote. "The minister and all spokespersons know they are not to speak to it." Another communications person later asked that the emails be deleted.

Two years later, the new Canadian Museum for Human Rights, a Crown corporation, decided not to use the term "cultural genocide" to describe Canada's treatment of First Nations, Métis, and Inuit. Its logic was that, not being a government department or court of law, it couldn't be the first public institution to use the term. It was following the example of the federal government. Three months after that, in October 2013, a provocative commentary by Phil Fontaine and prominent social activist and Liberal politician Bernie Farber appeared in the *Globe and Mail,* entitled "What Canada committed against First Nations was genocide. The UN should recognize it." It was published in anticipation of a visit from the Special United Nations Rapporteur for Indigenous People, Professor James Anaya. In it, Fontaine and Farber argue that Canada's historical treatment of Aboriginal peoples meets the UN definition of genocide.

Residential schools alone qualify as an attempted cultural genocide. A 1995 draft of the UN *Declaration on the Rights of Indigenous Peoples,* which Canada signed, protects against it. Cultural genocide is defined to include:

> *any action which has the aim or effect of depriving [Indigenous people] of their integrity as distinct peoples, or of their cultural values or ethnic identities; any form of population transfer which has the aim or effect of violating or undermining any of their rights; any form of assimilation or integration by other cultures or ways of life imposed on them by legislative, administrative or other measures; any form of propaganda directed against them.*

Until our government frankly acknowledges the truth of what it tried to do, in clear and certain terms, it is hard to imagine us moving beyond colonial systems of education and child welfare.

RE-TRAUMATIZING

Despite the size of the Indian Residential Schools Settlement Agreement, it is flawed in many ways. For one, the estates of former residents who have since died received no compensation, despite the fact that their descendants commonly experienced trauma because of the schools. Since the settlement, health historian Ian Mosby revealed the evidence of nutrition experiments conducted on residential schoolchildren. "Did the government know about these experiments when it negotiated the settlement?" Mosby wonders. "Did it negotiate in good faith?"

The most disturbing facet though is the process survivors have to go through to make a claim. Anyone who could prove having attended a residential school was eligible for $10,000 for the first year, plus another $3,000 for each additional year. Additional funds were made available for therapy, addictions counselling, and caregivers. But the method of proving attendance was painful, and a challenge for many survivors. Due to spotty government records, some survivors have been unable to find copies of their old school admission forms. Many have had to sit and describe memories of the school and remain consistent with details of abuse. But specific and detailed memories are challenging. Blackouts were common at Shubenacadie, a result of the severe abuse experienced. Some were taken to a school when they were only four years old, and are now elderly. It is a system designed to eliminate claims. As Joanne Henry, director of the Committee on Abuse in Residential Schools Society, puts it: "The government is not looking for one hundred ways to pay you. They're looking for one way not to." As of 2012, 51,188 residential school survivors had received less than what they put in for. To date, about 750 Mi'kmaw survivors have applied for the Common Experience Payment.

The process is much worse for those claiming compensation for abuse. "Survivors have to tell their story three to ten times," Daphne Hutt-MacLeod, a mental health services director at Eskasoni, explains. More than one hundred people in Atlantic Canada have been admitted to give testimony in this process, but the APC chiefs are lobbying for more time for survivors to apply. The initial deadline was September 19, 2012. Those admitted must, after decades of silence in many cases, publicly pick at painful, humiliating scabs for lawyers and adjudicators—and sometimes medical professionals—to learn what level of sexual abuse they qualify for. Often Elders will pray with survivors before they give their testimony. The adjudicators use a four-page checklist with a points system to determine how much money a survivor can potentially receive. The checklist is part of the fifty-paged Schedule D of the Independent Assessment Process and it is intimidating. Local First Nations groups are working to help survivors through this process. The form itself should come with a trigger warning: even someone who hasn't experienced abuse could easily suffer from reading it. And therefore some readers may wish to skip the following paragraph.

The first category on this form is, "Repeated, persistent incidents of anal or vaginal intercourse; Repeated, persistent incidents of anal/vaginal penetration with an object: 45–60 points." Also included are "One or more incidents of digital anal/vaginal penetration" and "One or more incidents of attempted anal/vaginal penetration (excluding attempted digital penetration)." Masturbation incidents score 26–35 points. Physical abuse categories include, "One or more physical assaults causing a physical injury that led to or should have led to hospitalization or serious medical treatment by a physician; permanent or demonstrated long-term physical injury, impairment or disfigurement; loss of consciousness; broken bones; or a serious but temporary incapacitation such that bed rest or infirmary care of several days duration was required." Examples are then provided. The form instructs adjudicators to add 5 to 15 percent to the score for verbal abuse, racism, or witnessing the abuse of another child.

The claimant is supposed to provide dates and times for each alleged incident, and the names of perpetrators—something even the public archives often lack. For survivors who may have blacked out as many details as possible, it's a fantastical test of memory. The form also explains that, contrary to Aboriginal cultures, "The format does not contemplate a narrative exposition of the evidence heard." "I'll lay dollars to doughnuts the victims of the Antigonish Archdiocese didn't have to go through that," Hutt-MacLeod says. "Some, not all, have even resumed destructive behaviours they've been

194 · INDIAN SCHOOL ROAD

away from for decades." It will be several years—until at least 2017—before this process is complete, and the Atlantic Chiefs are lobbying for an extension of the deadline. The average compensation will be around $18,000.

TRUTH AND RECONCILIATION

In 1991, responding to the Oka crisis, the Government of Canada established a Royal Commission on Aboriginal Peoples. The commission conducted 178 days of public hearings in 96 communities across Canada and consulted with numerous experts, posing the question: "What are the foundations for a fair and honourable relationship between the Aboriginal and non-Aboriginal people of Canada?" The commission's four thousand-page final report, released in 1996, set a twenty-year agenda for change. One of its recommendations was to hold a national inquiry on residential schools—echoing Phil Fontaine's demand in 1990. But it would take Nora Bernard's driving of the national class-action suit to finally result in a national inquiry of sorts to be facilitated by the Truth and Reconciliation Commission. It would be one of the few recommendations of the Royal Commission to be implemented. For 389 survivors of Shubenacadie, their families, descendants, and for staff of the religious organizations involved, the Truth and Reconciliation Commission provided the chance to put their stories on record, to be heard and acknowledged, in a series of daylong public events held in fall 2011 in Fredericton, Charlottetown, Indian Brook, and Eskasoni, as well as a four-day national event in Halifax.

The Halifax event drew nearly 2,000 people each day, including witnesses, commissioners, counsellors, church representatives, political representatives, school groups, and members of the general public. The event involved 175 volunteers, 40 TRC staff members, and 116 health support workers who gave all-day debriefing and self-care services due to the powerful emotions of the day. People participated in survivor sharing circles and panel discussions. Another 10,000 people watched webcasts online. In all, there were more than 50 ceremonies, sharings, activities, performances, and other activities. Participants gave 154 statements in all, 69 of them privately, 28 in sharing circles, 41 on panels, and another 10 during a formal dialogue on reconciliation. Six people made statements of reconciliation.

Survivor Lottie Johnson carried ashes from sacred fires lit at the national events in Inuvik and Winnipeg, and started the fire in Halifax. Survivor Patrick Etherington, his partner, and son walked more than 2,200 kilometres from Cochrane, Ontario, to Halifax, raising awareness about abuse at the residential schools.

Unfortunately, the attendance by non-Aboriginals was low. Journalist Tim Bousquet of *The Coast* observed that neither the prime minister, premier, nor mayor attended. "Halifax mayor Peter Kelly was in town—his City Hall office is across the street from the World Trade and Convention Centre, and his parking space is about 10 metres from the centre's front door, but there's no indication that Kelly crossed the street and spoke with the Truth and Reconciliation Commission," Bousquet wrote. "There were relatively few white faces present in the convention centre itself."

The stories the survivors shared were hard to hear—for church representatives, for the public, and for seasoned journalists. Many professionals cried at these events. But the stories, of course, were much harder to tell than hear. It would be the first time many survivors spoke of their experiences publicly. And even for those who had already spoken or written about their experiences, it had the potential to tear old wounds raw. Some testified that they had put hours of work, sometimes years, into assembling all their memories together into a statement they could say aloud. While much was laid bare, some things will always be too painful to share and were withheld. But although the stories were harrowing and painful, almost every survivor ended on a note of hope and pride, showing individual and collective resilience. They said the school was a systematic attempt to take away their culture. But it failed. "I am still here," was repeated many times, "still Mi'kmaw."

Most speakers had suffered not only during their residential school years, but for a long time afterward. Healing came through therapy, from devoted friends and family who refused to give up on them, or through embracing their cultural heritage and championing their rights: Mi'kmaw song, dance, drumming, language, and deeper ways of perceiving the world and being in it. Humour was essential. Some thanked Mi'kmaw artists like survivor Rita Joe for instilling cultural pride in them. Survivors also spoke of their unstoppable personal determination to spread the word about the rich history of their people, how it was strong enough to survive Canada's attempts to destroy it. Most were still on the healing journey. Many spoke of the need for a community-wide cultural revival, and for young people to learn the Mi'kmaw language from the Elders who still have it.

It took deep inner strength for survivors to sit before thousands and tell these personal stories, to expose the worst they'd been through and tell their truth. Some admitted that it hurt them all over again to do so, that they could feel the pain of it in their bodies. But testifying was part of the healing process. Forgiving was, for some, even harder. As one survivor put it: "Deep down I have to forgive myself first."

Fittingly, the day closed with an honouring ceremony for Nora Bernard.

MEN AND WOMEN OF THE CLOTH RESPONDING

"I have inherited a black mark…I have a long, long
way to go before I can understand your hurt."
—Tony Mancini, Catholic archbishop of Halifax to the
Mi'kmaw community at the TRC *Halifax session*

Only when settler Canada can acknowledge its shameful past with open eyes, without excuses, and apply the lessons in those mistakes to justice, shedding our "civilized" sense of superiority, will there be hope for Canada. The Shubenacadie Indian Residential School isn't just a historical fact. Although it is rarely discussed, it is a living history that resonates today. It is not enough to say that those who ran Shubenacadie, or even those who founded it, were part of a racist system. It is an accurate statement, but it falls short of the truth. These people were not passive floaters caught up in a racist stream. They were active players in a cruel and violent attempt at cultural genocide.

Since its formal apologies at Millbrook and Indian Brook more than twenty years ago, the Catholic Archdiocese of Halifax-Yarmouth has been reluctant to discuss Shubenacadie publicly. The Archdiocese did not consent to a formal interview for this book. Deacon Bob Britton, chancellor for the Archdiocese, chatted with me briefly over the phone and answered my first email. "Frankly I am not in a position to answer your questions," he wrote. "When I review our archival information we have little that relates to the origins, operations, and management of the school." This is in part because the Truth and Reconciliation Commission required that the churches hand over their records, which are to be entered into a database that will eventually be available online. Britton also told me that the Sisters of Charity were responsible for the "management of the school" and therefore had better records—or at least they did until their mother house burnt down in 1951. But priests appointed by the Archdiocese actually managed the school; Sisters of Charity nuns staffed it. And the school was open for another sixteen years after the fire, yet the Sisters of Charity and Archdiocese records of those years seem scant. What they *did* have now belongs to the TRC, and the TRC isn't ready to share.

When I asked what the Catholic Church has done since Shubenacadie closed to repair its relationship with Mi'kmaw and Wolastoqiyik communities, Deacon Britton noted that the Archdiocese started a mission parish at Indian Brook, called Saint Kateri Tekakwitha—after the Mohawk saint—in the early days of the residential school. Britton wrote that this parish and the one at Millbrook, Sacred Heart Church, "provide a visible presence of the church's mission—the proclamation of the Gospel and the care of the people of those two communities." No one returned my calls and emails to those parishes, seeking more details. But Rita Joe, in her autobiography, wrote fondly of Christmas Eve mass at her church in Eskasoni: "The Christmas songs were sung in English and Mi'kmaq....During the early part of the service, our priest spoke in Mi'kmaq—a full page of our language, we were so surprised that we clapped. The attempts of the priests and the nuns in the choir to speak our language always moves me."

Some survivors managed to find Sisters who had taught at the school—visiting them or exchanging letters—with varying results. Survivor Elsie Charles Basque, who was the first certified Mi'kmaw teacher in Nova Scotia and the first to work in a provincial public school, told journalist Darlene Ricker that she received an apology from one of her former Shubenacadie teachers. The Sister said she and her colleagues had no control over the system. Rita Joe and Isabelle Knockwood both wrote about their experiences contacting former teachers. Knockwood wrote that only some of the Sisters acknowledged the severity of punishments at the school. And even those who did felt the abuses were the fault of an individual or individuals, not a condemnation of the school itself.

One Sister wrote to Knockwood saying there was "so much ingratitude, exaggeration and negative remarks" from survivors, and little acknowledgement of the good things. "What about the meals, clean clothes, and care that was given when they were sick?" Another Sister wrote to Knockwood that she felt sympathy for the survivors because at a very young age they had been taken from home. She theorized that perhaps that experience alone had driven them to remember the worst things about the school—memories that had been magnified over time. "Over the years I have marveled at how well they did in spite of living in a different environment," she wrote.

Inspired by her friend Isabelle Knockwood's efforts, Rita Joe took her husband—also a Shubenacadie survivor—to see Sister Justinian in Halifax. Sister Justinian was at Shubenacadie from 1946 to 1955 and was one of Rita Joe's favourites. At the time of their reunion, the Sister was in her eighties and long retired. "When I walked into her room, Sister Justinian put out her arms for me, and I went into them," Rita Joe wrote in her autobiography. It was a tearful reunion. But Rita Joe's husband, Frank, could not contain his anger. He vented at Sister Justinian and Rita Joe scolded him in Mi'kmaw, reminding him how old this former teacher was. "We've got to forgive and forget," Rita Joe told him. Frank said his piece and then confessed he didn't hate Sister Justinian, he'd just been so badly hurt by the school and had naturally focused his anger on the adults who'd run the place. But Rita Joe wrote that she had always held sympathy for the Sisters, even as a child. In a sense, the couple well encapsulated the varied reactions to the school by survivors. Resentment, anger, and sometimes forgiveness and sympathy.

Survivors and researchers have questioned the Sisters of Charity, as an organization, several times about the school. In 1978, when journalist Conrad W. Paul wrote a series for *Micmac News* based on interviews with thirty survivors, he spoke with Sister Cathleen Dunne, then public relations director. "Any sister who served while Father Mackey was superintendent said he loved the children and did all he could to help them," she told him. "The sisters recall him as an extremely kind man." Sister Dunne denied the existence of a "dungeon" or "hole"—the closets where survivors remember spending days with only bread and water. Paul wrote of how *Micmac News* had to change printers to run the series. Their usual printer, the Dartmouth Free Press, would not run it without a signed release from the Sisters. "It was made quite clear that such a request could be and would be buried in red tape," Paul wrote. "[The Sisters of Charity] said we were not searching for the truth and implied that over thirty independent eye-witness accounts were lies," but refused to give him the other side of the story or release any documentation on the school.

In 1986 freelance journalist Heather Laskey contacted the Sisters of Charity for comment. She was working on a ten-minute documentary for CBC Radio. "Nobody'd done anything in the white press," Laskey says. "They knew about the school but they didn't care." The congregation again defended the Sisters' involvement in the school, saying they too had a difficult adjustment to make, that there had essentially been a massive culture clash in an isolated building with little understanding. One Sister told Laskey that unannounced nutritionists had visited the school twice while she worked there and given positive reports on the food. She also said that the children almost always became good readers. Sister Caroleen Browne, communications director, told Laskey the Sisters found some of the survivors' accounts "unfounded and exaggerated." She added that religious life used to be more rigid and harsher punishments more acceptable socially: "I believe the residential schools were an attempt to solve a problem, but it was a mistaken attempt." In 1995 Sister Mary Martin, on behalf of the order, told Dalhousie graduate student Marilyn Elaine Thomson-Millward the same thing.

In researching this book, I met with four Sisters of Charity and conducted detailed interviews and email correspondence with each of them. Their tone has softened considerably when describing survivor stories from Shubenacadie. "The Congregation as a whole, and individual Sisters, take all testimony seriously," Ruth Jeppesen, communications director, told me. She says the Sisters are "genuinely committed to the reconciliation process and have tried to ensure 'deep listening' throughout that process," that "some are certainly puzzled and saddened by some of the stories that don't fit with their own experiences."

As an organization, the Sisters of Charity has yet to issue any official apology for its role in the Shubenacadie Indian Residential School. Its first public statement on Shubenacadie came at the Truth and Reconciliation Commission in 2011—forty-four years after the school was shuttered. Sister Donna Geernaert made the statement: "It is with great sadness that we have listened to the stories of Residential School survivors," she said. "The history of these schools was not one of liberation. They were part of a system that was racist and oppressive. While we wish the past could have been different, our challenge today is to find the kind of education that will liberate." Sister Geernaert spoke at length of reconciliation efforts made by the Sisters, but didn't mention in her statement that the Sisters of Charity had been directly involved with the school as teachers, disciplinarians, and administrators.

The Sisters most survivors remember as being particularly violent, sadistic, and cruel are all long dead. In all, only three Sisters who taught at Shubenacadie survive—two locally and one in the United States. They are retired and elderly, and none of them were up for an interview, Sister Donna Geernaert told me. When I sat down with Geernaert, she knew little of Sister Mary Leonard, who along with Father Mackey is remembered as the school's most vicious adult during its early years. Like the Catholic Archdiocese of Halifax, the Sisters of Charity has little in the way of official records. What remains is being sent to the Truth and Reconciliation Commission, where it will not be made public until the entire database is complete. It could take a decade or more.

One document the Sisters of Charity would not share, TRC or no TRC, is the Annals, which the Sisters at the school kept. In the mid-1990s, Sister Mary Martin allowed graduate student Marilyn Elaine Thomson-Millward to view the Annals. According to Thomson-Millward, it was a journal of sorts with insights into what life was like at the school, and revealed much about the Sisters' attitudes to their work. Ruth Jeppesen sees it differently. "They're personal house records, nothing to do with the school," she says. "They would typically include things like the Sisters' prayer schedule… changes to guidelines and permissions…the kind of things that regulated their life as Sisters." In this book, I've had to rely exclusively on Thomson-Millward's excerpts and interpretations.

When I met with Sister Geernaert, she said that the Sisters of Charity had participated in a racist system. "I suspect in the 1930s we had no awareness that what we were doing was racist," she explained. "There was an inherent racism in the system no doubt. The federal government, possibly for the best possible motives, was trying to make Aboriginal people into white people." She also said that, in those days, the Sisters did whatever the archbishop asked of them. The Sisters at Shubenacadie had diverse experiences. Some wanted to be there and others found it difficult. "I've talked to Sisters that have been in the residential school both here and in Cranbrook," she said, "and I don't get any sense from them anything other than they liked being there. They appreciated the Native people." She recalled a conversation with one Sister who had taught at the residential school in Cranbrook, British Columbia—which was also taught by Sisters of Charity—in the last years it was open. She could not believe what she heard about residential schools in general. "Well, that wasn't us, was it?" this Sister said to Sister Donna. "Because our students were happy."

But it was.

Sister Geernaert said that other former teachers she's spoken with enjoyed the experience and felt good about it, that they had accomplished something. She stressed that not every survivor story is one of pain and sorrow. The worst of it, she felt, was the taking of children against a family's will. "I've talked to some of the Mi'kmaq who have been at the school and they went...because their parents wanted them to," she said. "And they probably had a different experience than those who were taken almost by force." She also said that "people who had very bad experiences" are the only ones who gave testimony at the Truth and Reconciliation Commission hearings throughout Atlantic Canada in 2011. "There were others that didn't have bad experiences and don't feel that they're in a position that they can actually talk about that...they would probably be ostracized." She said other survivors have told her they had good experiences.

For non-Aboriginal people, it is perhaps too easy to scapegoat the churches as mainstream society further secularizes, now that religion has met with popular criticism—bolstered by numerous sexual abuse scandals—and fewer and fewer people are involved with the churches. The churches were major players in that racist system, it is true. God's representatives on Earth perpetrated unspeakable crimes against children. The Catholic Church and its representatives ran Shubenacadie and are directly responsible for the abuses that happened there. But in the days of residential schools, at least until the late 1940s, most white Catholic Canadians shared with the nuns and priests a strong sense of cultural and racial superiority. It was that commonly held belief that allowed the horrors of Shubenacadie to be enacted by politicians, bureaucrats, and clergy.

RETURNING TO SPIRIT

"Reconciliation is a process which can't be demanded or rushed."
—Sister Donna Geernaert

The Sisters of Charity has been involved in the settlement process with other Catholic organizations and the federal government. It has raised and distributed funding for healing and reconciliation programs through its Moving Forward Together campaign. One Sister also played a role in organizing the TRC gatherings in the region. Internally, the congregation comes together once every six years to critically reflect on its missions and practices. At its last meeting, in 2008, the Sisters reflected on the dangers of unintentional complicity. "We talked about the importance of systemic change and recognizing how we can be complicit in a system that's unjust without realizing that we're complicit," says Sister Donna. But perhaps their most powerful initiative has been organizing a Returning to Spirit workshop.

Returning to Spirit was co-founded by Marc Pizandawatc, an Algonquian man from the Northwest Territories, and Sister Ann Thomson of the Sisters of St. Ann. The program happens in three phases. First, there are two separate but concurrent five-day workshops—one for non-Aboriginal people and one for Aboriginal people. Second, there are two separate but concurrent two-day workshops on communication. And finally, there is a three-day workshop where the Aboriginal and non-Aboriginal groups come together for sharing. The workshops focus on how residential school experiences linger in contemporary life, and how to move beyond healing and into a phase of reconciliation, bridging gaps between people and critically analyzing participants' beliefs about others.

Between May and September 2012, five First Nations people—including survivors or descendants of survivors of Shubenacadie—and five non-Aboriginal people participated in Returning to Spirit workshops in Tatamagouche, Nova Scotia. Sisters Geraldine Lancaster and Joan O'Keefe of the Sisters of Charity both participated. Sister O'Keefe also attended the Halifax and Indian Brook TRC events, and was disappointed there weren't more people there from the Catholic Church. "People didn't really know whether they should go or not," she says. "It wasn't advertised properly... people afterwards would talk to their friends from the United Church or

Anglican and they'd be saying 'how come you didn't go to some of it?'…
There was still room for more people." Sister Lancaster helped organize the
Halifax TRC event and participated in a TRC preparation event. "It was there
that I publicly expressed my sorrow for what had happened at the residential
school in Shubenacadie," she says. It was a powerful expression for her, but
nothing compared to Returning to Spirit. "After Returning to Spirit I stood
up and I had a broader, deeper meaning attached to my apology. I understood better what reconciliation really was."

During the first workshop, participants were asked to write their life stories in a stream-of-consciousness purge, never removing pen from paper,
"for I don't know how long," O'Keefe says. They had to read their deepest,
darkest memories to strangers, over and over again, until they had each
other's stories memorized, in an emotionally intense atmosphere. But in
doing so, they "let some of this stuff go," and they better understood how
even seemingly minor childhood pain haunts you. "Here I am at seventy
years old learning this about myself…I slept less and ate more." The Sisters
thought they were doing the workshop to learn how to help Mi'kmaq, but
it was themselves the Sisters had to learn about.

Lancaster was eager for the final session, the chance to sit knee to knee
with survivors and express her sorrow for "not knowing what was happening," for "feeling, as an adult, complicit even in things that happen today."
At the TRC events the Sisters had felt like spectators, and longed for the
chance to say how upset, touched, and concerned they were—that they
cared. Returning to Spirit gave them that chance. "Some of the women that I
met…I knew before, but I never knew they had been to residential school…
They never mentioned it," O'Keefe says. She told these women honestly
that when she first came to Nova Scotia she understood Shubenacadie to be
nothing more than a boarding school for First Nations children. She'd lived
with Sisters who'd taught there and they'd given no indication of anything
being amiss there. O'Keefe and Lancaster felt that the TRC session was about
truth, but not reconciliation. Returning to Spirit was a step toward true
reconciliation.

The Sisters heard from survivors that they needed to take what they'd
learned and tell other Sisters. As a result, they are working with Sister
Donna Geernaert to develop an education plan for the Sisters of Charity
in Canada and the United States, to help the organization understand its

role in the residential schools, the damage done, and its responsibility to reconcile. "Some still are struggling with it, to believe that it happened," O'Keefe says. "We, out of ignorance, let some awful stuff happen. How do we prevent that happening down the road and what can we do now? How can we be really respectful of the First Nations and their culture?"

As part of their reconciliation efforts, the Sisters have become involved in programming for First Nations communities. But they are careful to only do so when asked, rather than rush in with their own ideas. They were invited in 2012 to be part of Our Dreams Matter, a national movement for safe, comfortable schools with culturally based education for young Aboriginal people. First Nations schools get less money per student than provincial schools and no funding for "extras" like libraries, computers, or language training. And the unhealthy buildings of the residential school era, caused by Indian Affairs's penny-pinching, remain a problem. Today, First Nations students deal with mould, rodents, fumes, high carbon dioxide levels, and a lack of heat.

O'Keefe has attended court dates about Jordan's Principle, which calls on governments—at any level—to pay for whatever services are needed by an Aboriginal child in crisis, without arguing about whether the federal government or province is ultimately responsible. No child should be a victim of red tape. The principle was unanimously passed in the House of Commons in 2007, but neither the provinces/territories nor the federal government has followed it. In April 2013, Canada appealed a federal court decision enforcing the principle. The Sisters have also supported the Mi'kmaw Native Friendship Centre's Kitpu program for Mi'kmaw youth in Halifax. When O'Keefe saw on Facebook that the program had lost its funding and workers were scrambling to find new income, the Sisters stepped up. "I just have said I want to support in whatever way I can," O'Keefe says. "We also write to the Prime Minister or the Minister of Aboriginal Affairs to remind them of the commitment to equity in education and culture and health care."

MOVING EDUCATION

*"Education, which was once used to destroy our
culture, is now a tool to empower us."*
—Survivor testimony at the TRC

"INDIAN CONTROL OF INDIAN EDUCATION"

When the Shubenacadie Indian Residential School closed, there were still nearly eight thousand children in fifty-two remaining residential schools. Another four thousand children attended public schools but boarded in their old residential schools. The residential school system didn't formally end until 1969. It dwindled over the next two decades until only four federally run schools remained in 1988, but the last one, in Punnichy, Saskatchewan, would remain open until 1996.

The system was slow to wind down, but that didn't lessen Indian Affairs's enthusiasm for integration: it was a more cost-effective way to assimilate Indians. In 1969 the Department went all in on assimilation with its White Paper, an attempted final solution. It would abolish Indian Affairs and the entire reserve system, and eliminate "Indian" as a distinct legal status, cutting the Indians loose and forcing them to make their way—integrate, that is—into mainstream Canadian society. And it would make Indian education a provincial responsibility. Aboriginal peoples strongly resisted every aspect of the White Paper. In Nova Scotia, eleven Mi'kmaw leaders met with Indian Affairs officials for two days in 1970 at the Wandlyn Motel in Rockingham to discuss the idea of "placing Indian education under the jurisdiction of the provincial department of education," as had already been done in British Columbia, Manitoba, and New Brunswick. At this point,

679 Nova Scotia Mi'kmaw students attended provincial schools. Nationally, nearly 60 percent of Aboriginal students were attending provincial or territorial public schools.

Noel Doucette attended the meeting as president of the Union of Nova Scotia Indians. Charles Gorman was there as regional superintendent of Indian Affairs. Doucette was concerned by the Mi'kmaw experience in provincial schools so far. He complained that clergy still interfered with curriculum, and that teachers didn't care about Mi'kmaw students, or worse, were hostile to them, calling them "mentally retarded." White students called Mi'kmaw students "dirty Indians." School boards ignored Mi'kmaw parents because "they are not taxpayers." Doucette wanted more schools on reserves. It seemed integration always meant Mi'kmaw integrating into white society, never the other way. Gorman pointed out the difficulty in getting teachers, who were nearly all white, to work on reserves, where the pay was low. Eskasoni teachers threatened to leave if they didn't get a raise. There were many challenges with Mi'kmaw education, and neither the federal government nor the provinces seemed up to them.

Nationally, resistance to the White Paper from Aboriginal communities was fierce enough to kill the proposal within a few years. Its death knell came in the form of a 1972 National Indian Brotherhood (now the Assembly of First Nations) policy paper called *Indian Control of Indian Education*. John Knockwood and Peter Christmas of the Union of Nova Scotia Indians, and Barry Nicholas of the Union of New Brunswick Indians, played key roles in the development of this paper, which states: "We want education to provide the setting in which our children can develop the fundamental attitudes and values which have an honored place in Indian tradition and culture. We want the behavior of our children to be shaped by those values." Within months the federal government agreed to transfer management and control of education to First Nations, on their request. But in reality, changes were slow as usual and First Nations often found that the federal and provincial governments went ahead with agreements that overruled their interests. They sometimes blocked curriculum with First Nations perspectives. Indian Affairs provided few resources.

Almost a decade after *Indian Control of Indian Education*, Nova Scotia's minister of education, Terry Donahoe, assessed images of minority groups in the Nova Scotia school curriculum. "To the extent that the school program mentioned Blacks, Acadians, and Native peoples at all, it did so either in a condescending or romanticized way," he wrote. "And, too often, it left the impression that Blacks, Acadians and Native peoples were no longer significant presences in the life of this province, no longer groups with justifiable grievances to raise." Donahoe did not mention the Shubenacadie Indian Residential School, but his assessment of the challenges facing Mi'kmaw learners resonated with the overall integration policy in Canada: they were supposed to be invisible, and their problems supposedly solved. But not surprisingly, most Shubenacadie survivors, and Mi'kmaw students in general, struggled in the public schools.

Aboriginal leadership argued that it didn't have to be this way. Letting the provinces take responsibility for the education of culturally distinct people was no better than letting the federal government do it. The provinces were no better equipped to deal with the unique histories and cultures of First Nations—in fact, they had been providing prejudicial curriculum all along and helped create the very learning problems Mi'kmaq were dealing with.

MI'KMAW KINA'MATNEWEY (MK)

"Indigenous peoples have the right to establish and control their educational systems and institutions providing education in their own languages, in a manner appropriate to their cultural methods of teaching and learning."
– The United Nations Declaration on the Rights of Indigenous Peoples, *endorsed by Canada, November 2010*

In 1982 Eskasoni Elementary and Middle School, formerly a federal Indian day school, became the first to come under Mi'kmaw control. Several other schools on reserves followed suit. Wagmatcook First Nation (Cape Breton) started the first band-operated secondary school in Atlantic Canada in 1987. It wasn't a smooth transition, and even under band control some pre-service teachers complained that the Mi'kmaw school board suppressed the Mi'kmaw language. Since the creation of the *Indian Control of Indian Education* paper, only two Mi'kmaq from Wagmatcook had graduated from high school. The dropout rate was 96 percent. Parents had had enough, and worked and pushed until they got a band-operated high school. Their progress initiated a slow chain reaction. Eskasoni was next to get a high school. Ten years later, in 1997, after a highly publicized series of violent incidents between white and Mi'kmaw students at Hants County East Rural High School, the school principal sent every Mi'kmaw student home. Even though the latest incident had started when white students bullied a Mi'kmaw boy.

Jean Knockwood of Indian Brook, an educator, researcher, storyteller, and mother, had had enough of seeing Mi'kmaw youth hurt by racism. She decided to home-school her daughter. Soon other kids from the reserve wanted to join her "facility" and the operation mushroomed into dozens of students in a church basement. Indian Brook had agreed to integration with public schools after Shubenacadie closed, but the discrimination from white students, teachers, and the administration never stopped. It was almost as bad for the children's self-esteem as Shubenacadie once had been. Mi'kmaw students dropped out regularly, or got suspended.

Rather than send their children back into what many saw as a racist school system, the Indian Brook First Nation renegotiated its tuition agreement with the school board—it was paying thousands for each of its students per year—stating that if the board wanted First Nations tuition dollars it would have to send teachers to the reserve. The board complied, sending two substitute teachers. Parents gave input on the selection of teachers, who at that time were still mostly white. Parent-teacher meetings were potlucks held during the day so working single parents could go at lunch. Elders visited regularly, facilitating traditional talking circles to work through conflicts, and taught Mi'kmaw language, powwow, drumming, dancing, and beadwork. Mornings began with the "Mi'kmaw Honour Song."

The school Jean Knockwood started eventually became L'nu Sipuk Kina'muokuom, or Indian Brook House of Learning. Mi'kmaw teachers right from Indian Brook are common now. But even more significantly, the Indian Brook school eventually became part of a much bigger, band-operated system with thousands of students learning on reserve. It is called Mi'kmaw Kina'matnewey, "the whole process of learning." Around the same time Jean Knockwood was taking education into her own hands at Indian Brook First Nation, the federal Indian Affairs minister was meeting with Nova Scotia premier John Savage and nine of thirteen Nova Scotia

Mi'kmaw chiefs at Chapel Island/Potlotek First Nation. In February 1997 they signed the Mi'kmaq Education Act, which finally put education for kids on reserves fully into Mi'kmaw hands—including at Indian Brook, where the school Knockwood started was thriving.

The initiative actually goes back as far as 1991, when sexual abuse allegations at Shubenacadie and other residential schools were getting major media coverage. It was then that the Assembly of Nova Scotia Chiefs approached Indian Affairs proposing that a Mi'kmaq Education Authority be established, so that Nova Scotia Mi'kmaq could manage their own education. The authority later changed its name to Mi'kmaw Kina'matnewey, or MK. With education authority in hand, seventy-five MK stakeholders kicked things off with a symposium at the Oak Island Inn and Marina. They were building an education system from scratch. The eyes of Aboriginal educators across Canada were on them, and they had to be successful. How would this thing work? How would it be governed? And what would success look like?

Rita Joe wrote of a related conference held at a school gym in Eskasoni. "A lot of people passed on their concerns about the transfer of jurisdiction," she wrote. "They were heard by the *Saqmows* (chiefs) of the

Wagmatcook Chief Norman Bernard and National Chief Shawn Atleo at the Grand Opening of the new Wagmatcookewey School in 2013. Mi'kmaw Kina'matnewey

Maritimes, by the Indian Affairs officials and by other professionals. I felt so good that we are doing this." The participants came up with operational plans for each participating community. Most important was perhaps the concept of *Mawio'mi*, that all adult community members could attend meetings and work together to make decisions—either by vote or consensus.

There are now eleven band-run schools in Nova Scotia, another twenty or so (it varies from year to year) public schools with MK students, and MK is about the same size as the province's French school board, says its director of programs John Jerome Paul, a member of the Eskasoni First Nation and former teacher and principal. The change in jurisdiction has had a strongly positive impact. Nova Scotia Mi'kmaw children now stay in school longer and the high school graduation rate is the highest in the country among Aboriginal students. MK provides central education supports, sort of a more hands-off school board. On-reserve schools provide language immersion and Mi'kmaw-centred learning. In all, more than 2,900 students attend these schools and another 1,500 Mi'kmaw students go to public schools in Nova Scotia. Significantly, half the teachers in the MK system are Mi'kmaw. Twenty years ago, there were only a couple of dozen Mi'kmaw teachers in Nova Scotia. Now there are more than 200.

In the past two decades, more than a hundred Mi'kmaw-speaking students have gone on to complete a bachelor of education degree, mostly from St. Francis Xavier University, which has actively partnered with MK. Most Mi'kmaw graduates of ST. FX are fluent in the Mi'kmaw language. There are now on-reserve, part-time education degree programs available, with certificates in Mi'kmaw learning styles. Mi'kmaw language and culture are strongly encouraged here, and class discussions happen in English and Mi'kmaw. And that's the key. Mi'kmaw role models and mentors are as important as Mi'kmaw control of the education system. Culture permeates the building, in visible forms—such as drumming and dancing groups—but also in teaching styles. Teachers speak with pride of learning "the Mi'kmaw way." That is, how to take care of each other. Students who can afford it take turns bringing in snacks for everyone else. Discipline sometimes takes the form of a talking circle, expressing feelings about being teased and the power of words to hurt or help. One teacher told MK researchers that her desks are always placed in a circle.

Teachers also focus on Aboriginal content in the books they use and scrutinize Canadian history carefully. As one teacher told MK researchers, "When we talked about the Holocaust, I explained to my students that thousands and thousands of Native people also died because of genocide, but it isn't as publicly known." Some teachers encourage group work because they've observed that Mi'kmaw students tend to work better that way. Holistic thinking and storytelling are also encouraged, as is attacking essays from the middle and working backward and forward to conclusions and introductions—because the world doesn't actually work in straight lines. The traditional Mi'kmaw science is often discussed and taught—blended with the western science the curriculum still demands. One teacher spoke of an experiment using traditional medicine to inhibit bacterial growth. One class went moose hunting to learn traditional skills and make careful observations in nature. The learning is often hands-on.

MK has made tremendous and quick progress. But Mi'kmaw students still face barriers to academic success that most students don't have to deal with. In the provincial schools, 44 percent of Mi'kmaw students say their schools lack interest in meeting their needs; their teachers expect or want them to fail. These challenges are much less common in band-operated schools, but

The 2012 graduating class of Chief Allison Bernard Memorial High School celebrates academic success. Mi'kmaw Kina'matnewey

54 percent of students in those schools say they lack the resources they need to succeed. And yet, many are succeeding, at least to the point of graduating high school. An even greater challenge awaits those hoping to move on to community college or university.

POST-SECONDARY

The mountain Mi'kmaw learners are climbing in the lingering and wide wake of the Shubenacadie Indian Residential School, even decades on, is steep. MK has made incredible progress in a short time—more than five hundred Mi'kmaw students went to post-secondary school in 2012, an increase of 25 percent from the previous year. But only one university in Nova Scotia, Cape Breton University, has more than 2 percent Aboriginal students. In all, 12 percent of Nova Scotia Mi'kmaq between the ages of twenty-five and sixty-four have a degree, compared to 20 percent for the general population of Nova Scotia. Because of MK's success, the number of Mi'kmaw high school graduates eligible for university or community college goes up every year. But so do the costs of tuition and living expenses. Meanwhile, the amount of money Aboriginal Affairs provides for post-secondary education remains virtually flat. In all, there are about three hundred Mi'kmaq who currently qualify for post-secondary education but can't afford it. By comparison, about four hundred enrolled in university or college, and about one hundred graduated from post-secondary institutions in 2012.

Much like the residential schools, the federal government's refusal to invest more in Aboriginal education is hurting Aboriginal students. Even those who receive federal funding struggle to keep up with the high cost of education. Most Aboriginal students whose education is funded by Aboriginal Affairs fall a few thousand dollars short of actual tuition and living expenses. And in a move reminiscent of the Shubenacadie Indian Residential School, no funding is given for multiple visits home during the school year. Most Mi'kmaw families lack the financial resources to make up the shortfall, which makes even taking out student loans seem an insurmountable, long-term financial hardship. In 2002 Mi'kmaw and Wolastoqiyik (Maliseet) students at universities and colleges in New Brunswick and Nova Scotia told researchers with Atlantic Policy Congress and Indian Affairs that post-secondary financial support was insufficient and out of touch. Now, a decade later, a lack of funding remains the single biggest factor keeping Mi'kmaw learners out of post-secondary institutions.

But there are other challenges. Many Mi'kmaw university students have told researchers of discrimination on campus, insensitivity to Mi'kmaw culture in general, and a lack of First Nations role models at universities. Across Canada, Aboriginal people are underrepresented among university faculty, and the proportion decreases at higher administrative levels. The cultural knowledge that indigenous students bring to post-secondary institutions—traditional knowledge that is encouraged in a collaborative environment within MK—is often devalued within competitive environments on campus and in lecture halls. And there is still psychological residue from the residential school: formal education is strongly associated with assimilation. Aboriginal graduates sometimes feel isolated or ostracized in their own communities and lack role models who have graduated university. Aboriginal students are far more likely than other students to have dependants and childcare expenses, which are not funded. Leaving tight-knit, remote communities where they receive an education grounded in Mi'kmaw culture for a large, faraway, urban school where they become a visible minority can be enormously stressful.

Despite this situation, the first few years of MK saw a nearly 10 percent increase in its students going on to graduate from university or community college. First Nations students from the Atlantic provinces now attend post-secondary schools at a higher rate than their counterparts across Canada. A big factor in that change has been the tireless work by MK staff in building partnerships with St. Francis Xavier University, Cape Breton University, and Nova Scotia Community College, among others. These institutions have in turn reached out to Mi'kmaw high school graduates and accommodated their unique needs.

CBU responded by creating the Mi'kmaq Elmitek—"showing the path"—program. Elmitek goes beyond the usual first-year university transition-year program. Mi'kmaw students can complete off-campus classes in Indian Brook, Eskasoni, Membertou, and Wagmatcook. They need to be on campus only once a week during their first year, allowing them to remain connected with their communities. The university also started a four-year integrative science program with a focus on both Aboriginal and western science. And it created Mi'kmaw programs through its Mi'kmaq College Institute, now Unama'ki College, in business, law, natural resources management, and applied science. Meanwhile the School of Education at St. Francis Xavier has been working since 1995 to train Mi'kmaw teachers for band and provincial schools. "ST. FX really came to bat for us," says MK's programs director John Jerome Paul. "We've got 140 to 150 Bachelors of Education from that school." It's the people at any given school and their level of support for Mi'kmaw students that make all the difference. "The personal relationships with people at schools make it work. There have been really good people at ST. FX and we've been lucky."

LANGUAGE LOSSES

"Reconciliation will happen to me when I see my children studying their culture, studying their language."
—Margaret Ward testifying at the TRC

Mike Isaac of the Mi'kmaq Liaison Office of Nova Scotia's Department of Education travels the province in his work, speaking with band council leaders, educators, and students. He remembers, as a boy, having to stop speaking Mi'kmaw when he went to a Catholic school, and feeling that he had surrendered a piece of himself. "People don't value the language because they don't see it as something that will give them employment," he says. "Less and less young people are speaking Mi'kmaw because they don't see value in it." This attitude is a remnant of the colonial education system. The Mi'kmaw language thrived up until the 1950s, when nearly all Mi'kmaq spoke it. But the disruption caused by the residential and day schools, which forbid its use, caused significant loss of the language. To Isaac, the language is the Mi'kmaw identity. If you speak Mi'kmaw, he says, you "feel who you are as a people because our culture is embedded in our language. It's going to allow for that individual to have that sense of pride and dignity. They know exactly who they are."

In 1999 the Assembly of Nova Scotia Chiefs directed the recently formed Mi'kmaw Kina'matnewey to study Mi'kmaw language use in Newfoundland and Nova Scotia. Surveyors polled a remarkable three-quarters of Mi'kmaw households. At the time, Mi'kmaw was being taught mostly as a second language in schools on reserves. The researchers found that 55 percent of Mi'kmaw households used at least some Mi'kmaw language in the home. But the rest used only English. Only 43 percent of respondents could read Mi'kmaw and just 31 percent could write it. Eight percent said the reason they didn't use Mi'kmaw was due to the lasting impact of residential school. Others gave reasons that could also be indirectly attributed to the colonial education system. Seventeen percent said their children went to non-Aboriginal schools, and 15 percent said using English was the only way to succeed.

Eight years after that survey, in 2007, the Mi'kmaq Health Research Group and the Union of Nova Scotia Indians instigated a comprehensive study of the health of the Mi'kmaq on reserves. These researchers found that the vast majority of Mi'kmaw parents felt it was important for their children to learn the language. But only half of Mi'kmaw children understand it. Only one-third can speak it. And just 28 percent of Mi'kmaw youth use the language "in daily life."

If the Mi'kmaw language is to flourish among young people, skilled Mi'kmaw teachers must have access to good language-teaching tools. Thankfully there is a growing list of options for Mi'kmaw-language teachers. MK set out to publish as many books as possible in Mi'kmaw for students. "We're probably up around a hundred and working on the next hundred now," says John Jerome Paul, whose seven children have all grown up fluent Mi'kmaw speakers and have passed that on to their own children. Paul says that many of the program's students focused on language education and wrote Mi'kmaw-language stories as part of their studies. MK obtained funding to publish nineteen of those stories. Mike Isaac, who in addition to his day job writes children's books in English and Mi'kmaw, stresses the importance of having Mi'kmaw stories in the Mi'kmaw language. "You can translate *Hansel and Gretel* but there's no cultural relevancy," he says.

In October of 2013, Velvet Paul, the director of education for Shubenacadie First Nation, had her Mi'kmaw-language elementary school workbook, *L'nuey Klusuaqn Wi'katikn*, published, with an initial print run of two hundred. The first of its kind, the book has been so popular with teachers and students that almost immediately after its release she had to have another seven hundred printed. There are also now two dictionaries and a grammar book for the Mi'kmaw language. Trudy Sable and Bernie Francis are working with MK to develop an online atlas of Mi'kmaw place names, called *Pjila'si Mi'kma'ki*. MK is also creating an eight-thousand-word, interactive, online talking dictionary animated with photos, video, prayers, and the national anthem in Mi'kmaw at mikmaqonline.org. Fluent Mi'kmaw speakers are doing the voice work.

It is important to remember that Mi'kmaw wasn't the only language attacked by colonial education policies. If anything, the language of the Wolastoqiyik (Maliseet) of New Brunswick, Wolastoq, has suffered even greater losses, and is now severely threatened. There are now only sixty people left with Wolastoq as their mother tongue. Elders, language warriors, and academics are making efforts to document, promote, and preserve the language, in part through the development of basic Wolastoq-language curriculum.

John Valk, an associate professor of world view studies at the University of New Brunswick, is working closely with Elders Imelda and David Perley as part of a team that is interviewing Elders and recording their stories in a language bank. The goal is "the reversal of language death due to the assimilation policies by residential schools and ongoing provincial policies that limit the use of our beautiful Wolastoq language," Imelda Perley explains. But for that to happen, she says an inclusive language-education program is needed in public schools so that First Nations and other students can learn Walastoq or Mi'kmaw like they do French or English.

IMMERSION, IMMERSION, IMMERSION

While Mi'kmaw is in better shape than many other Aboriginal languages in Canada, the older generation, who know the language best, won't be around forever. Transferring their knowledge is a significant challenge. Sable and Francis, authors of *The Language of This Land, Mi'kma'ki*, believe there is a need for total Mi'kmaw immersion programs "for each and every community where possible." John Jerome Paul agrees. In Paul's telling, there are three ways to bring back the language: immersion, immersion, and immersion. "Language-maintenance programs don't work," he says. "See anyone who took regular French classes in school." See also Mi'kmaw students who take language classes in elementary school without being immersed: "By

Grade 5 or 6 they can tell you all the colours, count to a million, name all the animal names. But they cannot sit down with an Elder and have a conversation." Immersion is essential, and MK hopes that in time, with the proper resources, schools can have more of it.

MK has created language-immersion programs in three Mi'kmaw communities, with courses from daycare all the way to Grade 12. At Muin Sipu Mi'kmaq Elementary (Bear River), Acadia First Nation Youth Centre (Yarmouth), and Three Wishes daycares, children learn the Mi'kmaw language in song and dance and from puppet shows. At the preschool age they learn quickly how to count, sing songs, and name actions, animals, and colours in Mi'kmaw. Most elementary school immersion students can converse with Mi'kmaw Elders. They also read and write at the same level as high school graduates who have taken Mi'kmaw as a single course, rather than being immersed in it. On the whole, about 70 percent of MK immersion students are able to recover their language.

Immersion also restores in its students a sense of cultural pride—in their Mi'kmaw identity and values—that the Shubenacadie Indian Residential School once tried to kill, but only wounded. Some teachers have noticed that students use not only the language basics, but also nuanced cultural sayings, like *meskeyi* and *pepsite'lmiw*—"I'm sorry" and "don't disrespect me." These phrases are signs of the students' deepening understanding of the collectivist nature of their Mi'kmaw culture, that mutual respect is paramount to the good of the community. Students learn to take pride in their culture and have greater confidence and self-esteem as a result.

The next challenge is bringing the language back into everyday use. The residential school in Shubenacadie showed that without regular use, language is forgotten. "What's the use of teaching the student the language when the parents or community don't use it as a working language?" Mike Isaac says. But MK is careful to avoid replicating the paternalism of Indian Affairs, which has haunted the Mi'kmaq for too long. "We can't be prescriptive to communities," says John Jerome Paul. He doesn't think it's necessary anyway. He notes that many chiefs have made the language a community priority, or have passed policies saying Mi'kmaw is the working language of the reserve. Stop signs in Mi'kmaw can be found on some reserves and around band schools. But policy isn't always practice, and Paul emphasizes the enormous psychological challenge with speaking Mi'kmaw.

"The population is only fifty years removed from residential school," he says. "People were brainwashed, colonized by the English language to believe that Mi'kmaw won't help them. Now we have children asking, 'Why didn't you teach me my language?' Often we become intellectually committed, but we never do it if it's never a convenient time."

WAYS OF UNDERSTANDING

Mike Isaac of the Mi'kmaq Liaison Office, a former teacher, says that because Mi'kmaw culture has been devalued for so long, educators have limited knowledge or understanding of the Mi'kmaq. What little they know tends to be a historical image of hunter-gatherers. The complex post-contact history, the creation of reservations and centralization, early attempts to wipe out the Mi'kmaq, then the residential school—teachers, students, and the general public remain in the dark on these things. Isaac says it is hard for teachers to develop positive relationships with people from a culture they do not understand. And a positive relationship is essential if a student is to learn. That relationship is strongly linked to the content being taught. "It must be relevant to the student."

It's not a matter of turning all curriculum into Mi'kmaw curriculum, but rather making a consistent effort to link lessons to the traditional knowledge of the Mi'kmaq. In Isaac's experience, drawing those links works for Mi'kmaw and non-Mi'kmaw students. "Mi'kmaq say, 'Wow I didn't know our ancestors were chemists who understood the properties of matter,'" Isaac says. "And non-Mi'kmaq say, 'Wow I didn't know that about the Mi'kmaq.'" Relationship-building with Mi'kmaw students also involves making an effort to bridge cultural differences and learning styles. Non-Mi'kmaw teachers don't often see this. "If you're continuing to see the student...lacking in numeracy or literacy you don't challenge them and they won't step up." Isaac says that often teachers compliment Mi'kmaw students for barely passing, which sets the bar too low. Demanding so little creates a self-fulfilling prophesy; the student makes no great effort and continues to barely pass.

Lisa Lunney Borden feels that Mi'kmaw students often disengage from math because they have different ways of reasoning about it—a different world view—and don't see their culture reflected in the abstract way that mathematics is usually taught, without practical application. She's a professor in Saint Francis Xavier University's education department and the founder of Show Me Your Math, an organization that encourages First Nations students in Atlantic Canada to "explore the mathematics that is evident in their own community and cultural practices," often by talking with Elders about how they use math in their work. She also has Acadian ancestry and taught on a reserve for ten years, immersing herself in the community culture, becoming conversational in Mi'kmaw.

Lunney Borden notes that Mi'kmaw is a language based on verbs—action and motion, a state of flux. But Western mathematics is a static language. It describes things at rest. So, the concept of "straight" might better be translated to *pektaqtek*, or "it goes straight." A house can be described as a *kiniskwikuom*, "a dwelling that comes to a point." Mi'kmaw learners want actions but instead are given things. Simply describing things in a more action-oriented manner may make concepts much clearer for Mi'kmaw learners. "As I transitioned from asking noun-based questions such as 'What is the slope?' to asking verb-based questions such as 'How is the graph changing?' I found that students often understood better," Lunney Borden writes. Using concepts from Mi'kmaw culture can also help teachers. For example, division and multiplication can start with examples of "fair sharing," expressed by the root word *nemikatun* or "divide into parts." From there the reverse concept—multiplying—becomes clear.

On a deeper level, teachers can learn to understand math as a series of useful processes rather than something to memorize. Lunney Borden calls this the "verbification of mathematics." It helps if teachers understand Mi'kmaw, or at least the way it is structured and how that structure influences the way Mi'kmaw students think. In doing so, teachers are more likely to see areas where students may struggle to understand math concepts based on knowledge and thinking styles. This knowledge goes beyond merely taking Aboriginal Studies courses in universities. Teachers in Mi'kmaw schools told Lunney Borden that switching instruction from English to Mi'kmaw often increases student comprehension. Even Mi'kmaq who have been raised speaking English often use Mi'kmaw ways and patterns of thinking and expressing ideas, having been raised by Mi'kmaw speakers. Show Me Your Math, the program Lunney Borden started, has been working in MK schools since 2006, and in public schools serving Mi'kmaw communities since 2011. It engages students to seek out Mi'kmaw math in their communities. There have since been more than five thousand student projects. Through these projects, children learn that math is a skill their Elders have always used, even if it hasn't been recognized academically, and that it is an important part of their cultural heritage. This knowledge encourages them to learn both Mi'kmaw- and western-style mathematics.

Such efforts require teachers with an understanding of Mi'kmaw culture and the ability to connect with Mi'kmaw students. Without that, classroom misunderstandings rooted in cultural bias keep Mi'kmaw students from succeeding. For example, non-Mi'kmaw teachers sometimes feel disrespected by Mi'kmaw students if they don't look them in the eyes. In Euro-Canadian culture, you look someone in the eye to show respect and trustworthiness. In Mi'kmaw culture, you show respect to Elders by not looking them in the eye. How a teacher responds—if he raises his voice and shouts a demand for respect—can quickly, unwittingly, destroy all potential for learning.

To begin dismantling such cultural barriers, Mike Isaac would like to see more indigenous content in Bachelor of Education programs in universities, so they can better understand cultural differences and learn more about Mi'kmaw traditional knowledge and its connection to curriculum. "It's not taught in education programs how to understand Mi'kmaw students," he says. He recalls teaching a course in indigenous education at Acadia University in Wolfville, Nova Scotia. "Their jaws dropped," he says, because they had never before learned about laws and governance pertaining to the Mi'kmaq. He told his students that they couldn't possibly learn everything in a ten-week course, but that he hoped they'd learn to question what they heard about the Mi'kmaq in the media. He urged them to weave what they learned into their lessons, and told them it was possible to do so while meeting the required educational outcomes.

MI'KMAQ STUDIES

In 1996 Nova Scotia piloted a high school course in Mi'kmaq Studies, one of five options in the Canadian Studies stream. (Students need only one of the five to graduate.) With a curriculum that emphasizes tolerance and open-mindedness, the course was designed by a task force, including

Mi'kmaw and non-Mi'kmaw educators, in response to the misrepresentation of the Mi'kmaq in high school curriculum to that point. "It's pretty progressive," says Ben Sichel, who teaches the course at a Dartmouth high school. "There's an outcome that says students must understand the paternalistic nature of the Indian Act." The goal is to create a better understanding and appreciation of contemporary Mi'kmaw culture. But while the course focuses on Mi'kmaw culture, spirituality, education, governance, and historical and contemporary injustices, it fails to critique Canadian colonial history or contemporary racism. According to Sichel it has a reputation as an easy course. "Some students take it for the wrong reasons," he says.

The greater danger is perhaps that teachers without any education, background in, or exposure to Mi'kmaw people, history, or culture often teach the course. In 2011 Nova Scotia teachers told Pamela Rogers, a graduate student researcher in education, that there's a lack of interest in Mi'kmaw culture among teachers. When the province held a special professional development day on the subject, only twelve people attended. Sometimes teachers get stuck with it against their wills, and they resent it or are simply uninterested. "If done badly, it reinforces stereotypes," Sichel says, adding that if a non-Mi'kmaw teacher is going to be responsible for educating mostly non-Mi'kmaw kids about the Mi'kmaq, she needs proper training. He feels that Aboriginal Studies course content should be mandatory for all Bachelor of Education programs. When teachers take an interest, Sichel feels Mi'kmaq Studies can be a great course. He works hard to find and include contemporary readings and issues to discuss. Otherwise it is essentially a history course—though the history goes beyond pre-European contact and includes the long and complex relationship between the Mi'kmaq and Canadian governments.

Mike Isaac feels that however good the few courses in Mi'kmaq Studies in provincial schools may be, they are merely "snippets," not enough to understand a culture and the history of European-Canadian and Mi'kmaw relations. "The Mi'kmaq have been here thirteen thousand years, Europeans about six hundred," he says. "We know more about European history, values, and knowledge than they do the reverse." And as a result, Mi'kmaw students are tuning their teachers out at provincial schools.

Studies by Dalhousie's Victor Thiessen in 2009 and by the Province in 2013 show that Mi'kmaw students in provincial schools still score well below the provincial average on annual literacy and numeracy tests. At heart is a remaining inability to embrace the validity of Mi'kmaw science, math, and politics—the understanding of which was traditionally passed down orally, through stories like Muin and the Seven Bird Hunters. "A lot of those stories are gone and forgotten," Isaac says, along with their ability to instill pride among Mi'kmaw learners about their heritage and abilities. "There are a lot of people within Mi'kma'ki who are not proud of who they are because there's nothing positive ever taught or spoken about us as a people."

Isaac is gently pushing for the persistent use of indigenous knowledge to become deeply embedded into the curriculum for all students, Mi'kmaw and non-Mi'kmaw, Primary to Grade 12. He's not talking only about the song and dance and drum and regalia, but also the whole way of being and seeing. The more holistic Mi'kmaw way of understanding science, for example, is of great value. To date, Isaac works for an office that the Province chronically under-funds. The Mi'kmaq Liaison Office, which provides support to the education community for Mi'kmaw students in public schools, is supposed to have five full-time staff. "Most of the time there are two. So how can we provide that service?" he wonders. The same question applies to Mi'kmaw representatives on regional school boards: some boards have them and others don't. The representatives in place are vulnerable to budget cuts. At the same time, educators are benefiting from Mi'kmaw and Aboriginal knowledge. A few elementary and high schools use restorative justice circles in Nova Scotia, and the justice department is developing a pilot project to do the same at another hundred schools.

Many survivors, including Wayne Nicholas, say that Maritime students need to learn the history of the Shubenacadie Indian Residential School. The Truth and Reconciliation Commission recommends provincial education departments develop "age-appropriate educational materials about residential schools for use in public schools." The school at Shubenacadie was just one part of a colonial education system, which itself was one of many weapons in a failed attempt at cultural genocide. And while we no longer speak of assimilation, governments continue to treat First Nations peoples as a burden to be minimized and controlled. But if we don't learn this, we can't change it.

CIRCLING BACK

Five hundred years ago, the Europeans who arrived in what they called the "New World" missed an opportunity. Okay, maybe you can't pinpoint it to a moment. The French, in general, proved more open than the Brits to working with the Mi'kmaq and other First Nations they encountered here. Maybe that was a cultural difference between the two empires, but more likely the difference was the situation they encountered when they arrived. The French needed the Mi'kmaq to survive. The English found the Mi'kmaq working with their old enemies.

Despite their war-inspiring differences, the French and English shared a sense of manifest destiny: that God granted them the superiority to "discover," conquer, and tame all foreign lands. Indeed, it was each country's respective confidence in its own superiority that made each fight the other for domestic and foreign territory. Both countries' inability to see any other people, or ways of thinking and living, as worthy of respect, drove their pathological need to take land and resources for themselves. On some level, they believed they were giving back. Not recognizing the complexity of the societies they encountered or the effectiveness of those societies as they thrived in good health and contentedness for thousands of years, European leaders believed they were giving the gift of civilization. But that act of giving was actually another attempted theft, of culture. Our culture—the way we think and act—is who we are. In trying to steal other people's cultures, those early Europeans were trying to eliminate them.

I said this opportunity was missed and this theft attempted five hundred years ago, but both of these things have happened time and again through the centuries. They continue as our federal government forces European-Canadian legal systems—based more on checking things off a gruesome list than storytelling or sharing—onto victims of residential school abuse. They continue as the same federal government tries to force its singular vision of First Nations education on diverse peoples across Canada. These efforts are rooted in denial as we refuse to call this history what it was: attempted cultural genocide.

Residential schools are the most enduring and visceral example of Euro-Canada's violent attempted cultural genocide. We stole and culture-washed 150,000 children. At least 3,000 were killed. Based on Indian Affairs reports on disease, the real number of deaths is 30,000 or more. The survivors suffered lifelong injury. Many survived the school only to succumb to its ghosts, eventually taking their own lives to escape the pain.

As with any holocaust, fully understanding residential school is impossible. Even looking at one school, there are thousands of stories that often disagree with each other. Many stories have been lost. The school's creators are all dead, as are most of its teachers. The children have long since grown into adult versions of what they once were. Some are no longer with us. The ones who remain are now Elders. The foggy picture we get of the Shubenacadie Indian Residential School, from the archives and survivor stories, is one of much horror, an atrocity.

As with any other atrocity, there are more people to blame than fingers to point. It is perhaps satisfying to shun the church, as many survivors have done, or point at the cruel ways of dour nuns. We can condemn the impracticality of an archaic hierarchy of faith that isolates clergy inside a priest's inherently explosive God complex then put him in charge of children. We can also point toward a racist past, as mainstream Canadians often do. But in the school's thirty-seven years, the Maritime settler population never seemed to mind the idea of taking kids from their homes, communities, and cultures and making them live where they'd learn from nuns and priests to think and act white. The press described the school as a service to the "poor Indians," and the public applauded. When Father Mackey's brutal lashing and permanent scarring of nineteen boys made the news in 1934, the papers mocked the children for so audaciously complaining. The governments and churches were in fact enacting, in Shubenacadie and other residential schools, the will of the people—Euro-Canadian people anyway. When Shubenacadie's first students arrived, Canada was sixty-two years old. It was high time the Indians got with the program, and Shubenacadie would do the job.

Assigning blame is easy and there's lots to go around between federal bureaucrats and church representatives, RCMP officers, media representatives who didn't look deeply enough, child-welfare workers who were happy to let someone else take care of the Indians, scientists who saw starving, beaten down people as a research opportunity. The more you look at the school, the more you will find went wrong. And the more people involved. Ultimately, assigning blame becomes, while perhaps cathartic for some, less important than understanding that the residential school was based on supremacist assumptions that First Nations and Inuit peoples were outdated, a precursor to civilized man. And as long as those assumptions linger, bureaucrats, religious people, scientists, educators, bleeding heart social workers, journalists hunting out good stories, all of us are likely to be complicit in the next atrocity against a people we think need help, because we believe we are just a little bit, or a lot, further along in our development than they are.

We prefer to think that's all in the past. We shake our heads at the tragedy of it. What a horrible thing it was, and we thank God it's over. We now know better. We fail to acknowledge though that we—Euro-Canadians that is—have been the ones to benefit from colonial policies, including residential schools. We forget, or never learned, that we benefited from every policy that took First Nations land, pushed them onto reserves and into poverty, and forced them to try, in vain, to be more like us. We benefited from the land that was taken. And every dollar not spent on the reserves—for schools and other needs—was one spent on us.

We also fail to consider that all the steps forward in First Nations education and child welfare have been forced on the government by determined and resilient Aboriginal leadership. In the Maritimes, survivors of Shubenacadie pushed for the school to be closed in 1967. Nationally, survivors from many schools worked hard to create *Indian Control of Indian Education* first as a policy paper and next as a driving philosophy of change. Nora Bernard and many other fearless survivors pushed until the federal government finally acknowledged its role in the residential schools and created the Truth and Reconciliation Commission. John Jerome Paul and many other Mi'kmaq have been tireless language and education warriors, making Mi'kmaw Kina'matnewey the most successful First Nations education program in Canada.

Aboriginal Affairs, representing the interests of mainstream Canadians, has resisted most of these changes or pushed for more regressive policies. It continues to use its money to control First Nations. In that respect, nothing has changed since the residential school era. There is an often-quoted myth that Aboriginal people get all the benefits of a social welfare system without paying the costs. In reality, in terms of money spent per person, they are the most underserved demographic in Canada by a wide margin. As a result, while Canada consistently ranks in the top ten nations on all international standards of quality of life, the same standards applied to Aboriginal peoples in Canada would rarely put them in the top fifty.

When money is invested in reserves or systems supporting Aboriginal peoples, the supported are expected to surrender a degree of autonomy, to become more like the rest of us Canadians. It is the same, ongoing attempt at cultural theft. For 500 years, settler Europeans and their Canadian descendants have missed the chance to learn from and work with Aboriginal peoples as true partners. It would perhaps be naïve to expect that to change now. But then, surely no one on Mi'kma'ki 501 years ago expected giant ships to appear on the horizon and change everything.

If an organization of nuns whose members once terrorized, culture-washed, and abused First Nations children at either end of Canada can learn to follow the Mi'kmaw lead in reconciliation efforts, there is hope. If the victims of education as a tool of oppression can transform that tool to reclaim language and culture, there is hope. And if we can learn to recognize that Euro-Canada tried to destroy the hundreds of original cultures of this land, there is hope that we can end the ongoing attempts by our government to control and assimilate Aboriginal peoples, and move forward together along a more just, sustainable path.

SOURCES AND ACKNOWLEDGEMENTS

This book is possible in part because of the good work of those who have long contemplated the residential school system, and particularly the Maritime school. I wish to acknowledge *Micmac News* journalist Conrad W. Paul who, in 1978, in the face of formidable resistance from the Sisters of Charity and his newspaper's own printer, courageously blew the whistle on truths about the school that had been known but little discussed within the community for years. Freelance journalist Heather Laskey followed suit in the 1980s and was the first to bring survivor stories to the mainstream press, including CBC Radio.

In 1992 Isabelle Knockwood's germinal work on the school, *Out of the Depths*, was published. It was an account of experiences of survivors, including her story and those of the people she interviewed. It contains some of the most vivid descriptions of life at the Shubenacadie school for the children. Four years later, the Mi'kmaw poet Rita Joe released her autobiography, *Song of Rita Joe*, which added important personal details of life at the school and its long-term impacts on her life. These two works provide an important sense of life in a dreary institution for those of us who weren't there.

To understand how the school came to be, its reason for existence, the men behind it, the thinking of the churches and government bureaucrats, I drew from letters in Library Archives Canada, reports in the provincial archives, and important thesis work by numerous students over the decades, especially Marilyn Thomson-Millward, Kathleen Kearns, and Briar Dawn Ransberry. For their efforts and reports contextualizing the school's place in our history, I am grateful. I also relied on academic work of those striving to understand historical and contemporary Mi'kmaw childcare and education, including Pamela Rogers, Barbara Muriel Johnson, Roberta D. Clark, Jeff Orr, Fred Wien, and the twenty-four other authors of the critical Wen:de report, Jane MacMillan, Martha Walls, Nancy MacDonald, and Judy MacDonald.

I am particularly grateful to the many people who granted me their time, wisdom, perspective, and personal stories as I wrote this book. Wayne Nicholas opened up to me, a complete stranger, about his experiences at "Shubie," because he believes this shameful part of Maritime history remains too little known, and he hopes this book will be part of an ongoing effort to acknowledge and perhaps eventually reconcile. I much appreciate the honest assessments of Mi'kmaw education efforts from John Jerome Paul, who was also kind enough to recommend numerous useful reports and papers on the subject. Ben Sichel did the same, and along with Mike Isaac helped me understand efforts to improve education with Mi'kmaw content in Nova Scotia public schools. Lisa Lunney Borden and Stephen Augustin helped me better understand Mi'kmaw science and math, historically and contemporarily. And in an interview she granted several years ago, Jean Knockwood was the first to get me excited by the idea of on-reserve schools run by and for Mi'kmaq.

I'm also appreciative of Daphne Hutt-MacLeod's briefing on changes to fostering and adoption systems for Mi'kmaw children, and their relation to the truth and reconciliation process. Thanks also to Elizabeth MacDonald for answering my questions on behalf of the Department of Community Services, to Ian Mosby for explaining and expanding on his research findings on nutrition experiments conducted on children at Shubenacadie, and to Ruth Jeppeson and Sisters Donna Geernaert, Joan O'Keefe, and Geraldine Lancaster of the Sisters of Charity for taking the time to discuss the school and reconciliation efforts.

Many people helped me find the necessary resources to write this book. I want to note a couple of them here. Paul Bennett took the time to go through his personal "archives" and dig out a lot of useful books that provided important historical and national context on the Maritime school. And Heather Laskey spent a couple of afternoons with me talking about the book, and about her work as a freelance journalist writing about this school and an Irish industrial school based on the same model—with eerie similarities. Her insights were valuable. Moreover, she dug out all her old photos, transcripts, and notes for me and let me make copies.

Besides information, writing a book of this nature takes an incredible amount of time—usually unpaid for the most part. In writing this book I was fortunate to be awarded the Dave Greber Freelance Writers Award, which is, as far as I know, unique in Canada in that it provides money to writers when they need it most: while working on a new book. I can't thank enough Shirley Dunn and everyone involved with these awards and the Edmonton LitFest for their support.

And I'd be remiss not to thank, once again, the great people at Nimbus Publishing, specifically Patrick Murphy, for his belief in this project and his ongoing gentle wisdom pushing things forward, and my brilliant editor Whitney Moran, who I've come to think of as a LEGO Master Builder with her magic for moving things around until they make the most possible sense. Without the intelligence of these two sensitive souls, this book wouldn't be.

The same is true, as with everything I do, of my family and community of friends. I'm so enriched by them and lucky to have so many of them in this region and beyond. Thank you all for your curiosity, questions, and interest, and for always seeming eager for the next book, no matter how hard its subject.

Lastly and mostly, thanks to Daniel Paul. Many years ago I was blown away by *We Were Not the Savages*, his fundamental history of Mi'kma'ki and Euro-Canadian-Mi'kmaq conflict and relations. I hurt my neck nodding so hard as I read it. For decades, he has relentlessly tugged the rug of myopic Canadian history out from under our feet, forcing us to see a much darker, less glorious reality, and a much more complex one, too. I thank him for that, for sharing his thoughts and knowledge on the residential school, for pointing me toward valuable resources, and for writing the foreword for this book.

FURTHER READING

Introduction: Why and How

A National Crime: The Canadian Government and the Residential School System, 1879 to 1986 by John Milloy (Winnipeg: University of Manitoba Press, 1999).

"Indian residential school historical record threatened by TRC, Aboriginal Affairs bumbling: Auditor General" (Aboriginal Peoples Television Network, April 30, 2013, aptn.ca).

"Ottawa fears admission it purposely destroyed Indian residential school files would lead to court fights: documents" by Jorge Barrera (Aboriginal Peoples Television Network, May 1, 2012, aptn.ca).

Out of the Depths: The Experiences of Mi'kmaw Children at the Indian Residential School at Shubenacadie, Nova Scotia by Isabelle Knockwood (Black Point, Nova Scotia: Roseway Publishing, 2001).

I: Before Shubenacadie

Accounting for Genocide: Canada's Bureaucratic Assault on Aboriginal People by Dean Neu and Richard Therrien (Halifax: Fernwood Publishing, 2003).

The Betrayal of Faith: The Tragic Journey of a Colonial Native Convert by Emma Anderson (Boston: Harvard University Press, 2007).

The Capuchins in America by Reverend Otto Jeron (United States: Catholic Theological Union, 1906).

Come Over and Help Us: The New England Company and Its Mission 1649–2001 by Neil Hitchin, Ph.D. and the Governor and Court of the New England Company (Ely, England: St. Pancras Publishing and Research and St. Edmundsbury Press, 2002).

Cornwallis: The Violent Birth of Halifax by Jon Tattrie (Lawrencetown, Nova Scotia: Pottersfield Press, 2013).

Conversations with a Dead Man: The Legacy of Duncan Campbell Scott by Mark Abley (Vancouver: Douglas & McIntyre, 2013).

"Education in Quebec in the 17th Century" by James Douglas, Jr., Literary and Historical Society of Quebec (Quebec City: *Transactions*, New Series, No. 25, 1903).

The Education of Indian Children in Canada: A Symposium Written by Members of Indian Affairs Education Division, with Comments by the Indian Peoples (Toronto: Ryerson Press, 1965).

The Federal Indian Day Schools of the Maritimes by W. D. Hamilton (Fredericton: The Micmac-Maliseet Institute/University of New Brunswick, 1986).

Indian Education in Canada Volume 1: The Legacy edited by Jean Barman, Yvonne Hébert, and Don McCaskill (Vancouver: University of British Columbia Press, 1986).

Indian Education in the North West by Rev. Thompson Ferrier (Toronto: Department of Missionary Literature of the Methodist Church, 1906).

integrativescience.ca: a website for the Institute of Integrative Science & Health at Cape Breton University. It has a series of enlightening short videos and other multimedia, including English and Mi'kmaw versions of a video of the Mi'kmaw story Muin and the Seven Hunters, as well as a video explaining the concept of "Two-Eyed Seeing," featuring Elder Albert Marshall and Elder Murdena Marshall.

L'sitkuk: The Story of the Bear River Mi'kmaw Community by Darlene A. Ricker (Lockeport, Nova Scotia: Roseway Publishing, 1997).

The Language of this Land, Mi'kma'ki by Trudy Sable and Bernie Francis (Sydney, Nova Scotia: Cape Breton University Press, 2012).

Micmac Indian Medicine: A Traditional Way of Health by Laurie Lacey (Halifax: Formac Publishing, 1977).

Mi'kmaq Medicines: Remedies and Recollections Second Edition by Laurie Lacey (Halifax: Nimbus Publishing, 2012).

"Missing Children & Unmarked Burials: Research Recommendations" prepared by The Working Group on Missing Children and Unmarked Burials (Winnipeg: Truth and Reconciliation Commission, 2009).

"Out of the Ruts of Nova Scotia Education: Mi'kmaw Doors of Education Emerge" by Barbara Muriel Johnson (Ph.D. dissertation, Halifax: Dalhousie University, 2000).

"'part of that whole system': Maritime Day and Residential Schooling and Federal Culpability" by Martha Walls (Brandon, Manitoba: *Canadian Journal of Native Studies*, 30.2, Winter 2010: 361–385).

Report on Industrial Schools for Indians and Half-Breeds by Nicholas Flood Davin (Ottawa: Minister of the Interior, March 1879).

Report on the Indian Schools of Manitoba and the Northwest Territories by P. H. Bryce (Ottawa: Indian Affairs, Government Printing Bureau, 1907).

Shingwauk's Vision: A History of Native Residential Schools by J. R. Miller (Toronto: University of Toronto Press, 1996).

"Telling 1922's Story of a National Crime: Canada's First Chief Medical Officer and the Aborted Fight for Aboriginal Health Care" by Adam J. Green (Brandon, Manitoba: *The Canadian Journal of Native Studies* 26.2., 2006, 211–28).

"The New England Company and the New Brunswick Indians, 1786–1826: A Comment on the Colonial Perversion of British Benevolence" by Judith Fingard (Fredericton: *Acadiensis*, 1.2, 1972, 29–42).

The Story of a National Crime, Being an Appeal for Justice to the Indians of Canada; the Wards of the Nation, Our Allies in the Revolutionary War: Our Brothers-n-Arms in the Great War by P. H. Bryce, M.A., MD (Ottawa: James Hope & Sons, Limited, 1922).

They Came for the Children: Canada, Aboriginal Peoples, and Residential Schools (Winnipeg: The Truth and Reconciliation Commission, 2012).

"Transforming Mathematics Education for Mi'kmaw Students Through Mawinkinutmatimk" by Lisa Lunney Borden (Ph.D. dissertation in Education Studies, University of New Brunswick, 2010).

We Were Not the Savages: A Micmac Perspective on the Collision of European and Aboriginal Civilization Third Edition by Daniel N. Paul (Halifax: Fernwood Publishing, 2006).

II: The Shubenacadie Indian Residential School

Most of the information about the creation of the school and its management comes from files at Library and Archives Canada in Ottawa and from the thesis and dissertation work of Marilyn Thomson-Millward (né O'Hearn) and Kathleen Kearns.

"A Case Study of the Residential School at Shubenacadie, Nova Scotia" by Marilyn Elaine O'Hearn (M.A. thesis, Halifax: St. Mary's University, 1989).

"Administering Colonial Science: Nutrition Research and Human Biomedical Experimentation in Aboriginal Communities and Residential Schools, 1942–1952" by Ian Mosby (University of Toronto Press: *Social History* 46.91, May 2013).

"Beyond the Banality of Evil: Three Dynamics of an Interactionist Social Psychology of Tyranny" by S. Alexander Haslam and Stephen Reicher (University of Exeter, University of St. Andrews, Society for Personality and Social Psychology, Inc., 2007).

The Catholic Diocesan Directory of Nova Scotia (Halifax: The Archdiocese of Halifax, 1936. Available at Nova Scotia Archives.

The Catholic Encyclopedia: An International Work of Reference on the Constitution, Doctrine, Discipline, and History of the Catholic Church edited by Charles G. Herberman (New York: Robert Appleton Company, 1907).

"Charges Unfounded" by the editorial writer (Halifax: *Chronicle Herald*, September 24, 1934).

Charity alive: Sisters of Charity of Saint Vincent de Paul, Halifax, 1950–1980 by Mary Olga McKenna (Lanham, Maryland: University Press of America, 1998).

"Contesting the 'Nature' Of Conformity: What Milgram and Zimbardo's Studies Really Show" by S. Alexander Haslam and Stephen D. Reicher (School of Psychology, University of Queensland, St. Lucia, Australia; University of St. Andrews, Scotland, 2012).

Directory for the Sisters Employed in the Charitable Institutions of the Sisters of Charity by Mother Mary Berchmans (Halifax: Sisters of Charity, 1925 [this book is stamped inside with "Sisters of Charity Shubenacadie, N.S."]).

"Hard to erase bitter memories of school days filled with fear" by Heather Laskey (Moncton, New Brunswick: *Atlantic Insight*, February 1988, 23).

"The History of the Shubenacadie Indian Residential School, 1929–1957" by Kathleen Kearns (B.A. Hons. thesis, Sackville, New Brunswick: Mount Allison University, 1990).

Journey From the Shadows video by Madeline Yakimchuk (Sydney, Nova Scotia: Gryphon Media Productions, Atlantic Policy Congress of First Nations Chiefs Secretariat, M/ Carroll Consulting, 2010).

The Lucifer Effect: Understanding How Good People Turn Evil by Philip Zimbardo (New York: Random House, 2008).

Quiet Rage: The Stanford Prison Experiment, 1992, by Ken Musen and Philip Zimbardo: www.youtube.com/watch?v=exVZ7O2XDCE.

"RCMP 'herded' native kids to residential schools" (Halifax: CBC *News*, October 29, 2011).

"Researching the Devils: A Study of Brokerage at the Indian Residential School, Shubenacadie, Nova Scotia" by Marilyn Elaine Thomson-Millward (Halifax: Dalhousie University Ph.D. dissertation, 1997).

"Residential school survivor robbed of her childhood" by Pat Lee (Halifax: *Chronicle Herald*, October 27, 2011).

"Residential school survivors share horrific experiences" by Raissa Tetanish (Truro, Nova Scotia: *Truro Daily News*, October 12, 2011).

"Residential School Survivors Share Their Stories: Truth and Reconciliation Commission hears testimonials at Eskasoni" by Joyce MacDonald (Halifax Media Co-op, October 31, 2011).

"Residential school survivor tells of abuse at Indian Brook hearing" (Halifax: CBC *News*, October 12, 2011).

"Teach Your Children Well: Curriculum and Pedagogy at the Shubenacadie Indian Residential School, Shubenacadie, Nova Scotia, 1951–1967" by Briar Dawn Ransberry (M. A. thesis, Halifax: Dalhousie University, July 2000).

"The Shubenacadie Indian Residential School," Parts 1, 2, and 3 by Conrad Paul (Membertou, Nova Scotia: *Micmac News*, 1978).

The Sisters of Charity: Halifax by Sister Maura Powers (Toronto: The Ryerson Press, 1956).

"Seeking truth in Charlottetown" (Charlottetown: *The Guardian*, September 30, 2011).

Song of Rita Joe: Autobiography of a Mi'kmaw Poet by Rita Joe with the assistance of Lynn Henry (Sydney, Nova Scotia: Breton Books, 2011).

TRC Coverage (Halifax Media Co-op, *The Coast*, CBC, *Chronicle Herald*, etc.).

"Truth commissioners come to Fredericton" (Halifax: CBC *News*, September 8, 2011).

"Truth and Reconciliation Commission Held in Eskasoni" (posted at *eskasoni.ca* October 14, 2011).

"Truth & Reconciliation: Thursday October 27: Transcript of Tim Bousquet's Twitter feed" by Tim Bousquet (Halifax: *The Coast*, October 30, 2011).

"When School Becomes Prison" script by Heather Laskey (aired on *Maritime Magazine*, CBC Radio Halifax, October 12, 1986).

III: ONE YEAR FROM ANOTHER

"Chief Noel Doucette: inspirational role model" by Daniel Paul (Halifax: *Halifax Herald*, October 4, 1996).

"Education Key To Future Of N.S. Micmac Population: Education and Poverty Don't Mix" by Stan Fitzner (Halifax: *Chronicle Herald*, September 1, 1965).

"Former Indian School For Welfare Project" (Halifax: *Chronicle Herald*, January 16, 1968).

"Indian Education in Nova Scotia" by G. G. Currie (B.A. thesis, Sackville, New Brunswick: Mount Allison University, 1947).

"The Hawthorn Survey (1966–1967), Indians and Oblates and Integrated Schooling" by Robert Carney (Winnipeg: Canadian Catholic Historical Association Study Sessions, 50, 1983, 609–630).

"The Oblates of Saint Peter's Province in Nova Scotia (Canada) 1948–2003" by Carl Kelly (*Vie Oblate Life* 63.1, 2004, 33–55).

IV: After Shubenacadie

Aboriginal Peoples in Canada: First Nations People, Métis and Inuit. Analytical document: National Household Survey 2011, published by the Minister of Industry (Statistics Canada, 2013).

"Addressing Mi'kmaq Family Violence" by L. Jane MacMillan (Antigonish, Nova Scotia: St. Francis Xavier University, 2011).

"A legacy of Canadian child care: Surviving the sixties scoop" by Christine Smith (McFarlane) (Regina: *Briarpatch Magazine,* September/October 2013).

Aski Awasis/Children of the Earth: First Peoples Speaking on Adoption edited by Jeannine Carrière (Winnipeg: Fernwood Publishing, 2010).

"Decolonizing Mi'kmaw Education Through Cultural Practical Knowledge" by Jeff Orr, San Salom/John Jerome Paul, and Kelusilew/Sharon Paul (Montreal: *McGill Journal of Education,* Fall 2002, 37.3, 331–54).

"Federal official wanted emails deleted outlining plan to stonewall on residential school genocide questions" by Jorge Barrera (Winnipeg: Aboriginal Peoples Television Network, January 13, 2012).

First Nations Post-Secondary Education and Training Literature Review and Best Practices: Leading towards recommendations for comprehensive post-secondary planning and evaluation framework for Mi'kmaw Kina'matnewey by Jeff Orr, Crystal Roberts, and Megan Ross (submitted to Mi'kmaw Kina'matnewey and Indian and Northern Affairs Canada June 16, 2008).

The Globalization of Addiction: A study in poverty of the spirit by Bruce Alexander (Oxford: Oxford University Press, 2008).

"Health and the health care delivery system: the Micmac in Nova Scotia" by Peter Twohig (M.A. thesis, Halifax: St. Mary's University, 1991).

The Health of the On Reserve Mi'kmaq Population prepared by Dr. Charlotte Loppie and Dr. Fred Wien on behalf of the Mi'kmaq Health Research Group and the Union of Nova Scotia Indians (January 7, 2007).

How the Cougar Came to be Called the Ghost Cat/Ta'N Petalu Telui'tut Skite'Kmujewey Mia'wj by Michael James Isaac (Halifax: Roseway Publishing, 2010).

Indian Control of Indian Education: Policy paper presented to the Minister of Indian Affairs and Northern Development by the National Indian Brotherhood/Assembly of First Nations (1972).

"Indians tell of roadblocks to education" (Halifax: *Mail-Star,* March 20, 1970).

"In Nova Scotia, a Mi'kmaw Model for First Nation Education" by Jennifer Lewington (Canadian Education Association: *Education Canada* 52.5, 2012, 14).

Learning about Walking in Beauty: Placing Aboriginal perspectives in Canadian classrooms (Toronto: Canadian Race Relations Foundation, Coalition for the Advancement of Aboriginal Studies, 2002).

The Lost Teachings/Panuijkatasikl Kina'Masuti'l by Michael James Isaac (Halifax: Roseway Publishing, 2013).

Mi'kmaw Kina'matnewey Annual Report 2012–2013.

Mi'kmaw Kina'matnewey Oak Island Education Symposium (Nov. 19–Dec. 3, 1999) Summary Notes.

Multiculturalism: A handbook for teachers edited by Peter L. McCreath (Halifax: Nova Scotia Teachers Union, 1982).

Native Children and the Child Welfare System by Patrick Johnston (Ottawa: Canadian Council on Social Development, 1983).

"People to People, Nation to Nation." *Highlights from the Report of the Royal Commission on Aboriginal Peoples* (Ottawa: Minister of Supply and Services Canada, 1996).

"Problematizing social studies curricula in Nova Scotia" by Pamela Rogers (Montreal, Quebec: McGill University M.A. thesis, June 2011).

"Reflections of a Mi'kmaq social worker on a quarter of a century work in First Nations child welfare" by Nancy MacDonald and Judy MacDonald (Ottawa: *The First Peoples Child & Family Review* 3.1, 2007, 34–45).

"Retooling schooling: Four projects that are revolutionizing the way we teach and learn" by Michelle Miller, Chris Benjamin, and Anna Kirkpatrick (Regina: *Briarpatch Magazine*, September 2009).

"Statement of Apology—to former students of Indian Residential Schools" delivered by The Right Honourable Stephen Harper on behalf of the Government of Canada (June 11, 2008).

"Statement of the Government of Canada on Indian Policy 1969" (Ottawa: Published under the authority of the Honourable Jean Chrétien, Minister of Indian Affairs and Northern Development Ottawa, 1969, Queen's Printer Cat. No. R32-2469).

"Stories of Aboriginal Transracial Adoption" by Simon Nuttgens (DeWinton, Alberta: *The Qualitative Report*, 18.3, 2013, 1–7).

The 500 Years of Resistance Comic Book by Gord Hill (Vancouver: Arsenal Pulp Press, 2010).

"A Tribute to Nora Bernard—a proud lady who said 'no more'" by Daniel Paul (Halifax: *Chronicle Herald*, January 3, 2008).

Unsettling the Settler Within: Indian Residential Schools, Truth Telling, and Reconciliation in Canada by Paulette Regan (Vancouver: University of British Columbia Press, 2011).

"The 'Verbification' of Mathematics: Using the grammatical structures of Mi'kmaq to support student learning by Lisa Lunney Borden (Fredericton: *For the Learning of Mathematics* 31.3, November 2011, 8–13).

"We are Mi'kmaw Kina'matnewey": An Assessment of the Impact of the Mi'kmaw Kina'matnewey Self Government Agreement on the Improvement of Education for Participating Mi'kmaw Communities by Jeff Orr and Coralie Cameron (submitted to Mi'kmaw Kina'matnewey and Indian Affairs Canada, June 1, 2004).

"Wen:de: We Are Coming to the Light of Day" by Cindy Blackstock, Tara Prakash, John Loxley, and Fred Wien (Ottawa: First Nations Child and Family Caring Society of Canada, 2005).

"What Canada committed against First Nations was genocide. The UN should recognize it" by Phil Fontaine and Bernie Farber (Toronto: *Globe and Mail*, October 14, 2013).

"What's the word for…? Is there a word for…? How understanding Mi'kmaw language can help support Mi'kmaw learners in mathematics" by Lisa Lunney Borden (Queensland, Australia: *Mathematics Education Research Journal* 25.1, March 1, 2013, 5–22).